Judicial TYRANNY

the new kings of america?

By MARK I. SUTHERLAND

WITH

JAMES C. DOBSON, Ph.D.

—

BENJAMIN D. DUPRE', ESQ.

—

DON FEDER

—

WILLIAM J. FEDERER

—

DAVID C. GIBBS III, ESQ.

—

AMBASSADOR ALAN KEYES

—

US ATTORNEY GENERAL EDWIN MEESE

—

DAVE MEYER

—

CHIEF JUSTICE ROY S. MOORE

—

HON. HOWARD PHILLIPS

—

REV. RICK SCARBOROUGH

—

PHYLLIS SCHLAFLY, ESQ.

—

ALAN E. SEARS, ESQ.

—

MATHEW D. STAVER, ESQ.

—

HERBERT W. TITUS, ESQ.

Judicial TYRANNY - the new kings of america?
by Mark I. Sutherland, et. al.
revised edition

Mark I. Sutherland
PO Box 270033
St. Louis, MO 63127

Library of Congress

POLITICS / LAW / CURRENT AFFAIRS
ISBN 0-9753455-6-7 paperback $24.99
ISBN 0-9753455-8-3 hardback $29.99

Amerisearch, Inc., P.O. Box 20163, St. Louis, MO 63123,
1-888-USA-WORD, 314-487-4395 voice/fax
www.amerisearch.net

For

Our Children

Who Will Inherit

What We Leave Behind

CONTENTS

PREFACE 9

1. A CONSTITUTIONAL CRISIS
U.S. Attorney General Edwin Meese 11

2. THOU SHALT HAVE NO GOD BEFORE US
Benjamin D. DuPré, Esq. 13

3. THE POWER OF OUR TRUE HISTORY
Dave Meyer 27

4. A CHRISTIAN AMERICA?
David C. Gibbs III, Esq. 35

5. WHAT LAW?
Ambassador Alan Keyes 45

6. WHO IS AMERICA'S SOVEREIGN?
The Honorable Howard Phillips 55

7. THE RULE OF LAW
Chief Justice Roy S. Moore 61

8. JUDICIAL ATHEISM
Rev. Rick Scarborough 79

9. REDEFINING THE RULES
Mark I. Sutherland 85

10. AMERICAN OLIGARCHY
William J. Federer 95

11. IT'S A JUDGE ISSUE
Phyllis Schlafly, Esq. 105

12. JUDICIAL ORDERED MURDER?
James C. Dobson, Ph.D. 115

13. INTERNATIONAL LAW?
Alan E. Sears, Esq. 131

14. JUST SAY NO TO JUDICIAL TYRANNY
Don Feder 135

15. THE SOUL OF AMERICA
Rev. Rick Scarborough 141

16. WHEN IN THE COURSE...
Mathew D. Staver, Esq. 153

17. THE POWER OF EACH STATE
Herbert W. Titus, Esq. 163

18. THE FINAL MOMENTS OF CONFLICT
Ambassador Alan Keyes 179

19. TO IMPEACH OR NOT TO IMPEACH?
Mark I. Sutherland 197

20. WHAT DO I DO NOW?
Mark I. Sutherland 203

DECLARATION OF INDEPENDENCE 209

CONSTITUTION OF THE UNITED STATES 217

AMENDMENTS TO THE U.S. CONSTITUTION 235

About The Authors 251

Acknowledgments 261

Endnotes 263

PREFACE

We live in the greatest nation on Planet Earth, but it is becoming more and more apparent that in order to keep it great, the people must do something to stop the federal courts that are daily setting themselves above the law and dictating to us how we should live, and what we should think.

This book is designed to bring you up to speed on the ongoing struggle against an over-reaching judicial branch, without overwhelming you with legal double-speak. It is written in plain American, and presented in bite-sized pieces. It features some of our nation's most prominent leaders in the battle for continued liberty and freedom in our nation.

It is my prayer that you will study the principles in this book and apply them to how you vote, how you view the role of government, and how you react when the next judge throws out the will of the people in favor of the latest social engineering project.

To bring our nation back from the elites in black robes that wish to redefine everything we are, it is going to take work. But by picking up this book you are taking the first step, and together we can turn our nation around.

Edmund Burke, the famous British politician who supported our War of Independence while serving in the

British Parliament, stated a simple truth that still applies to us today. He said, "The only thing necessary for the triumph of evil is for good men to do nothing."

Americans have done nothing for too long, and we are paying the price today. But it is not too late. The fight has only just begun.

Thank you for becoming part of the solution. Thank you for standing with us.

Faithfully Yours,

Mark I. Sutherland

1.

A CONSTITUTIONAL CRISIS

By U.S. Attorney General Edwin Meese

In 1787, the founders gave us the U.S. Constitution, which combined a number of relatively new ideas for that particular point in time.

The founding fathers were very much concerned about governmental power and possible oppression, having just gone through the "War for Independence," and they did not want to give up the freedom that they had won so dearly in the 1770's.

This was why they developed a series of checks and balances to present the country and protect the freedom of the people.

The founders had a couple of particular things in mind to protect our freedoms. One was the separation of powers, which was designed to diffuse governmental power among three separate branches. The other was an independent judiciary.

Prior to that time the king's judges, in the early days of our country before we became the United States Of America, were pretty much mouthpieces for the monarchy. If the king didn't like their actions, he simply removed them from office or lowered their pay.

An independent judiciary, however, was to be protected in two ways. One was lifetime appointment for federal judges, and secondly, the judges' compensation could not be reduced during his or her time in office.

Well, during the past seventy years, about a third of our country's history, there have been some changes in what the original founders had in mind.

First of all, we have had courts that have warped legislative functions.

Second, we have some in the Senate who are seeking to influence and control the decisions of the courts. They are trying to prevent constitutionally faithful judges from being appointed by our president.

And they are seeking to intimidate, coerce and dominate the courts by extracting promises from judicial nominees as to how they would decide cases before they are even confirmed.

That is why the current battle that is going on in Washington over judicial appointments is so important, not just to this administration, not just to the political warfare that is taking place today, but to the future of our constitution and the future of our nation's existence as a democratic republic.

So, I don't think I am exaggerating to say that we have a constitutional crisis at the present time.

2.

THOU SHALT HAVE NO GOD BEFORE US

How Chief Justice Roy Moore Broke the First Commandment of Judicial Tyrants

By Benjamin D. DuPré, Esq.

THE SUPREME JUDGE OF THE WORLD

In 1776, the American people, "with a firm Reliance on the Protection of Divine Providence," rejected the "absolute Tyranny" of King George III's monarchy.[1] "A Prince," we said, "whose Character is thus marked by every act which may define a Tyrant, is unfit to be the Ruler of a free people."[2]

In declaring our independence of Great Britain, we relied upon the truth that "Governments are instituted" to secure "certain unalienable rights"—rights with which "all Men...are endowed by their Creator."[3]

When oppressed by the tyrannical commands of a ruler, America in 1776 appealed to "the Supreme Judge of the World for the Rectitude of our Intentions."[4]

In modern America, our judicial "rulers" decree that we may no longer publicly appeal to God as sovereign over man or government—there is no "Supreme Judge of the World" to which these judges are accountable. This was the "new commandment" given to the American people by a federal judge in the Alabama Ten Commandments trial of 2002, and I was there.

INTO THE JUDICIAL BUILDING

My first job out of law school was a law clerk position with the Alabama Supreme Court's Chief Justice, who had become well-known (and Chief Justice) because of his heroic defense of a small, wooden rendition of the Ten Commandments that he refused to take off his county courthouse wall in Gadsden, Alabama.

On July 31, 2001, I packed my 1989 Pontiac Bonneville to the roof and drove toward Alabama, excited about the prospects of working with a judge who understood natural law, Constitutional law, and the limited role of the judiciary. I had no idea just how much I would come to better understand the significance of such things in my new job and through the example of my new boss.

That very evening, while I was on the road to Alabama and the start of my legal career, Chief Justice Roy Moore was installing a granite monument—with the Ten Commandments on top and historical references to God on the sides—in the Alabama Judicial Building, sparking a national debate about the proper role of God and religion in government. The "Ten

Commandments Judge," it seemed, was still practicing what he preached.

THE TRIAL

"God save the United States and this Honorable Court." With those preliminary words acknowledging God, the federal court came to order in the October 2002 trial to determine whether Chief Justice Moore could acknowledge God through his Ten Commandments monument.

Those of us on Chief Justice Moore's side of the courtroom hoped the preliminary invocation for Divine blessing was sincere and not a mere ceremonial formality. (We also did not fail to note the ironic monument prominently featured outside this federal courthouse: a golden bust of a Greek goddess of justice named Themis, situated between two waterfall "scales of justice.")

The Chief Justice had been brought before federal judge Myron Thompson because he actually believed that a state official had the right to acknowledge Almighty God (as opposed to false Greek gods), and that God really could "save the United States," including Alabama, from the moral depths to which it had plummeted. To that end, Chief Justice Moore had placed the Ten Commandments monument in the rotunda of the Alabama Judicial Building to acknowledge God as the moral foundation of our country's laws and justice systems.

The case encompassed more than just the issue of whether the Ten Commandments could be displayed in a government building, and it featured more than just the American Civil Liberties Union (ACLU) & Co. versus Chief Justice Moore. Those of us who were a part of the trial—including Judge Thompson—understood that much more was at stake: the meaning and authority of the Constitution, the proper role and limited power of civil government, and the right of a state and its officials to acknowledge Almighty God and His sovereignty.

Chief Justice Moore, by acknowledging the sovereignty of *God* over men and governments (including judges), had gone too far. Judge Thompson would have none of it because, as any good tyrant knows, a competitor for sovereign power must not be tolerated—especially One of a Divine Nature.

In opening statements, Judge Thompson was told that Chief Justice Moore's purpose in "placing the Ten Commandments monument in the Supreme Court of Alabama" was "to acknowledge God's law and God's sovereignty."[5]

But those words were first argued, not by Chief Justice Moore's attorneys, but by the lead attorney for the *plaintiffs*: Morris Dees, head of the so-called Southern Poverty Law Center, which had brought the lawsuit together with the ACLU and Americans United for Separation of Church and State. Dees's intent, of course, was to paint Chief Justice Moore's actions as unconstitutional and even as extremist. But at least he got the whole point of the monument and correctly explained it to the judge.

Herb Titus, in his opening statement on behalf of Chief Justice Moore, eloquently explained what was at stake in the case.

> "This is a case about freedom versus censorship. This case is part of a movement underway across the nation to misuse the Establishment Clause as a sword to sensor the historic relationship between God and our government by prohibiting the open and public acknowledgment of God by our elected government officials.

While those who lead this movement claim that God must be censored from the public square in order to protect religious liberty, the opposite is the case.

For the public acknowledgment of God as the source of our liberties is absolutely essential if we are to preserve those liberties. As the Declaration of Independence attests, if the source of individual rights is not God, then our rights are not inalienable, and if you take God out of the equation, then the all-powerful state is unchecked by any higher law."[6]

Amazingly, Judge Thompson interrupted Mr. Titus shortly after he had begun his opening statement, something that trial judges *rarely* do. "Am I to understand, then," Judge Thompson interjected, "that the essence of the argument is the monument was placed in the Supreme Court building *so that God would be a check on the actions of the state*?"[7]

From the outset, Judge Thompson realized that the message of this Ten Commandments monument and the beliefs of the Chief Justice that installed it were threatening the scope of his power as a federal judge by recognizing an Authority higher than his own, by actually acknowledging God as *God*.

Morris Dees was also concerned about the message of the monument. When Chief Justice Moore took the witness stand, Dees interrogated him:

"Q. Do you agree that the monument, the Ten Commandments monument, reflects the sovereignty of God over the affairs of men?

"A . Yes.

> "Q. And the monument is also intended to acknowledge God's overruling power over the affairs of men, would that be correct?
>
> "A. It reflects those concepts, the laws of nature and of nature's God. . . .Yes."[8]

Chief Justice Moore's testimony was thorough and educational. (It should be required reading for every law student.) He reiterated many of the same themes that he had touched upon when he unveiled the monument (and in speeches thereafter): that there was a moral foundation to our law that was being eroded, especially in the courts of our land; that the law of God provided that moral standard for our law; that America and her several states historically and presently acknowledged God and His sovereignty throughout our governmental institutions and practices; and that our sense of, and right to, liberty and justice will be lost if we cease to acknowledge that we are "one nation under God" because the government will have assumed the role of ultimate sovereign. He explained at trial:

> "I put the monument in the building for the purpose of restoring the moral foundation of law. And to do that, one must recognize the source of those moral laws, which is God. And when you recognize the source of those moral laws, it returns the knowledge of God to the land, the source of your life, liberty, property. And so the purpose was to restore the moral foundation."[9]

By acknowledging God, Chief Justice Moore argued, he was following similar, constitutionally-sound examples throughout our country, such as the Declaration of Independence, the Pledge of Allegiance, our national motto, and even the prayer at the beginning of court (even Judge Thompson's court).

Likewise, the same Alabama Constitution that granted him authority as Chief Justice established the state's justice system (of which he was the head) "invoking the favor and guidance of Almighty God." He simply had to acknowledge that God upon Whom the Alabama justice system was based or else he would not be faithful to his oath to Alabama's Constitution. The Ten Commandments monument similarly acknowledged God; it was not a "law respecting an establishment of religion," which the "Establishment Clause" of the First Amendment prohibits.

Chief Justice Moore's team reminded Judge Thompson that he was also under the Constitution, the "supreme Law of the Land." The Establishment Clause of the First Amendment states that "Congress shall make no law respecting an establishment of religion."

This is the law that the plaintiffs accused Chief Justice Moore of violating. Chief Justice Moore and his attorneys argued that an acknowledgment of God (like the monument) does not violate the Establishment Clause because it is not, of course, a "law" and it is not "respecting an establishment of religion," under the proper and traditional definition of the word "religion."

James Madison and the Virginia Constitution (even to this day) defined "religion" as "the duties we owe to our Creator and the manner of discharging them."[10] Thus, religion encompasses duties that we fulfill and methods of fulfilling those duties, not simply acknowledging God as sovereign. Under any reading of the words of the First Amendment, therefore, the Ten Commandments monument did not violate it.

The primary concern we had was whether Judge Thompson would actually understand the argument that a state and its officials have the right to acknowledge God, His sovereignty, and His laws as the moral foundation of our own—or that Judge Thompson would at least recognize that as the main issue in this case. Morris Dees and the plaintiffs seemed to understand what was at stake. Moreover, Chief Justice Moore had testified extensively about the right to acknowledge God. Our answer came in closing arguments.

Judge Thompson stated in closing arguments, "And so the monument itself, then, if I'm understanding you correctly, is this acknowledgment of God and in itself serves, then, as a check on the state and what the state can and cannot do?"[11] Steve Melchior, one of the Chief Justice's attorneys, agreed. Shortly thereafter, Judge Thompson said to Melchior, "I think we can all agree that the monument acknowledges God."[12]

Just to make sure there was no misunderstanding, Melchior laid the issue bare before Judge Thompson: "so right now sitting square before this District Court, no games or anything like that, is: can the state acknowledge God?"[13] Judge Thompson's response was encouraging:

> "I think that is basically it. You know, I would almost think I would have to start my opinion that way. The issue is, can the state acknowledge God? I think you said it. And I think perhaps in many ways I doubt the plaintiffs will disagree with you on that."[14]

That evening and in the days thereafter, Chief Justice Moore would often exclaim, "You know, Judge Thompson understands the issue! He really got it!" We were encouraged and a bit amazed that the judge was able to see clearly that the acknowledgment of God and His sovereignty over man was at stake in this case. Some of us even held out hope that his decision would be in our favor.

REX LEX

When Judge Thompson issued his decision that the monument was unconstitutional, we were sorely disappointed. When we actually read the opinion, we were stunned. The monument was not unconstitutional, Thompson held, simply because the Ten Commandments were on it; what made it unconstitutional was that Chief Justice Moore placed the monument in the Alabama Judicial Building "with the specific purpose and effect, as the court finds from the evidence, of acknowledging the Judeo-Christian God as the moral foundation of our laws."[15]

Judge Thompson certainly understood what Chief Justice Moore had done, and he did not like one bit of it.

> "[T]he court disagrees . . . that, *as a matter of American law*, the Judeo-Christian God must be recognized as sovereign over the state, or even that *the state* may adopt that view. This is an opinion about the structure of American government, rather than a matter of religious conscience, that the court feels fully comfortable refusing to accept."[16]

Judge Thompson felt "fully comfortable" rejecting the sovereignty of God over the state, and he dismissed any such notions as the Chief Justice's own subjective religious beliefs:

> "[W]hile the Chief Justice is free to keep whatever religious beliefs he chooses, *the state* may not acknowledge the sovereignty of the Judeo-Christian God and attribute to that God our religious freedoms."[17]

Judge Thompson could not recognize that God was sovereign over him – no tyrant would – and through the guise of the United States Constitution, he made sure Chief Justice Moore would not get away with publicly acknowledging God either. Chief Justice Moore simply could have surrounded the Ten Commandments with other historical documents and portrayed it as a stale "secular" museum display that would not have threatened Judge Thompson's reign.

Instead, Chief Justice Moore had given God's law a prominent position on top of the monument, all by itself, as a clear acknowledgment of God's superiority. At the end of his opinion, Judge Thompson made just that point, reiterating that the problem with the monument was not the presence of the Ten Commandments, but that through it Chief Justice Moore recognized God as sovereign over man:

> "If all Chief Justice Moore had done were to emphasize the Ten Commandments' historical and educational importance (for the evidence shows that they have been one of the sources of our secular laws) or their importance as a model code for good citizenship (for we all want our children to honor their parents, not to kill, not to steal, and so forth), this court would have a much different case before it.
>
> But the Chief Justice did not limit himself to this; he went far, far beyond. He installed [the monument] with the specific purpose and effect of establishing a permanent recognition of the "sovereignty of God," the Judeo-Christian God, over all citizens in this country. . . . To this, the Establishment Clause says no."[18]

Judge Thompson's misuse of the Establishment Clause to effect the removal of the monument was as stunning as his attempt to remove God as sovereign. Judge Thompson refused to define the word "religion" in the First Amendment, but nevertheless concluded that Chief Justice Moore had violated the First Amendment. He said it would be "unwise, and even dangerous" to define the word "religion."[19] In other words, he could not define religion, but Chief Justice Moore had established it! By his own admission, he was not applying the law in the case, but his own judicial power.

Chief Justice Moore argued in vain that Judge Thompson had no authority under the First and Tenth Amendments to order him to remove the monument, and that Chief Justice Moore would violate his own oath to the Alabama and United States constitutions if he removed the granite acknowledgment of God.

But a judge who has denied the sovereignty of God is hardly inclined to subject himself to the law. Judge Thompson ordered the monument removed and intimidated other state officials to remove the monument he deemed "impermissible" because it acknowledged the sovereignty of God.

ARBITRARY POWER

"Tyranny" was defined by the English philosopher John Locke as "the exercise of power beyond right, which no body has a right to."[20] Locke, whose 17th-Century writings heavily influenced the Founding Fathers, rightly observed that "wherever the power, that is put in any hands for the government of the people, and the preservation of their properties, is applied to other ends, and made use of to impoverish, harass, or subdue them to the arbitrary and irregular commands of those who have it; there it presently becomes tyranny, whether those that thus use it are one or many."[21]

Whether as "one or many," whenever judges interfere with the inalienable right to acknowledge God and His sovereignty, they "exercise power beyond right" and, like our last and former king, establish a regime of tyranny over the people and civil servants of this country.

Whenever those in government cease to acknowledge the sovereignty of God or his moral law, man becomes the ultimate sovereign and government is accountable to no one and no higher law.

If the 20th Century has taught us anything, it is that atheistic, communist regimes produce the cruelest acts and most tyrannical of governments, denying the sovereignty of God and the dignity of every man. In the 1950's, America responded to last century's tyrannical atheism with the affirmation that we are "one nation under God" and that our national motto is "In God We Trust."[22] Will we halt the judicial erosion of references to God and His sovereignty or, as the late President Ronald Reagan once warned, will we become simply a nation "gone under"?[23]

By his own admission, Judge Thompson banished the Ten Commandments monument because it acknowledged a power higher than his own. Having rid himself of any accountability to the Highest Authority, therefore, it was an easy task for Judge Thompson to reject the authority of the highest human institution over him—the Constitution. But Judge Thompson was hardly forging new ground; rather he was following the lead of the United States Supreme Court and much of the federal judiciary.

In a 1958 case called *Cooper v. Aaron*, the Supreme Court held that its own interpretations of the Constitution—not the Constitution itself—were the "supreme law of the land."

Despite their oaths to the Constitution—not other judges—most federal judges elevate the opinions of judges above the words of the Constitution itself. Judge Thompson was merely enforcing the orthodoxy of supremacy that most federal judges hold to. They are jealous sovereigns, and they tolerate no God before them. "Where-ever law ends," warned John Locke, "tyranny begins."[24]

Tyranny will continue unchecked only so long as the people oppressed by it do not recognize it as tyranny. I have witnessed arbitrary judicial action in our land, and I will not shrink from calling it what the Founding Fathers would have called it: tyranny. In one sweeping case, a federal judge in Alabama rejected both the "Supreme Judge" and the "Supreme Law" of the land. As in 1776, such acts rightly "define a Tyrant" and one "unfit to be the Ruler of a free people."

IN GOD WE TRUST

Those concerned about judicial tyranny can easily become disheartened in the midst of repeated apparent defeats. After all, Chief Justice Moore lost his federal case, refused to remove the acknowledgment of God, and was himself removed from office for such a stand. But the big picture is that God never relinquishes His sovereignty, and man will always be tempted to "be as gods."[25]

The crucial question is not whether God, in fact, *is* sovereign, but whether men and governments instituted among them will rightly *acknowledge* Him as sovereign (*i.e.*, as God). Our first President, George Washington, reminded America of a self-evident truth, that "it is the duty of all nations to acknowledge the Providence of Almighty God, to obey His will, to be grateful for His benefits and humbly to implore His protection and favor."[26]

In God we *must* trust.

3.

THE POWER OF OUR TRUE HISTORY

By Dave Meyer

Eight years ago a missionary gave me a book that transformed my life. Before this time I was a good Christian because of my knowledge of the Word of God, but a helpless and hopeless citizen because of my ignorance of the heritage that had been passed down to me. It was there all along, but I could neither appreciate it nor help to maintain it because I had almost no knowledge of it.

I soon learned that almost all Christians were in the same condition I was in – total ignorance concerning our heritage. How could this be? How could our past be totally forgotten – wiped out with little or no knowledge of it? It almost seemed impossible. How could we forget this God-inspired story – His-Story – of how this nation had been birthed and established, how it had grown from its fragile beginnings to the most powerful nation on the face of the earth?

WHAT WAS THE PRICE?

1. The men and women that sacrificed their lives, families, and fortunes because of their vision.

2. The wars that were fought to gain and maintain our independence.

3. The miracles that our God had performed to assure this freedom that we all enjoy and yet take so much for granted.

Why was I, a good Christian, uninformed? I soon found out while reading *America's Providential History* and then many other books on our heritage.

1. Why I was ignorant;
2. That my ignorance was not by accident;
3. That almost all Christians know very little, if anything, about our powerful Christian heritage.

As I read about our history, it became very clear to me that Satan's goal was to remove all evidence of God, and eventually God Himself, from our history first, and finally our nation. As I studied the true history of our country, I began to see Satan's step-by-step plan to destroy this nation going back to 1870, when a Harvard Law School Dean by the name of Christopher Columbus Langdell introduced the philosophy of positivism, which is relativism used in the legal sense.

The goal of this philosophy was to do away with the system by which our nation had been governed since its conception, which was a government based upon laws formed by the absolute standards of God's Word.

According to constitutional scholar and law professor John Eidsmoe, this philosophy is characterized by the following five major theses:[1]

> 1. There are no objective, God-given standards of law, or if there are, they are irrelevant to the modern legal system.
>
> 2. Since God is not the author of law, the author of law must be man; in other words, the law is law simply because the highest human authority, the state, has said it is law and is able to back it up.
>
> 3. Since man and society evolve, therefore, law must evolve as well.
>
> 4. Judges, through their decisions, guide the evolution of law.
>
> 5. To study law, get at the original sources of law – the decisions of judges.

It is clearly evident that this philosophy has denied the absolute standards of God's Word and ignored our Constitution, which is based on these standards. This idea, which was introduced so many years ago as a seed, has grown into a monster that is trying to destroy our government and, ultimately, our way of life.

Evidence of this is clearly seen in the evolving anarchy of our judicial system. Just two examples, and there are many, are:

Benjamin Cardozo (1870-1938), appointed to the Supreme Court in 1932, openly refused to be bound by a concept of transcendent laws or fixed rights and wrongs:

> "If there is any law, which is back of the sovereignty of the state, and superior thereto, it is not law in such a sense as to concern the judge or lawyer, however much it concerns the statesman or the moralist."

Like many of his predecessors, Cardozo also encouraged the Court to eliminate the use of its foundational precedents. He even condoned the prospect of the Court departing from its traditional role and instead, assuming the function of lawmaker. As he explained:

> "I take judge-made law as one of the existing realities of life."[2]

Reflective of this same philosophy, Charles Evans Hughes (1862-1948), the Court's Chief Justice from 1930 to 1941, declared that:

> "We are under a Constitution, but the Constitution is what the judges say it is."[3]

These decisions and statements are just a few of many from our past that have reshaped our judicial system; from a system where unelected, appointed officials' jobs were to interpret, or make judgment, according to the original intent of the Constitution to a system where they now establish law as they desire.

The Constitution clearly defines by whom, and how, this nation is to be governed. It identifies the three branches – legislative, executive, judicial - and clearly defines the boundaries of each one. And the responsibility of each branch is to make sure these boundaries are maintained.

For instance, in the U.S. Constitution, Article 1, Section 8 defines the responsibilities of Congress. One of these responsibilities is Congress shall have power to make all laws. Since this is how the Constitution reads, no other branch but Congress can make laws. Furthermore, if either of the other two branches does make laws, they are in direct violation of the Constitution. This violation is a fact today in some judicial decisions. What can we as law-abiding citizens do?

According to the preamble of the Constitution, we (meaning each citizen) have both the authority and responsibility to hold the elected officials of this government accountable. The preamble to the U.S. Constitution reads:

> "We the people of the United States, in order to form a more perfect Union, establish justice, insure domestic tranquility, provide for the defense, promote the general welfare, and secure the blessings of liberty to ourselves and our posterity, do ordain and establish this Constitution for the United States of America."

As you can see, we the people ordained and established this Constitution. Therefore, we the people are responsible to see that it is maintained, as President Abraham Lincoln stated in the famous Gettysburg Address. His final words were that this nation under God shall have a new birth of freedom and that the government of the people, by the people, shall not perish from the earth.

Well then, why are we as citizens not taking our authority and fulfilling our responsibility? As I mentioned in the beginning of this chapter, I was, and almost all Christians are, ignorant of their heritage and the legacy that has been left to them. I also mentioned that this ignorance was not by accident, but planned systematically, step by step. Much of our history has been revised and/or removed from our history books. Our entire godly heritage has been extracted to the point that, by comparison, a history book from 100 years ago and a history book from today are almost unrecognizable as being about the same history.

The reason for this is two-fold. First, our vision is found in our true history, and the Bible in Proverbs 29:18 says, "Where there is no vision, the people perish."

Secondly, the Bible says in Hosea 4:6, "My people are destroyed for lack of knowledge." Satan, through people, has been on a mission to destroy our nation, and his primary tool, as has been the case throughout all history, is ignorance. His means of operation is deception. Therefore, he is known as the Great Deceiver. Who is easier to deceive than those that are ignorant?

All we have to do is look at the last sixty years of our history to recognize this deception.

In 1947, the judicial decision of the separation of church and state, was based upon the twisting of the First Amendment of the U.S. Constitution. The First Amendment in reality reads "Congress shall make no law respecting an establishment of religion or prohibiting the free exercise thereof," and is the only place in the Constitution where it forbids Congress to make a law.

As I shared earlier, Article 1, Section 8 of the U.S. Constitution reveals that Congress shall have the power to make all laws, with the exception of the restriction in the First Amendment that states, "Congress can make no law concerning an establishment of religion or the free exercise thereof." The actual text of the First Amendment forbids the acceptance of this gross misinterpretation of the amendment that the judiciary has forced upon us. Without opposition by the public in general, and the body of Christ in particular, we opened the door for Satan to begin to dismantle the authority and power of the Church, one right at a time.

The specific purpose of the first part of the First Amendment was to protect the church from the government. But what was meant for the protection of the Church was twisted and now has become a weapon against the Church. This happened as a result of a lack of understanding of the Constitution - the governing document of the country - by the church.

As a result of this, lie became truth, and the rest is history. Prayer was removed from school, and then followed the Ten Commandments. The mention of God was removed from history books; and war memorials could no longer have crosses to mark gravesites. Nativity scenes were removed from public sites, etc., etc. All this happened with almost no opposition. Why? Because we were ignorant.

Well, I said all that to say this: we must not be ignorant any longer. If we are, we only have ourselves to blame. We will be accountable to God and our children, for they will reap from our diligence or failure.

Psalm 1:1-2 says, "Blessed (happy, fortunate, prosperous, and enviable) is the man who walks and lives not in the counsel of the ungodly [following their advice, their plans and purposes], nor stands [submissive and inactive] in the path where sinners walk, nor sits down [to relax and rest] where the scornful [and the mockers] gather. But his delight and desire are in the law of the Lord, and on His law (the precepts, the instructions, the teachings of God) he habitually meditates (ponders and studies) by day and by night."

As you will notice in the first part of Psalm, this person was blessed (happy, fortunate, prosperous and enviable) because he educated himself in the Word of God, and as a result, learned to take action as revealed in the second part of verse 1. He did not live in the council of the ungodly, nor did he stand submissive and inactive in the path of sinners. Remember, you need to make a decision for right (omission is submission). Nor did he sit down where the scornful and mockers gather. Also remember silence is acceptance.

As I close this chapter, I want to express my thankfulness for the knowledge that I now possess of this incredible adventure with which God has blessed each person who has been granted the privilege to live in this nation. My only regret is that I did not possess this knowledge long ago. It has changed my life, increased my faith, and brought me great joy.

We, at Joyce Meyer Ministries, offer this knowledge to you through these books on the true history and godly heritage of your country. Also, through our web site, at www.joycemeyer.org, you can learn how to fulfill your responsibility as a Christian and a citizen. Duty is ours; the results belong to God.

4.

A CHRISTIAN AMERICA?

By David C. Gibbs III, Esq.

It cannot be emphasized too strongly or too often that this great nation was founded, not by religionists, but by Christians; not on religions, but on the gospel of Jesus Christ! For this very reason peoples of other faiths have been afforded asylum, prosperity, and freedom of worship.

—Patrick Henry (attrib.)

America today is a nation of people struggling to find their roots, but unable to do so because they refuse to recognize that those roots are sunk deep into the soil of Biblical revelation. This struggle to find our roots is primarily being fought today in the judicial arena. Whether America thrives or flounders in the 21st Century will primarily depend upon who wins the battle for the courts in this generation.

For one hundred fifty years after the Declaration of Independence proclaimed freedom from England, Americans and their leaders universally recognized the Biblical foundations that formed the basis for our nation's legal system. America's last great act under this Biblical heritage was the freeing of the slaves following the Civil War.

President Abraham Lincoln rightly understood in the mid-19th Century that God alone was the grantor of America's rights. He understood that the Almighty had given these rights to every person in all times and in all places, including African slaves who had been brought to America against their will. By the close of the 19th Century, however, America's leading jurists had set themselves on another course—one that was intended to obscure and deny a recognition of the hand of God in this nation's legal system.

Prior to 1900, American lawyers studied the law using a book by William Blackstone, *Commentaries on the Laws of England*. The first one hundred forty pages of this book outlined the Biblical precepts and principles that controlled the law. The rest of the book noted how this Biblical law was being interpreted in England. America's Founders used Blackstone's principles to undergird the legal system of their newly emerging nation. In fact, Blackstone's four-volume *Commentaries*, published by 1767, just a decade before the Declaration of Independence, became more popular in America than in England. America was a blank slate for the emergence of a new legal system based entirely on the principles of the Biblical God.

After 1900, legal trendsetters like Christopher Columbus Langdell at the new Harvard Law School deliberately substituted evolutionary legal principles for the fixed, immutable and unchanging laws of God that had previously been universally accepted in American jurisprudence. Charles Darwin had published his earth-shattering book promoting evolution, *Origin of the Species*, in 1859. The biology principles outlined in that book almost immediately began to infiltrate into other areas of learning. One of these areas was the law, where some jurists had already been seeking a way to eliminate God from the legal equation.

By the 1870s, Oliver Wendell Holmes, Jr. saw the solution to an American legal system without God in the evolutionary principles of Charles Darwin. Holmes, who was lauded as a great legal philosopher and jurist, boldly announced in the 1870s that there was no "brooding omnipresence in the sky" (i.e. God) that mankind was obligated to be subordinate to in the legal arena. Holmes' ideas were heralded by other legal thinkers of that day as a new, modern theory destined to leave behind the religious underpinnings of the past which these jurists believed were holding back progress in the law.

By the beginning of the 20th Century, elite academics in new law schools were well underway toward undermining the authority of God in the law. Legal educators were abandoning the Biblical principles that had been memorialized in the Declaration of Independence, enshrined in the Constitution, and taught in Blackstone's *Commentaries*. Lawyers began to attend law schools that ignored Blackstone and taught a far-reaching, progressive legal theory of case precedents that permitted the law to evolve, expand and grow in whatever shape these jurists desired.

This was the beginning of judicial tyranny in America. Judges no longer saw themselves as subordinate to God's law, but believed they could alter the law for themselves in any way they saw fit.

After this deliberate judicial move away from God, American jurisprudence coasted for half a century on the collective Biblical memory of the past. But, after a Supreme

Court case in the 1930s that officially abandoned all law based on religion, this memory became increasingly faded and jaded. By the 1960s, American culture began to join the chorus of these evolutionary, anti-God legal philosophers. Since then, the God of the Bible that guided and inspired the Founders and American jurists for nearly two centuries has been gradually pushed out of America's legal system.

HOW DO WE KNOW THESE THINGS?

It is clear from an objective reading of our founding documents that the language of Thomas Jefferson in the Declaration of Independence, of James Madison in the Constitution, and of the original constitutions of all 13 colonies prior to 1776 mirrored the language used by William Blackstone. His *Commentaries* were published in the 1760s, just in time for the American experiment in freedom. These *Commentaries* sold more copies in America than in England, where the law was already moving away from these Biblical moorings.

The *Commentaries on the Laws of England* outlined the development of English law, which began as far back as 1000 A.D. When Jesus did not return at the first millennium as many expected, the church had to reorient itself toward discovering how mankind could best live in a protracted worldly society. Medieval thinkers began to formulate a political and legal system for the long haul, first using canon (church) law and then developing (civil) law from that religious legal base.

These deeply religious thinkers and medieval scholastics recognized that the Bible contains a double revelation of God—a revelation of faith, by which to guide man in his relationship to God, and also a revelation of morals, by which to guide man's relationship to others in society. The development of this legal adaptation of God's fixed and immutable moral laws dealing with the organization of societies in all times and in all places occurred over a period of several hundred years. It was this law that Blackstone finally set down in writing in his *Commentaries*, complete with Scripture references on almost every page. And it was this book that inspired the Founders and educated every generation of lawyers and judges in America for its first one hundred fifty years.

WHAT WERE THE BIBLICAL PRINCIPLES THAT UNDERGIRDED AMERICA'S FOUNDING?

First and foremost, Blackstone, the Founders, and all early American lawyers and judges recognized that God had created a people for Himself, entirely dependent, not only upon the physical laws of the universe, but also upon equally applicable moral laws. God's moral laws are as immutable and fixed as the laws of gravity and physics, said Blackstone.

Following these moral laws in society, Blackstone noted, is essential for the happiness of mankind. The "pursuit of happiness" language in the Declaration of Independence found its basis here. Mankind had also been given life (personal security) and liberty (personal freedom) as part of the image of God bestowed upon Adam and Eve, but clouded by sin at the Fall. If sin had not entered the world, Blackstone noted, Adam and Eve could have discerned the natural moral laws (natural law) of the universe in the same way that mankind can discover the physical laws set in motion by God through pure scientific endeavors. But because sin entered the picture in the Fall, God was obligated to supplement His natural law (referred to as "the laws of Nature" in the Declaration of Independence) with an additional written revelation in the Bible ("the law of . . . Nature's God" in the Declaration).

Thus equipped, mankind is able to discern those moral precepts and principles of government that best lead to the happiness of mankind living together in human societies. The "pursuit of happiness" enshrined in the Declaration of Independence was a phrase recognizing that mankind's happiness depends upon a right understanding and implementation in society of the fixed, immutable, and unchanging moral laws of God. No law enacted by man, Blackstone said, was legitimate unless it reflected the moral law of God as revealed in the Bible. That is the primary reason, for instance, why murder, adultery, theft, and lying are wrong. These basic principles are found in the Ten Commandments – the basis for both Biblical faith and American law.

All governments must be grounded in God's moral revelation in order to function properly. Therefore, all societies must be based upon God's foundational principle of families, beginning with one man and one woman united for life. That, for example, is the real reason why homosexual marriage is wrong for all societies. That is also the primary reason why today's homosexual advocates and many judges who support this movement are so intent on simultaneously undermining Biblical faith in America through judicial tyranny expressed in an invented legal principle of "separation of church and state," which was judicially imposed beginning with a United States Supreme Court decision in 1947.

The Supreme Court's support of abortion in 1973 is illegitimate for the same reason. Supreme Court justices do not have the authority to contradict God's moral code and call it law. The erroneous legal reasoning by the Supreme Court in *Roe v. Wade,* nevertheless, as well as in its recent rulings on homosexuality and even the Pledge of Allegiance, are merely the logical culmination of one hundred years of an evolving legal philosophy that began heading down the wrong road in 1872 when Oliver Wendell Holmes, Jr. declared the death of God in the legal world.

Abraham Lincoln still recognized America's foundation in the moral law of God when he declared in his 1859

Presidential campaign that slavery and the Supreme Court's decision upholding it in the *Dred Scott* decision were not law because they contradicted the moral law of God. The Founders had declared the equality of all mankind in the Declaration of Independence, but a paradox was created by the 3/5 compromise in the Constitution, a measure intended by the North to lessen the political strength of Southern slave states by counting slaves as only 3/5 of a person for apportionment purposes.

This paradox was finally eliminated by the Fourteenth Amendment, which recognized that all men truly are imbued with the image of God and are, therefore, all guaranteed the rights of life (personal security), liberty (to perform their duties to God) and the pursuit of happiness (the freedom to conform to God's laws which was recognized as the only path to true happiness). Some legal commentators have noted that the third inalienable right (the pursuit of happiness) also involves the right to own property, another foundational right recognized in the constitutions of the original thirteen colonies. In no case, however, did the pursuit of happiness ever imply the licentiousness that characterizes its understanding in modern American law.

William Blackstone and America's Founders recognized that these three rights (life, liberty and the pursuit of happiness) are inalienable because they are part of the image of God given to mankind at Creation. Therefore, like the legal concept of inalienable property, citizens are not able to sell, give away, or otherwise divest themselves of these rights. These rights are a foundational part of what it means to be a human being created in the image of God. These rights are recognized, not bestowed, by government.

Today, American jurists have begun to adopt the legal reasoning of Europe's Enlightenment jurisprudence, which argued then and argues still, that the rights of citizens are not bestowed by God, but by the state. If our rights are granted by the state, however, they are not inalienable because the state can take them away (witness the legalization of abortion in which the state has purported to take away the inalienable right to life of tiny humans created in the image of God, who are, for the moment, hidden from view within their mother's wombs). Blackstone correctly argued that no law of man is a valid law if it contradicts the moral laws of God. That is the only legitimate basis upon which to oppose the legalization of abortion or of homosexual marriage. The moral law of God was the basis for all law in the Declaration of Independence, America's Articles of Incorporation, and in the Constitution, America's Bylaws.

It is absolutely amazing to consider how strange this basic American legal philosophy now sounds in a nation where every citizen is considered "free" to live his life in any sort of licentious manner. But Blackstone and America's Founders believed that all rights and all freedom must be based upon the recognition of every citizen's individual duty owed to the Biblical Creator God. Every American freedom granted in the Declaration of Independence was originally recognized by the Founders as arising from a corresponding individually owed duty to God.

Every man created by God is duty bound to subordinate himself to God. America was founded specifically to protect and defend the rights of every citizen to carry out this duty to God the Creator, as each sees fit. Included in man's duties to God are the duties that God-fearing men owe to one another when they live together in society.

But the Founders never envisioned the existence or protection of any rights, such as the alleged right to pornography or sexual license, that were not grounded in mankind's individual duties owed to the Biblical God. On the other hand, the Founders did envision the protection of the religious expression of every individual in America because God does not force faith on anyone. Faith is a free gift of God to be received or rejected. That is why Buddhists, Muslims, and atheists are just as protected in America as Christians, and they are every bit as able to practice their own faith or lack thereof on our shores.

One of the most important principles expounded by Blackstone was that law may only be imposed on an inferior by a superior. God is the only superior able to impose moral laws upon mankind. That imposition is primarily what many modern citizens and jurists are seeking to avoid today in our new American law. Since every man is equally subject to God, the Creator and Sustainer of the universe, individual government officials may only impose their own ideas of the law in areas where God has not clearly spoken. One popular example would be whether to set the speed limit at 50 or 60 miles per hour (called municipal law by Blackstone).

God did not discuss modern superhighways and speed limits in His Biblical law, so the people are free in these areas (called "indifferent" areas by Blackstone) to decide the law for themselves. However, where God has clearly spoken in His Word, such as in the organization of societies by family units and in the prohibition of murder and theft, any laws imposed by governments or judges that are contrary to the moral laws of God are illegitimate. That is the Biblical basis upon which America was founded. It is a heritage we barely remember in 21st Century America, but which we urgently need to celebrate and reclaim if we intend to protect and maintain our unique and free nation and our precious system of government and law.

Judicial tyranny sets itself up against the laws of God and seeks to organize society by its own rules. We Americans must return our legal system to Godly principles if we expect our nation to endure for another two hundred fifty years as it has for the past two hundred fifty.

In order to do that we must oppose judicial tyranny and promote judges who respect God's law and who seek to preserve the laws of God that were incorporated by our Founders into the legal fabric of our society. It is only when we again submit our nation to God's laws that freedom can be protected for all our citizens and our nation can continue to be the America we have all known and loved.

David C. Gibbs, III, has appeared on Larry King Live, Prime Time America, Open Line and was the attorney for Terri Schiavo's family in the alarming case of her being starved to death. To contact the legal missionary ministry of the Christian Law Association, please call (727) 399-8300 or visit www.ChristianLaw.org.

5.

WHAT LAW?

By Ambassador Alan Keyes

Adapted from a speech given
August 16, 2003 in Montgomery, AL

I have to begin with a confession — which is really appropriate for a Catholic, I guess, making a confession! And I have to say that very often I stand before crowds and I believe that I speak from some knowledge that I've gained over the years, and from some meditative thought. But today, here we are in the midst of a crisis. A federal judge recently threatened the chief justice of the state of Alabama. And that judge told the justice he had to remove the Ten Commandments from the courthouse.

Now all these people have been running about telling us that if we stand against the pronouncements of this judge, that we're somehow breaking the law; that we are somehow showing contempt for the Constitution. I've got to tell you, for all my life I have done my best to stand for a few things. Chief among them is respect for Almighty God and all that He enjoins upon us with His blessings and His gifts and wealth and power and responsibilities that He has showered upon our nation. So implied in that respect for Him and His Authority has been respect for the Constitution of the United States.

And I want to tell you, I would not stand anywhere where my standing could be construed in a way that undercut or damaged the Constitution of this country, on which I believe our liberties depend.

But there is something I don't understand. This is my ignorance, because I've thought about it. I've read a fair amount about the Constitution and our ordered liberty, about institutions and laws, and so forth.

Will somebody point out to me the law that this federal judge is basing his decision on? Because if I'm breaking the law and if Judge Moore is breaking the law, I'd like to know which one it is. I'd like to know who passed it. I'd like to know where it's written.

They tell me that if somehow or other I don't respect this doctrine of the "separation of church and state," that I am therefore disrespecting the Constitution. I sat down again the other day and I scoured the Constitution. The Constitution is not a very long document, by the way; you can get through it in a fairly short time. That was the brilliance of our Founders. It didn't take them 100,000 pages. It's not like the treaty that established the World Trade Organization that 10,000 people couldn't get through in 10,000 years.

No, you can sit down and read the Constitution in a short session. I scoured it. I looked through it once, I looked through it twice, and I looked through it a dozen times. I didn't find a single mention of this separation of church and state.

Religious establishment is forbidden? Is that right? No, that's not what's forbidden. The First Amendment actually says, "Congress shall make no law respecting an establishment of religion, or restricting the free exercise thereof." It is forbidden for Congress to touch this question. It is forbidden for Congress to address it. It is forbidden for Congress to deal with it. If Congress is forbidden to make a law, how can this judge enforce a law that Congress cannot have made?

Let's read it again. "Congress shall make no law respecting an establishment of religion, or restricting the free exercise thereof." Now, I want to stop there because, you know, I'm middle-aged now. And I've got to tell you, as you age – when you're young it's bad enough. As you get a little older, this business of exercise becomes a real challenge. It has been for me. And I still have a son young enough that I've got to be encouraging him to get his body ready for high school and get out there and run and work. And you've got to lead by example. So exercise has been much on my mind.

One thing I've noticed about it, as much as I wish it were not so, is that simply sitting back in my easy chair thinking about it doesn't help. Having a firm opinion about it, believing deeply in exercise - that doesn't make my body stronger. Last time I looked, exercise means that you've got to get up out of the chair and act on what's in your heart. You've got to live it out in what you do, in what you say, in how you act, in how you govern your life.

All the liberals in this country have tried to put us in a "privacy" box where freedom of religion means the freedom to privately believe as you choose. That is not accurate; that is not remotely adequate. The free exercise of religion means that we have the right in our families and in our schools and in our communities and in our governments and in our states to live according to the Word of God.

And what I don't understand is that for most of our country's history it never occurred to judges in courts to assert any differently. It was never a question that folks didn't have the right to read the Bible at the workplace, teach it in the schools, openly respect the Law of God in their laws. It was so far from occurring to them that they acknowledged Scriptural Law as one of the foundations of our life and freedom. And in many decisions, including decisions by the Supreme Court on polygamy and so forth, it was explicitly cited as one of the bases for our understanding of law.

It's also true that this free exercise of religion was very deeply important to the people who founded the country. Why do you think many of the first colonies were founded, Massachusetts and other places like this? Religious liberty, of course. People were fleeing from war and tyranny and persecution over religious conviction and profession in Europe.

Now, what kind of persecution was it? It wasn't just the persecution of "I'm going to throw you to the lions if you don't believe what I believe." No. What they were doing in Europe in those days on one side and the other was looking at folks and saying, "I'm the sovereign; I'm the national power. And in your cities and in your provinces, you must act according to my religious belief." And there were cities and there were towns and there were provinces and there were states that stood up and said no, and they fought and the blood ran red for their right to live in communities that were governed by laws that reflected their faith.

If nothing else today, I think all of us of Christian faith and belief and conscience, and all of those who stand on a ground of Biblical tradition, all of those who believe that we cannot live without the law and rule of that God we invoke when we claim our rights, all of us must stand and make clear to the courts and to the Congress and to the president and to every power that exists that we remember now what our freedom of religion is supposed to be. And we shall demand that we be granted again what the tyranny of the courts has sought to wrest from us, the freedom to live in communities that are governed by laws that reflect our beliefs.

Our Founders were wise, though, because they looked at the terrible wars that had taken place in Europe and they didn't want it to happen here. And they realized that the root of those conflicts had been the effort of national sovereigns to impose their religious beliefs and practices on people and states and provinces and localities beneath their civil administration. So what did they do? They put an amendment in the Constitution with the wording we've talked about, wording intended to tell the Congress and thereby the national government that the whole business of religious belief, that whole business of any regime, any attitude concerning, establishing, or restricting the free exercise of religion, to be imparted through law, that all of it was none of the federal government's business.

Now, that does give rise to the possibility that there might be states in which there may be required a religious test or oath of office. There might be states in which there may be established churches where instructions are given to schools to teach the Bible. There might be places where you and I might disagree with the religion some folks wanted to put in place over their communities. But guess what the Founders believed? They believed that people in their states and localities have the right to live under institutions they would put together to govern themselves according to their faith.

Today there is, I believe going on right now, a violation of the Constitution.

There is, I believe, a lawless act against which we must stand, it is the lawless act of the federal judges who seek now to wrest from us that religious liberty which is ours, not merely by right of the Constitution, but by grant and right of the Creator God.

We have the right to our religious liberties within our communities and our states. And one clear confirmation we have that this is so, that the First Amendment didn't intend to destroy this right - and that in fact such communities could exist, such states could exist - is that at the time the First Amendment was passed, at the time our founding generation put it on the books in the first place, there were a majority of states — former colonies organized around religious affiliation and identity — where religious tests and oaths of office, and in fact, established churches, remained in effect.

Do they mean to tell us that the very people who wrote and passed the amendment then went back home to live in contradiction of its terms? This is a lie and it's time we threw this lie back into their teeth.

So does this mean I believe in religious persecution against non-believers? No, I don't; quite the contrary. But I think that what we are faced with now is an effort to set the stage for religious persecution against people of faith. Because these radical secularists claim that they are acting in order to oppose somehow the imposition of religious beliefs. But no, what they are doing in the courts, what the judges are doing when they toss out the Ten Commandments, toss out against the will of the people in the states and communities, the people's desire to show their reverence for Almighty God — what the judges are doing is imposing a uniform national regime of disbelief and atheism on the people of this country. They are doing exactly what the Constitution of the United States forbids.

Now folks want to tell me that if the judge violates the Constitution and in the decision wrests my rights of free exercise away, then I have no recourse, Judge Moore has no recourse, the people of Alabama have no recourse; we've just got to sit back and take it.

And I'm hard-pressed. I look at the history of the country and I'm scouring the pages to see where it says that that is so, and what do I stumble across but a Declaration of Independence that says when there is a long train of abuses that are destroying our rights, the Founders said that it is not only our right, it is our duty to oppose them. That's what I see.

We stand here today in a great tradition, not as our lying critics would have it - in the tradition of those who defied the courts in order to oppress and destroy the rights of their fellow human beings - but in the tradition of those who stood against unjust laws in order to stand for the rights of all our people. This is where we stand. But even as it was the case that those who stood against slavery and for civil rights, they stood in fact on the solid ground of American truth and constitutional principle. So it is today.

And I think we have to be clear. Despite the historical fact that the rights of the people have been at times wrongly invoked in their states in the name of institutions that trampled on the rights of individuals does not mean that it is always wrong to appeal to our constitutionally protected "states rights." It does not mean it is right today to stand silent while the rights of the people of the state of Alabama are trampled by a tyrannical and arbitrary federal judge.

If we can act alike, if we can act with knowledge and precision, if we can act with care and courage as we defend our liberty in this place, then it could be here today that finally we draw the line against those who seek to abuse the color of law in order to destroy the substance of liberty.

What if this happens? What if that happens? What if they come and try to take down the Ten Commandments? What if it goes to the Supreme Court and they decide differently? What then? And as I have said to folks, we've just got to know our Constitution. First of all, there is a person in this country who could solve this problem fairly easily. I have pondered the limits of authority and the proper powers of our co-equal branches of government deeply, when I was running for president a long time ago, and people used to ask me questions about distortions and remedies in our institutions of liberty.

Just imagine we wake up tomorrow and George W. Bush, having read about the Ten Commandments battle in Alabama as president of the United States says, "Okay, the judge says, Judge Moore you're breaking the law. I'm sending you this, and let it be known to everybody in the country that I pardon you now for this offense and I pardon all people in their states of all such offenses, because I believe that they are acting according to their constitutional right."

The president could solve this problem in a word, in the proper exercise of his constitutional authority in defense of our constitutional right. So might the Congress, by cutting off the funds to enforce it, as some have introduced into the Congress, by disestablishing the courts that dare to assault the rights of the people in their most fundamental guise. All these are possible courses of action, but what they should remind us of is that we live in a constitutional order in which no branch was supposed to be the absolute tyrant over the others, not the courts over the Congress and the president, not the president over the others. If the president decides that the courts are wrong, it is up to the Congress to stand against it, and if they stand with him, then the Constitution has been served.

We have three branches of government, and I hope that all Americans will stand to call on the president and call on the Congress to take courageous action, finally to put the bridle on these unruly courts. We can make the difference, but we know that what is at stake is not just the symbolic display of the Ten Commandments, it is the reverence that we must hold for them in our hearts if we are to fulfill this nation's promise of true, responsible self-government. For self-government in the end cannot come from the external impositions of law and police forces and military forces. True self-government begins where our Founders knew it began, where our Lord knew it began. True self-government begins in the heart.

And it is the heart of a people governed by respect for the Ten Commandments and the Word of God written upon their hearts. It is the heart of such a people that fits them for a freedom that will endure.

6.

WHO IS AMERICA'S SOVEREIGN?

By The Honorable Howard Phillips

Adapted from a speech given
August 16, 2003 in Montgomery, AL.

It is always disappointing to me when a politician or a judge, who is after all a politician in black robes, puts his personal ambitions ahead of his oath of office and his duty, not just to his constituents, but also to God Almighty. I'm fed up with politicians who with false pride proclaim that they will set aside their personal principles, whether the issue is *Roe v. Wade* or the Ten Commandments, in order to appease the powers that be who control their confirmations and even their appointments.

My friends, this is a crucial moment in the history of the American republic. God may choose to use the unblemished character and the undaunted courage of one faithful man to bring about a turning point in our jurisprudence and in our culture, back to biblical morality and forward to a restoration of a constitutional design and the system of liberty set forth by America's founding fathers.

James Madison was, in addition to being our fourth president, a member of the 1787 constitutional convention and one of the chief architects of that great document, the Constitution. Madison is attributed with the statement, "We have staked the whole future of American civilization, not upon the power of government, far from it. We have staked the future of all our political institutions upon the capability of mankind for self-government, upon the capacity of each and all of us to govern ourselves, to control ourselves, to sustain ourselves, **according to the Ten Commandments of God**."

Law is always the will of the sovereign. The overarching question we face today is, "who is America's sovereign, and what is his law?" Chief Justice Roy Moore knows the correct answers, but federal judge Myron Thompson flunks the test. The Holy Bible makes clear that Jesus Christ is our sovereign. He is King of Kings, Lord of Lords and the ruler of all nations.

America's founding fathers understood and acted on this biblical truth. In our Declaration of Independence they proclaimed that we are endowed by our creator with certain unalienable rights, and they enunciated the truth that government derives its just powers from the consent of the governed. In the very first article of the Constitution of the United States, the framers established the principle of accountability, investing all legislative powers therein granted in a Congress with an appointed Senate representing the states and an elected House representing the people.

Those who framed our great Constitution acknowledged that, as God's creatures, we must hold the federal government accountable to us, so that as God's stewards, we can be accountable to Him.

That is our duty, and the Constitution recognizes the fact of the duty we owe our creator and provides the means for us to do our duty. The provisions of the Constitution cannot lawfully be amended by judicial fiat or edicts from the bench. Indeed, Article V of the Constitution spells out the only authorized procedures for amending the Constitution. Nowhere does the Constitution authorize federal judges to change even a single word in the document or to disregard the plain meaning of its text.

In fact, Article VI of the Constitution makes explicitly clear that the Constitution and the laws made pursuant to it are the supreme law of the land. All judicial officials, including Judge Myron Thompson (who ordered the removal of the Alabama Ten Commandments monument) and the judges of the U.S. Eleventh Circuit Court of Appeals (who supported that order), have sworn oaths that bind them to support the Constitution as it is written, not as they would personally prefer it to be written.

As you know, the First Amendment says Congress will make no law respecting an establishment of religion or prohibiting the free exercise thereof. Clearly, if the words of the framers are honored, Congress has no authority to restrict the establishment of biblical religion in the state of Alabama, and neither has any federal judge such authority.

Congress may not interfere with the free exercise of religion nor may any federal judge interfere with the free exercise of religion. The Tenth Amendment stipulates that the powers not delegated to the United States by the Constitution nor prohibited by it to the states, are reserved to the states respectively or to the people. No federal court has had delegated to it any authority whatsoever over the placement of the Ten Commandments Monument in the Alabama Judicial Building.

Read this carefully, my friends: Judge Thompson has violated his oath of office by disregarding the words of our

U.S. Constitution and by corruptly attempting to usurp the authority of the elected chief justice of the Supreme Court of the state of Alabama. And so have the federal judges on the Eleventh Circuit Court of Appeals broken their oaths of office. Each of these federal judges has shown contempt for the Constitution. That is why we hold them in contempt. And that is why we call upon them to resign or to be removed from office.

When the true history of these times is written, school children will learn that these men are the Benedict Arnolds of American jurisprudence. Each of them should be stripped of their robes as an example to others who in their official capacities seek to supplant constitutional truths with their private anti-Christian prejudices.

The good news is that the Constitution has remedies for misconduct by federal judges. Article III, which places the judiciary in a position subordinate to the Article I Congress and the Article II executive, provides that inferior courts – and they've proven themselves inferior – such as those in which Judge Thompson and his Eleventh Circuit collaborators are installed, are ordained and established by the Congress.

By the same token, the Congress has the clear authority to remove the claims of jurisdiction and to disestablish those courts that are arrogantly and presumptuously anti-constitutional. Article III goes on to provide that federal judges shall hold their offices during "good behavior". No reasonable person could argue that when Judge Thompson breaks his oath to the Constitution and when his rulings are sustained by judges of the Eleventh Circuit Court of Appeals, that any of these men have manifested good behavior, which among other things was intended to mean fidelity to the Constitution and fidelity to the oaths which they swore before God.

Even without resort to impeachment, Congress may by legislation disestablish a court and by simple majority vote remove a federal judge for failing to manifest good behavior. If we are to maintain respect for the institutions of our federal republic, lawbreakers and oath-breakers must be removed from positions of responsibility.

Judge Moore has kept his oath to the Constitution of Alabama and to the Constitution of the United States. He has upheld the law. He has obeyed his duty to God, to the people of Alabama and to the citizens of the United States of America. I urge President George W. Bush, when the next vacancy occurs on the Supreme Court of the United States, to nominate to fill that position on the Supreme Court the man best qualified in our entire nation to uphold the Constitution of the United States and the laws of God on which that Constitution is premised.

I speak of that great patriot, that exemplary jurist, God's man for these times, the Honorable Roy Moore.

May God bless Judge Moore and his family, may God bless the people of Alabama, may God bless you, and may God bless America.

7.

THE RULE OF LAW

By Chief Justice Roy S. Moore
with John Perry

At the entrance to Washington Hall, the main dining facility for cadets at the United States Military Academy at West Point, New York, is "Constitution Corner." Located adjacent to a statue of George Washington riding a magnificent stallion, Constitution Corner reminds visitors and cadets of the purpose of the academy: To provide leaders "of principle and integrity so strong that their oaths to support and defend the Constitution will unfailingly govern their actions."[1]

The plaque on Constitution Corner, entitled "Loyalty to the Constitution," informs all who visit there that the "United States boldly broke with the ancient military custom of swearing loyalty to a leader. Article VI require[s] that American Officers thereafter swear loyalty to our Basic Law, the Constitution."[2]

Article VI of the Constitution is not only binding on officers in the military, but also on all executive, legislative, and judicial officials of both the state and federal governments. Article VI provides that "this Constitution, and the Laws of the United States which shall be made in Pursuance thereof...shall be the supreme Law of the Land; and the Judges in every State shall be bound thereby."[3]

In other words, the Constitution is our basic law, and all judges are bound to its clear meaning and its express terms. It is our "rule of law," and no judge can alter or disregard that law. That is exactly why all judges, including the justices of the United States Supreme Court, take an oath to uphold and support the Constitution of the United States.

Likewise, the express provisions of each state constitution that do not conflict with provisions of the U.S. Constitution also become a "rule of law" to which judges and other state officials in that state are bound. Judge Myron Thompson's order to remove the Ten Commandments monument because it acknowledged the Judeo-Christian God was clearly unlawful.

The express purpose of the First Amendment to the U.S. Constitution was to allow the freedom to worship God and to prevent the federal government (including the federal courts) from interfering with that right of the states and the people. All states acknowledge God in their own state constitutions, and Alabama is no exception. In fact, in the Alabama Constitution, the recognition of God is the basis of its justice system.

When Judge Myron Thompson ordered me to remove the Ten Commandments monument, he not only issued an unlawful order; he also ordered me to do something that violated my conscience and my oath to the Constitution of the United States and the constitution of the state of Alabama. Judge Thompson placed himself above the law. As a cadet at West Point, and later as a company commander in Vietnam, I knew the importance of following orders. The success or failure of a mission and the lives of others depend on strict adherence to the chain of command.

That principle of obedience to superiors is also crucial to the proper functioning of a court system. Nevertheless, the principle of obedience to superior officers is based on the premise that the order given is a lawful one. In the court-martial trial of Lieutenant William Calley, a unit commander at My Lai in Vietnam who killed more than one hundred innocent civilians, Calley defended himself by claiming that he was just following the orders of his superior, Captain Ernest Medina.

Nevertheless, Lieutenant Calley was court-martialed. The military tribunal that considered his appeal rejected his defense by saying that an order to kill civilians, even if given by a superior officer, did not excuse Calley's conduct because such orders are clearly unlawful.[4]

That is exactly the principle stated on the plaque at Constitution Corner at West Point. It states: "Our American Code of Military Obedience requires that should orders and the Law ever conflict, our officers must obey the law. Many other nations have adopted our principle of loyalty to the basic law."[5] Lieutenant William Calley's conviction confirmed that the basic law remained intact. When people who are sworn to support the law disregard it and issue orders which they think are "the law," we are governed by the rule of man, not the rule of law!

The United States did break boldly with ancient customs and practices on July 4, 1776, when it declared independence from Great Britain and established a nation under the authority of the "Laws of Nature and of Nature's God." In 1776, the American colonies knew well the history of tyrannical rule in England. On June 15, 1215, on the field of Runnymede, King John was forced to sign the Magna Charta, which consisted of a preamble and sixty-three clauses that bound the king to observe certain rights and liberties of the people.[6]

Not long afterward, in 1256, a noted legal scholar and judge, Henry de Bracton-who is considered the "Father of the

Common Law"-explained that "the king must not be under man but under God and under the law, because law makes the king."[7] De Bracton continued, "Let [the king] therefore bestow upon the law what the law bestows upon him, namely, rule and power for there is no rex [king] where will rules rather than lex [law]."[8]

This principle is displayed even today. Carved in stone above Langdell Hall at Harvard University are the words Non sub Homine sed sub Deo et lege ("not under man but under God and law"), to remind us that the governing authorities, whether king or president, are not under man, but under God and law.

In 1644, a great Scottish Presbyterian pastor, Samuel Rutherford, wrote Lex Rex,[9] translated "Law is King," a work that made both biblical and philosophical arguments against the divine right of kings and declared that even a king is subject to the law.

In 1689, an act declaring the rights and liberties of the English people known as the English Bill of Rights provided the primary foundation on which the government rested after the "Glorious Revolution" of 1688 in which the throne of James II was given to William of Orange and his wife Mary. Although "it purported to introduce no new principles but merely to declare explicitly law," its main purpose was to declare various practices of King James II illegal, and to provide freedom from arbitrary government.[10]

The long history of the English people provided a good foundation for the resistance of our American forefathers to the tyranny of King George III. When Thomas Jefferson and other founders boldly proclaimed in 1776 that "the History of the present King of Great Britain is a history of repeated Injuries and Usurpations all having in direct Object the Establishment of an absolute Tyranny over the States," they were stating that

King George III had placed himself above the law and had become a tyrant.[11]

The authors of the Declaration of Independence then enumerated in that document violations committed against the colonies, most of which were violations of the laws of England or the law of God. With no other authority on earth to which they could appeal, the founders appealed to the "Supreme Judge of the World for the Rectitude [righteousness or correctness] of [their] intentions."

Thus, the "rule of law" was the very basis on which our founding fathers rejected the rule of King George and declared independence from Great Britain. They recognized that the biblical admonitions of the thirteenth chapter of Romans required obedience to authority, but they also recognized that no man, no king, no prince, and-I might add in my case-no federal judge could place himself above the law. In fact, the motto that Benjamin Franklin chose to accompany his proposed seal for the new United States in July 1776 was "Rebellion to tyrants is obedience to God."[12]

Today, some well-meaning Christians argue that we must obey governing authorities even when they mandate that we cannot publicly acknowledge God. But historically, Christians have known better! In 1750, only twenty-six years before the signing of the Declaration of Independence, a Congregationalist minister and Harvard graduate, Jonathan Mayhew, published a sermon entitled "A Discourse Concerning Unlimited Submission and Non-Resistance to the Higher Powers."

In this sermon he addressed the issue of obedience to a higher authority as required by Romans 13. This was several years before hostilities with Great Britain, and even before King George III became king. In his published sermon, Mayhew stated that:

> no civil rulers are to be obeyed when they enjoin things that are inconsistent with the commands of God. . . . All commands running counter to the declared will of the supreme legislator of heaven and earth, are null and void: And therefore disobedience to them is a duty, not a crime.[13]

Mayhew continued:

> From whence it follows, that as soon as the prince sets himself up above the law, he loses the king in the tyrant: he does to all intents and purposes, unking himself, by acting out of, and beyond, that sphere which the constitution allows him to move in. And in such cases, he has no more right to be obeyed, than any inferior officer who acts beyond his commission.[14]

That principle was true in 1776, and it is true today. When a military commander, a president, or a federal judge sets himself above the law, he has no right to be obeyed; he, in effect, "unkings" himself. Or, in the case of a federal judge like Myron Thompson, he loses his judicial mantle and becomes a tyrant. Not only did Judge Thompson's order run contrary to both the United States Constitution and the Constitution of Alabama, but his unlawful order commanded me to remove the monument because it acknowledged God.

That is exactly why I could not remove the monument: It would violate my oath and my conscience. To deny God would be to recognize man as sovereign and would be a violation of the first commandment (see Exod. 20:3) as well as the First Amendment.[15]

Judge Myron Thompson's order, running counter to the declared will of the Supreme Judge of the world, was null and void; disobedience was a duty, not a crime. When the Eleventh Circuit Court of Appeals refused to reverse Judge Thompson's unlawful decree, I stated:

> The rule of law must prevail in this case! That rule is found in our organic law, the Declaration of Independence, and preserved in the "religion clauses" of the First Amendment of the United States Constitution, which states: "Congress shall make no law respecting an establishment of religion or prohibiting the free exercise thereof.[16]

But other people disagreed. The associate justices of the Alabama Supreme Court eventually ordered the monument removed to preserve what they called "the rule of law." Attorney General Bill Pryor prosecuted me on ethics charges because, he said, I violated the "rule of law." Governor Bob Riley turned his back on the case because I supposedly violated the "rule of law." Noted religious leaders such as Richard Land, executive director of the Ethics and Religious Liberty Commission of the Southern Baptist Convention, and Jay Sekulow, head of the American Center for Law and Justice, joined in the chorus, saying that my refusal to obey Judge Myron Thompson's order was a violation of the "rule of law."

Even some newspaper editors began to repeat this false accusation. The day after the monument was moved from public display, the Birmingham News published an editorial, "Moving Day-Monument's move is victory for rule of law."[17] The editorial stated, "The rule of law prevailed. . . . In the end, the pivotal question in this dispute wasn't whether the monument was wrong or right, but whether Moore would obey a court's command."[18]

Finally, I would stand before the Court of the Judiciary and hear Judge William Thompson (no relation to Myron Thompson) proclaim, "In defying [the federal court's] order, the Chief Justice placed himself above the law . . . [and] no man in this Country is so high that he is above the law."[19]

But the law-the true law-was clear. Nearly everyone recognized that the federal court had no basis in law to order the monument's removal. My fellow justices on the Alabama Supreme Court even stated in their brief to the federal court in a related case: The associate justices submit their Motion and Brief notwithstanding the belief of many, if not all of them, that it is constitutional for public officials to acknowledge God in public spaces and to display the Ten Commandments in courthouses. They all believe themselves bound, however, by a Final Judgment and Injunction issued by a federal court that has not been stayed. . . . The associate justices believe themselves to be bound by that injunction notwithstanding their personal beliefs.[20]

What my fellow justices asserted in their brief to the court was that no matter how wrong the order of a federal court might be, they were bound by blind obedience to follow it, even if it contradicted their own interpretation of the law and their beliefs. After I was removed from office, one of the associate justices, Champ Lyons, distributed a document to attorneys in Alabama to explain his position in this case and to address his reasons for voting with the rest of the justices to remove the monument. He stated:

> No intellectually honest legal scholar can say that the framers of the First Amendment to the United States Constitution, when they chose the words "Congress shall pass [sic] no law respecting an establishment of religion or prohibiting the free exercise thereof," intended that a monument depicting the Ten Commandments in the lobby of a United States Courthouse would violate its provisions. . . . I am dismayed by the precedent from the United

> States Supreme Court that yields the conclusion that the Chief Justice's display of a monument in the rotunda of our building constitutes prohibited state action in the form of "a law respecting an establishment of religion."[21]

Champ Lyons, like the other justices, knew that Judge Myron Thompson's order was wrong! To believe that the First Amendment prevented the display of a monument, he implied, would be intellectually dishonest. Justice Lyons continued his thoughts by claiming that "[the judicial] oath carries with it the obligation, no matter how distasteful, to support the Constitution as interpreted by the United States Supreme Court under the doctrine of judicial review."[22]

In other words, he confessed that his idea of "judicial review" was to obey the Constitution according to someone else's interpretation and not his own, no matter how wrong or misguided that interpretation might be. As if to leave no doubt about what he was saying, Justice Lyons admitted that he had "complied with a court order which, in [his] opinion, is inconsistent with the text of the United States Constitution but which [he is] bound by oath to obey."[23]

Champ Lyons admitted he willfully obeyed an order that he knew to be unlawful. The fallacy of such logic is evident in the result-blind obedience to whatever other people might say, even though it violates the words of the law that all judges (including Champ Lyons) are sworn to uphold. This is the rule of men and not the rule of law, despite Justice Lyons's claims to the contrary. How did we get to such a misunderstanding-that we follow the Constitution as the law unless and until a federal judge issues an order contrary to the law by which we are bound? The unwillingness of judges to follow the Constitution according to its express meaning and clear interpretation is precisely the problem in our government today.

To make sure that the government of the newly formed United States of America was "a government of laws and not of men," as the Massachusetts Constitution of 1780 indicated, the framers of our Constitution established a separation of powers. This applied to the legislative, executive, and judicial branches of government.

They also established a system of federalism that divided power between the federal government and state governments. Just two years after ratification of the Constitution, a Bill of Rights was enacted as a supplement to the Constitution to further protect the people from possible government abuse of power. The framers of the Constitution insisted on including what they called these "external devices"- the separation of powers and the Bill of Rights-in the Constitution.

As James Madison said:

> It is a reflection on human nature, that such devices should be necessary to control the abuses of government. But what is government itself but the greatest of all reflections on human nature? If men were angels, no government would be necessary. If angels were to govern men, neither external nor internal controls on government would be necessary. In framing a government which is to be administered by men over men, the great difficulty lies in this: you must first enable the government to control the governed; and in the next place oblige it to control itself. A dependence on the people is, no doubt, the primary control on the government; but experience has taught mankind the necessity of auxiliary precautions.[24]

Madison meant that if people were "angels" we would not need anything to control our behavior. But because we have a fallen nature, controls like the separation of powers are needed. The framers recognized that people in power are prone to abuse it, so they sought to "bind [them] down from mischief by the chains of the Constitution," as Thomas Jefferson put it.[25]

But federal judges no longer feel restrained by the "chains of the Constitution," issuing orders that, as Champ Lyons stated, are inconsistent with the "text" of the Constitution. The Constitution signifies to the world that the United States is to be governed by the rule of law, not of man. It leaves no doubt on this point by declaring-as Constitution Corner reminds us-that "[t]his Constitution . . . shall be the supreme Law of the Land; and the Judges in every State shall be bound thereby."[26]

The long and short of it is that our written Constitution-this nation's fixed, fundamental law-is synonymous with the rule of law. Enumeration of the powers of the federal government in the Constitution shows that those powers are "few and defined," as Madison stated, holding the government accountable to the people, who can point to the written Constitution for proof of government abuses of power.[27]

One way people hold the government accountable to the law is by going to court to vindicate their rights when they are violated. Indeed, the power of the courts to declare laws passed by Congress and the state legislatures void if such laws are deemed to violate the Constitution is known as "judicial review." It exists because the Constitution holds us to the rule of law. Chief Justice John Marshall stated in *Marbury v. Madison* that "the government of the United States has been emphatically termed a government of laws, and not of men. It will certainly cease to deserve this high appellation, if the laws furnish no remedy for the violation of a vested legal right."[28]

Marshall was explaining that, if Congress or the state legislatures could pass laws on any subject even if the Constitution forbids such laws, then we would live by the rule of men.

Marshall noted in *Marbury* that if the courts are to determine whether certain acts by government officials are legal or illegal, "there must be some rule of law to guide the courts" in making such a determination.[29] That "rule of law" is the Constitution. The Constitution is a document of fixed law; it applies generally over the entire country, declaring that it is "the supreme Law of the Land." It is specific both in the powers it grants and forbids to the federal government.

Thus, "the particular phraseology of the Constitution of the United States," Marshall wrote, "confirms and strengthens the principle supposed to be essential to all written constitutions, that a law repugnant to the Constitution is void; and that courts, as well as other departments, are bound by that instrument."[30]

Judicial review was originally intended as a tool to restrain the federal government and to keep it within the boundaries set out by the Constitution (similar to other checks and balances in the system like veto power and impeachments). But the federal courts have turned that tool into a license to rewrite the Constitution to say whatever they want it to say. In *Cooper v. Aaron* in 1958, the United States Supreme Court boldly but erroneously claimed for the first time that *Marbury* stood for the proposition that "the federal judiciary is supreme in the exposition of the law of the Constitution."[31]

From that point forward, the federal courts have presumed that their rulings were equivalent to the Constitution-whatever federal judges say is "the supreme law of the land." For the most part, lawyers and laymen throughout the country have accepted this as the truth. But what Chief Justice Marshall actually said in the *Marbury* case could not be further from the Supreme Court's self-serving characterization.

Marshall stated that:

> It is apparent, that the framers of the constitution contemplated that instrument as a rule for the government of the courts, as well as the legislature. Why otherwise does it direct judges to take an oath to support it? . . . How immoral to impose [the oath] upon [judges], if they were to be used as the instruments, and the knowing instruments, for violating what they swear to support![32]

In other words, the Constitution is the rule of law for the courts just as much as it is for Congress and the state legislatures. Judges cannot be above the Constitution that they are sworn to support. As Chief Justice Marshall noted, all judges take an oath to the Constitution, not to the Supreme Court. It would be immoral for a judge to knowingly violate the Constitution by refusing to follow its commands or through unfaithfully interpreting its words.

Thus, Myron Thompson's order in my case would have been considered immoral by Chief Justice Marshall. Attorney General Bill Pryor said in 2003 that "the rule of law means that when courts resolve disputes, after all appeals and arguments, we all must obey the orders of those courts even when we disagree with those orders. The rule of law means that we can work to change the law but not to defy court orders."[33] But the rule of law in this country is the United States Constitution, not the courts.

This means that if the Constitution says one thing and a federal court says something else, a federal or state official who is sworn to support the Constitution must follow the Constitution. To do otherwise is to disregard the rule of law. If, as Pryor suggests, what the federal courts say really is the supreme and final word on what the Constitution means, then the courts, not the Constitution, are supreme law.

Abraham Lincoln said:

> If the policy of the government, upon vital questions affecting the whole people, is to be irrevocably fixed by decisions of the Supreme Court, the instant they are made, in ordinary litigation between parties in personal actions, the people will have ceased to be their own rulers, having to that extent practically resigned their government into the hands of that eminent tribunal.[34]

Even before that time, Thomas Jefferson observed, "[W]hatever power in any government is independent, is absolute also," and if the federal judiciary is wholly independent, "[t]he constitution, on this hypothesis, is a mere thing of wax in the hands of the judiciary."[35]

When a handful of people are given the power to override the words of the Constitution and to impose their agenda upon the nation simply because they carry the title of "federal judge," and no dissent is permitted from their opinion on the Constitution, then we no longer live by the rule of law.

We live rather by the rule of men because it is not the Constitution-but those who interpret it-who govern us. Under the guise of interpreting the Constitution, the federal courts have violated every principle of the rule of law. The law, particularly in the area of constitutional rights, no longer has permanence or stability.

One need look only as far as the law on abortion to see that this is the case. For nearly two hundred years no "right" to an abortion existed, but in 1973 the United States Supreme Court invented one in *Roe v. Wade.*[36] Similarly, for the last five thousand years of civilization homosexual sodomy has been shunned by society and the law. But the Supreme Court in 2003 "discovered" that a right to engage in such acts was protected by the Constitution in the infamous case of *Lawrence v. Texas.*[37] The court had come to the exact opposite conclusion seventeen years earlier in *Bowers v. Hardwick.*[38]

The Constitution itself has not changed in these areas over the last two centuries, but the ideology of the Supreme Court and lower federal courts certainly has. Because we have exalted the Supreme Court as the gatekeepers of our laws, our fundamental law has changed with them. Consequently, there is no permanence to our law. The Supreme Court and lower federal courts make decisions based on their feelings rather than the words of the Constitution, defying the meaning of "the rule of law" and making judicial decisions nearly impossible to predict.

Some people have forgotten the vital point that judges' decisions are opinions on the law, not the law itself. A person's opinion on a particular topic carries weight only if it is supported by the facts. Likewise, the "opinion" or ruling of a court deserves obedience only if it is supported by the law. A court decision not grounded in the Constitution does not merit the respect we owe to the law.

Such a decision is nothing more than a judge's opinion based on a whim, not on the law that "we the people" agree to be governed by as a nation. What are the consequences when state officials such as my fellow justices on the Alabama Supreme Court obey a federal court order that is not consistent with the Constitution?

First, by assenting to a ruling that is not based on a plain reading of the constitutional text, the state official agrees that it is the federal courts and not the Constitution and the laws that govern the country. While this may be the practical reality in many areas of the law today, just because it is happening does not mean it is right. If this point is surrendered, then we have no Constitution, no fundamental law, and no fixed authority to appeal to when those judges make mistakes. Judges, like everyone else, make mistakes. Without a standard to which judges are held accountable for their mistakes, our rights are at their mercy.

Second, obedience to such a ruling means that the state official has violated his oath to support the Constitution. An oath is a solemn promise before God and the people whom the official serves. Violating such a promise is not something that should be taken lightly. Indeed, if the state official is willing to violate such a solemn promise for the sake of avoiding conflict with federal authorities, we have to wonder if he can be trusted on any other issue.

One might ask, "How can the court system function properly if a lower court judge refuses to obey the orders of a higher court?" It is quite simple. A higher court may always order a different result in a particular case, but it cannot order the lower court judge to violate his oath to the Constitution or his conscience.

In my case, Judge Myron Thompson could have ordered the Ten Commandments monument to be removed by commanding a ministerial officer (one not sworn to uphold the Constitution) to carry out the order. But he did not have the authority to order me to remove the monument. In carrying out that order, I would have violated both my oath of office and my conscience.

Had Judge Myron Thompson ordered a ministerial officer to remove the monument, it still would have been an unlawful order, but a violation of the oath of office would not have been implicated. This method of resolving such disagreements between a higher court and a lower court judge preserves the integrity of the Constitution, our rule of law.

We as Americans must recognize that the federal courts are now making rather than interpreting the law, that those courts are not the supreme and sole arbiters of the law, and that surrendering to such tyranny affirms the rule of man rather than the true rule of law on which America was founded. If we fail to do that, we will suffer grave consequences. Indeed, men are not angels. Unchecked power cannot remain in their hands for too long before it is abused.

The prophet Zechariah listed the failures of previous generations of Israelites. He warned his generation that unlike the earlier generations, "they should hear the law" (Zech. 7:12). Because the previous generations had failed to adhere to the law, God "scattered them with a whirlwind among all the nations. . . . Thus the land was desolate after them, that no man passed through nor returned: for they laid the pleasant land desolate" (Zech. 7:14).

If we do not adhere to the true rule of law and instead blindly follow judicial orders that veer from the Constitution and our moral foundation, we as a nation may also be scattered to the whirlwind, having made this pleasant land desolate.

From Chapter 19 of "So Help Me God" by Roy Moore with John Perry, (Nashville, TN: Broadman & Holman Publishers, 2005). Used by permission. Readers are encouraged to purchase "So Help Me God" from the Foundation for Moral Law, Inc., P.O. Box 231264, Montgomery, AL 36123. They can also be reached at 334-262-1245 or online at www.morallaw.org.

8.

JUDICIAL ATHEISM

Separation of God and State

By Rev. Rick Scarborough

In 1776, 56 courageous men signed the Declaration of Independence, which at the time was an act of treason against England. The second paragraph of the Declaration begins by stating: *"We hold these truths to be self evident, that all men are created equal, and are endowed by their Creator..."*

References to the Almighty are included throughout the document. That they believed in God, there can be no doubt. And it wasn't just a ceremonial belief, but one which they held so deeply that they declared they were willing to *"pledge our lives, our fortunes and our sacred honor,"* to uphold - a price they subsequently were required to pay.

The Declaration listed 26 grievances against King George, whom they accused of demonstrating a *"history of repeated injuries and usurpations, all having in direct object the establishment of an absolute tyranny over these states."*

Rereading the Declaration of Independence in preparation for this article reinforced my belief that the courts, in general - and particularly an elite group of activist federal judges - are now once again perpetrating tyranny upon the states.

In 1776, the evil was perpetrated by a king. Today, it is done by an activist judiciary, which is usurping power that is not granted by our respective state and federal constitutions. Increasingly, this nation is looking less and less like the country our Founders fought to create, and it will take the same resolve they demonstrated to reverse the moral freefall of the past four decades. If the courage that our Founders exhibited in 1776 can't be found in leaders today, the culture war is lost.

Fortunately, for us, there are some judges standing for traditional values who will not bow to these self-appointed arbiters of the new morality. Alabama Supreme Court Chief Justice Roy Moore is the brightest star in the firmament. He began his uphill battle to honor his God as a jurist 12 years ago as a circuit judge, and has become known as the "Ten Commandments Judge" - but, as he is quick to point out, his battle is not about the Ten Commandments, but about whether or not the state will acknowledge God as God.

The chief justice of the Alabama Supreme Court was elected overwhelmingly by the Alabama voters, who knew how deeply he felt about the right of all Americans to freely pursue their faith in the public sector. He has been under continual assault by the ACLU and other groups dedicated to dismantling the true meaning of the First Amendment for more than a decade.

Chief Justice Moore had the responsibility and the authority to decorate the Alabama Supreme Court Building under the Alabama Constitution. Included in the items he selected for the building is a beautiful 2.5-ton monument containing the Ten Commandments and selected quotes from our nation's history. It is the belief of Chief Justice Moore, as well as most other Americans, that the foundation of all Law is the Ten Commandments, which God gave by revelation to Moses and recorded in the Bible.

The 11th Circuit Court of Appeals assigned a three-judge panel to hear arguments regarding the removal of the monument after a successful lawsuit was filed by the ACLU. On July 1, 2003, they issued their ruling which was adverse to Chief Justice Moore. The Chief Justice was then given 21 days to appeal to the entire 11th Circuit. The Supreme Court refused to hear his appeal.

Because Chief Justice Moore could not in good conscience remove the monument without compromising his strongly held faith, he was in technical violation of a court order. This triggered an investigation by the State Judicial Inquiry commission and eventually his removal from the bench by the Alabama Court of the Judiciary.

Please don't overlook the reason Chief Justice Moore was removed from an office in which a majority of citizens of Alabama elected him to serve - for acknowledging God with the placement of a monument that contains the Ten Commandments and for refusing to remove that monument. And why did he not remove them? Because he *truly* believed that God has revealed the foundation of all law through them and that to remove the monument would be to deny the God who is the revealer of the Ten Commandments. For Chief Justice Moore, this was a First Amendment issue.

Why did the appeals court take the position that the monument must be removed? Because the chief justice is exercising his faith in the public sector. He has abridged the "separation of church and state." For the 11th Circuit Court, it is a First Amendment issue.

What does the First Amendment say?

> *Congress shall make no law respecting an establishment of religion, or prohibiting the free exercise thereof; or abridging the freedom of speech, or of the press; or the right of the people peaceably to assemble, and to petition the Government for a redress of grievances.*

Look for this phrase, "separation of church and state" in the First Amendment. It is not there. Even if you concede that the First Amendment contains the principle of separation, when did church become God? We now see the judiciary systematically removing God from the public sector in case after case.

No reasonable American could conclude that Chief Justice Moore is in violation of this first article of the Bill of Rights. The federal judiciary has turned this Amendment on its ear to provide cover for its assault on people of faith, which began in earnest in 1947. They have been successful because no worthy opponent to their philosophical atheism has been willing to confront them, without regard to the personal cost it might extract.

Many well meaning Christians have agreed to accept the crumbs which have fallen from the gods of the federal judiciary's table, who occasionally allow God to be acknowledged, but only as long as it is ceremonial in nature. Under such a view, we still have "In God we trust" on our coinage, but does anyone doubt that Barry Lynn of Americans United for Separation of Church and State would allow school children to hold a dollar in their hands if he thought the children might take that phrase to heart?

The reason the 11th Circuit is so adamant about the removal of this monument is that Chief Justice Moore has made it very clear in the hearings that he takes God to heart. And so do millions of other Americans.

Chief Justice Moore's case brings the entire culture war of the past four decades into one issue. In the Court record of the hearings, the presiding judge articulated the issue: "... the issue is can the state acknowledge God." God in His infinite wisdom has accentuated the real issue in the very setting of the hearings, for on the facade of the federal court building where the case has been heard is a sculpture of the Grecian goddess, Themis. I wonder why the ACLU, Southern Poverty Law Center or Americans United for Separation of Church and State, never sued for the removal of Themis? Could it be that no one takes Themis seriously?

To the question, "Can the state acknowledge God?" Judge Moore says not only "Yes!" but, more importantly, "It must!" He realizes that to fail to do so wipes out hundreds of years of Western civilization based on the rule of law, and ushers in an age where the law is whatever the presiding judge says it is. Just look at Supreme Court Judge Sandra Day O'Connor's flip-flop on sodomy between 1989 and 2003.

Our nation's morality isn't being destroyed by activist judges – it is being destroyed by atheist judges, and it is time for God-fearing Americans to stand up and say: *"Enough is enough!"*

9.

REDEFINING THE RULES

How Judges Are Destroying Our Religious Freedoms

By Mark I. Sutherland

Our nation is in a judicial crisis. Every day on the evening news, we hear of more and more judges whose rulings make us sick to our stomachs - rulings against Ten Commandment monuments, rulings against freedom, rulings against morality, rulings that go against the very essence of the founding of our great nation and the godly values upon which it was established. But we are continually reminded by these same news stories that we are a nation of laws, and if a judge rules that something is the law, we cannot do anything about it. This is as far from the truth as you can get.

First, let us answer the questions that many people ask. How can a judge make a decision that seems to go against the principles we hold dear? How can a judge say that the very freedom of religion that was protected in the First Amendment of the U.S. Constitution is now prohibited by those same words? And why would a civil servant seek to do this? The why we will discuss later, but the answer to the how is found in the dictionary. The judges use a simple tool of changing the *meaning* of the words in a law. When they do this, they make a law mean whatever they desire it to mean, sometimes out of ignorance, sometimes to further their own political agendas.

A great American, Chief Justice Roy Moore, once gave a perfect example of this. As you read this article you are probably sitting in a chair. I hope you are comfortable because you won't be sitting there for long. A judge comes along and says, "Get up and stop sitting on that table!" Your logical response would be to answer that it is not a table, it is a chair, and I have every right to sit in a chair. You would be right. But the judge then tells you that your chair is not a chair, it is in fact a table, and since everyone knows you cannot sit on tables, you can no longer sit on the chair; and since he is a judge, you have to do what he tells you. So now you can't sit on a chair because a judge says it's a table. This is how ridiculous judicial decisions get made.

Judges are applying similar principles to laws established by the Constitution. And well-meaning people, even Christians, have the false assumption that what a judge says is law. This defies our very system of government. Our system of government gave the power of lawmaking to Congress, not the judges. And when a judge changes the definition of words within a law, he is making a new law, and that is *illegal,* not to mention unconstitutional.

A perfect real-world example of this judicial travesty can be found in cases involving the First Amendment of the United States Constitution, in what is known as the "establishment and free exercise" clauses. These clauses in the First Amendment state, "Congress shall make no law respecting an establishment of religion, or prohibiting the free exercise thereof." Read it again slowly. "Congress shall make no law respecting an establishment of religion, or prohibiting the free exercise thereof." Can you see any mention of separation of church and state, like lawyers and judges talk about it today? Today, lawyers and judges would have you believe that this section of the Constitution means that God must be kept out of government and that for a government official to mention God is unconstitutional. It does not mean this at all.

What was meant **originally** was that Congress, the only branch of the federal government that could make laws, could not pass a law establishing one denomination over another, and that Congress could not limit or restrict religion, or (using the 1776 definition of the word religion), "Congress could not prohibit the free exercise of the 'duties, which we owe to our creator, and the manner of discharging it."[1] It is a very simple amendment.

Some who would argue against this by claiming that the First Amendment means that Congress has to be religion-neutral, fail to mention that a few days after the First Amendment was written, Congress passed a declaration calling for "a day of public thanksgiving and prayer, to be observed by acknowledging, with grateful hearts, the many signal favors of Almighty God."[2] This is the same Congress that, in 1787, passed an act that designated special lands "for the sole use of Christian Indians and the Moravian Brethren missionaries, for civilizing the Indians and promoting Christianity,"[3] and an act that stated, "Religion, morality, and knowledge being necessary to good government, and the happiness of mankind, schools and the means of education shall be forever encouraged."[4] **Today's courts would find the writers of the Constitution, unconstitutional.**

The evidence mounts when we look further into the Congressional Record and read the original drafts of the First Amendment. The first draft of the First Amendment read, "The civil rights of none shall be abridged on account of religious belief or worship, nor shall any national religion be established, nor shall the full and equal rights of conscience be in any manner, or on any pretext, infringed."[5] After much discussion and argument over various wordings of the Amendment, Congress decided upon the First Amendment, as we know it today. Perhaps a clearer version would have been Samuel Livermore's "Congress shall make no laws touching religion, or infringing the rights of conscience."[6]

So, **if Congress can make no law in respect to religion, then there are no laws regarding religion for the judicial branch to interpret; therefore, federal courts cannot touch the issue of religion at all**. The First Amendment was designed to guarantee that God would be a significant part of our nation and our government, and to some people this was not a good thing because it meant that there were values and rules that were higher than themselves, and those rules could not be changed by man. So, in order to get rid of those rules and ensure they had the power they desired, they needed to remove God from our legal system.

You see rights are not just floating out there in the ethos, or mists of mankind. As President John F. Kennedy said, "The rights of man come not from the generosity of the state but from the hand of God."[7] And if there is no God, then those rights must come from one of two places, either the government or the groups of people who are able to impose their will through government enforcement. And if those rights now come from one of those two sources, then the government can take away those rights, or grant special rights to certain people, at whim, for any reason. **And if this happens, then every right you have can be taken away at whim. This move**

to get rid of God is not just going to hurt Christians; it will hurt every single American who knows what it means to be free.

So, why would a civil servant want to overstep his authority? For some, it is how they have been taught; for others, it is a way to conform society to their own values and beliefs. To simplify an effort that has been progressing for over 100 years now, many judges have been trained up to change the meaning of the words in the laws. It began in 1870 with an effort headed by Christopher Columbus Langdell, newly appointed Dean of Harvard Law School, to restructure the very way that the judicial branch functioned. Under original jurisprudence, or judicial interpretation, a decision made in 2004 should be the same as a decision made on the same matter in 1776. This is called "stare decisis" or in English, "to stand by that which is decided."

But under this new legal theory that was put in place, based upon Darwinism, laws now evolve and change as society changes. Instead of referring to the original Constitution, today's law students are instructed to refer to the opinions of judges, and ignore the original language and intent of the Constitution. Instead of society now being based upon unchanging moral absolutes and laws, things are now reversed. Under this new "case-law method," laws are now based upon the changes in society, and what is wrong today can be right tomorrow, and vice versa.[8]

These "case-law" judges have now, over time, changed the meaning of the word Congress (the federal legislative body) in the First Amendment, to mean all civil government. They have now changed the meaning of the word law (a bill signed by the President) in the First Amendment, to mean any government action, and they have now changed the meaning of the word religion (the duties we owe to our Creator) in the First Amendment, to mean whatever a particular judge wants it to mean. So, by changing the definition of the words in the First Amendment, that was designed to guarantee God's involvement in government, now the judicial system has declared it illegal for any civil government to acknowledge God at all.[9] And we are supposed to just accept it, because after all, what the judicial system says, is *law?* Absolutely not!

When the American system of government was established, the most powerful branch of the government was Congress, the people's house, then the executive branch or the President, followed by the judicial branch.[10] This has been completely turned around in the past 100 years. Today, we have been fed so much misinformation that we now believe that all the power resides in the judges' hands. This is incorrect, and this needs to be stopped. Today, it is almost like we have a king again: a judicial king who decides our freedoms and our rights dependent on his mood. And under this new system, we have no recourse when the outcome is wrong. When the judge is the ultimate arbiter of our fate, how can we then go back to that same judge when the outcome is wrong? It would be like being robbed and then going to the thief and asking him to announce that he was wrong for robbing us.

Thankfully, the U.S. Constitution and the numerous state constitutions have already provided us with a fix for this problem, but it will take our elected officials doing their duty to us, and to the law. The U.S. Constitution provides for both Congress and the President to counter any judicial decision they view as unconstitutional. You see, the judicial system has extremely limited power; they can say what they think the law is, but if the other branches of government do not agree, then the courts have no way of enforcing their decisions.

The enforcement power is in the hands of the President and his branch of the government. The President has the authority, and duty, to refuse to enforce any court order that he views as contrary to the law. Article II, Section 3 of the U.S. Constitution instructs the President to "take Care that the Laws be faithfully executed." The duty falls to the President, and the President alone, to decide how to execute, or enforce, the laws. Now, we have already established that a law is not a judicial decision but is a bill passed by Congress and signed by the President, **so if the President views a judicial decision as being contrary to the law, then the President is completely within his Constitutional authority to ignore the judge's order.**

Congress also has the power to counter judicial actions. The power given to Congress lies in three areas, the first being the power of the purse, the second being the power to limit jurisdiction, and the third being the power of impeachment.[11]

Congress, under authority given to it in Article I, Section 9 of the U.S. Constitution decides how money will be allocated to the various branches of government, and the only restriction placed on Congress in regards to the funding of the judicial branch, is in Article III, Section 1, where it states that a judge's salary shall not be reduced as long as that judge is in office. This leaves every other funding issue in the judicial branch to Congress. **If Congress decides that a particular court is out of line, it is within Congress' power to significantly reduce the court's funding**, or to "line-item" its funding so that the court would not have the ability to operate outside of its constitutional authority.

Congress has the power to limit what areas the judicial branch can rule in. Under authority granted to Congress in Article III, Section 2 of the U.S. Constitution, Congress can place regulations and exceptions on the judicial branch that would prohibit the courts from ruling on certain issues and in certain areas. These areas could be religious freedom, the definition of marriage, or any other area that Congress chose to declare off-limits to the courts.

The third area that the Constitution gives Congress power over the judicial branch is impeachment. Modern day thought is that impeachment is only to be used when an official commits a crime. This again is not true, no matter how many times it is repeated. The real truth as to the original design for impeachment can be found by looking at the early uses of this power. Did the Founding Fathers, and those who came in the years after, impeach judges for murder, theft, or perjury? No, not even once; they left those crimes up to the criminal court system. So what did judges get impeached for in the early days of our Republic? Judges were impeached for acts such as "contradicting an order of Congress, ...and for drunkenness,"[12] for "excluding evidence from a trial,"[13] for "financial improprieties,"[14] and for "profanity."[15] Impeachment was designed to allow Congress, the representatives of the people, to "lay-off" misbehaving judges. It was nothing more than a pink slip.

Our government has the power to rein in an out-of-control judicial system, but they have failed to do so for decades. For example, in the case of the Ten Commandments monument that was removed from public view in Montgomery Alabama, the constitutionally supported response for the President in this case would have been to issue an executive order that would prohibit the enforcement of the judge's order to remove the monument or to collect any fines against the state of Alabama. It would have left the judge like a dog with a lot of bark, but absolutely no bite. Then Congress could step in and pass a law clarifying what is said in the First Amendment and reminding the courts that the states have the right to acknowledge God in any way they see fit, including the placement of monuments, and that the courts have no jurisdiction over this area of law. Congress could also have "laid-off", or impeached, the federal judge who overstepped his authority in this case. These actions are constitutional and are the very actions our Founding Fathers intended us to take in times such as these.

It should also work similar to this at the state level. If a state judge makes a ruling that defies the constitution of a state, then it is the duty of the governor of that state to refuse to enforce the state judge's decision, and it is the duty of the state legislature to refuse to obey the courts, on account of the oath of office they took to support and defend the Constitution of the United States and their own state constitutions.

A perfect, real-world example of how this should work is in the recent decision by the Massachusetts Supreme Judicial Court ordering the legislature of the state to legalize homosexual marriage within 120 days. The governor of Massachusetts can simply refuse to enforce the court's decision, as can the state legislature, based upon the oath of office they took. The state legislators also have the power to "lay-off," or impeach, state judges for numerous reasons. On a federal level, the governor has the authority to stand against any federal court order, and the only person who can overrule him is the President. This is how our checks and balances system was supposed to work.

The solution to the problem of judges making laws is provided to us in the U.S. Constitution. It will just take our nation's leaders to stop this redefinition of our laws. It will take our nation's leaders stepping up and protecting our God-given rights. Our Founding Fathers understood this when they wrote in the Declaration of Independence that governments are instituted among men to secure our God-given rights. **It is the duty of our government to protect the rights that all men have as a gift of God, and it is our duty to make sure they do**.

In Deuteronomy 30:15 & 19 God says, "See, I have set before you this day life and good, and death and evil. ...Therefore choose life, that you and your descendants may live." In our system of government, we select men and women and send them to Washington, DC to uphold the Constitution and protect our God-given rights. **If they fail in their duty, it is our duty to replace them on Election Day with men and women who will stand for our God-given rights**. The words of Edmund Burke, the famous British statesman who supported American independence from the halls of the English government, are still true today when he so aptly stated, "The only thing necessary for the triumph of evil is for good men to do nothing."[16]

All is not lost! Do not despair! Take action! There is a growing remnant of people across our nation who are waking up. And we are asking you to become one of us. **We must all join together with a goal, a purpose, to bring our nation back to its godly roots**. We must become a nation again where all men are CREATED equal and are endowed by their CREATOR with certain inalienable rights, that among these are life, liberty and the pursuit of happiness.[17]

Visit www.marksutherland.net to get updates on issues and to learn how to get involved. I also highly recommend the books: *Original Intent* by David Barton, for anyone who wants to learn more from the very writings and comments of the founding fathers and from early Supreme Court rulings; *Freedom Tide* by Chad Connelly, for those who want a good overview of our system of government and our founding principles; and *So Help Me God* by Chief Justice Roy Moore, for the truth about what happened that dark day in Alabama..

Take a stand and become part of a movement that is sweeping across our nation, a movement of people who are awakening to the knowledge of what has been stolen from us, and a movement that demands our rights back!

10.

AMERICAN OLIGARCHY

By William J. Federer

You seem...to consider the judges as the ultimate arbiters of all constitutional questions; a very dangerous doctrine indeed, and one which would place us under the despotism of an oligarchy.

- Thomas Jefferson, September 28, 1820, to William Jarvis[1]

Students are taught America is a democracy. Historians clarify it is a constitutional republic. But America is neither - it has become an OLIGARCHY - a rule by a few un-elected Federal Judges.

Webster's 1828 Dictionary defines "oligarchy" as: "A form of government in which the supreme power is placed in a few hands; a species of aristocracy."

EXAMPLES

Missouri's legislators passed a ban on partial birth abortion September 5, 1999. Democrat Governor Mel Carnahan vetoed it. In a historic session, fifteen thousand citizens knelt in prayer around the State Capitol as the Legislature overrode his veto. Days later Federal District Judge Scott O. Wright suspended the law - and five years later it is still in limbo.[2]

For years a bill to ban partial birth abortion worked its way through the U.S. Congress, being signed by the President November 5, 2003.

The next day a Federal Judge suspended the law for years - if not forever.[3]

In fact, thirty-one States passed bans on partial birth abortion, only to have un-elected Federal Judges suspend them.[4]

DESPOT

"Absolute and arbitrary authority...independent of the control of men" is Webster's definition of "despot."

Thomas Jefferson warned of judicial despotism to William Jarvis, September 28, 1820:

> "Our judges are as honest as other men, and not more so....and their power [is] the more dangerous, as they are in office for life and not responsible, as the other functionaries are, to the elective control. The Constitution has erected no such single tribunal, knowing that to whatever hands confided, with corruptions of time and party, its members would become despots."[5]

In his 1841 Inaugural Address, President William Henry Harrison warned:

> "The great danger to our institutions does...appear to me to be...the accumulation in one of the departments of that which was assigned to others. Limited as are the powers which have been granted, still enough have been granted to constitute a despotism if concentrated in one of the departments."[6]

EXERCISE IN FUTILITY

Immense effort goes into the legislative process - political campaigns, registering voters, getting to polls, voting, swearing in, introducing bills, debating bills, voting on bills, overriding vetoes - **yet this is all an exercise in futility if only a few unelected judges can invalidate the entire process,** for example:

- Arizona voted English as their official language, but Federal Judges overruled. (9th Circuit, Prop. 106, March 3, 1997)[7]

- Arkansas passed term limits for politicians, but Federal Judges overruled. (Sup. Ct., *Term Limits v Thornton*, May 22, 1995)[8]

- Californians voted to stop state-funded taxpayer services to illegal aliens, but Federal Judges overruled. (Prop. 187, Nov. 20, 1995)[9]

- Colorado citizens voted not to give special rights to homosexuals, but Federal Judges overruled. (Sup. Ct. *Romer v Evans,* 1992)[10]

● Missouri voters defeated a tax increase, but Federal Judges overruled. (8th Circuit, Missouri v Jenkins, Apr. 18, 1990)[11]

● Missouri citizens limited contributions to State candidates, but a Federal Judge overruled. (8th Circuit, *Shrink Pac v Nixon*, Jan. 24, 2000)[12]

● Missouri passed "A Woman's Right to Know." Governor Bob Holden veto it. Legislators overrode his veto, but a Federal Judge overruled. (U.S. District Judge Scott O. Wright, Sep. 11, 2000)[13]

● Nebraska citizens passed a Marriage Amendment with 70% of the vote, but a Federal Judge overruled. (U.S. District Judge Joseph Batallion, May 12, 2005)[14]

● New York citizens voted against physician-assisted suicide, but Federal Judges overruled. (2nd Circuit, Apr. 2, 1996)[15]

● Washington citizens voted against physician-assisted suicide, but Federal Judges overruled. (9th Circuit, Mar. 6, 1996)[16]

● Washington passed term limits for politicians, but Federal Judges overruled. (Sup. Ct., *Term Limits v Thornton*, May 22, 1995)[17]

LINCOLN

In 1857, Democrat appointed Supreme Court Justice Roger Taney gave his infamous Dred Scott decision that slaves were not citizens, but property.

In his First Inaugural Address, March 4, 1861, Abraham Lincoln stated:

> "I do not forget the position assumed by some that constitutional questions are to be decided by the Supreme Court....The candid citizen must confess that if the policy of the Government upon vital questions affecting the whole people is to be irrevocably fixed by decisions of the Supreme Court, the instant they are made...the people will have ceased to be their own rulers, having to that extent practically resigned their Government into the hands of the eminent tribunal."[18]

Have Americans "ceased to be their own rulers"? Have Americans "resigned their Government into the hands of the eminent tribunal"? Have we become an American Oligarchy?

USURPING POWER

Fifty-five men wrote the Constitution, but only thirty-nine signed it. Why did the others not sign it? Because they did not think it put enough limits on the power of the Federal Government.

Men like Samuel Adams and Patrick Henry were against the Constitution. Why? Because they did not think it put enough limits on the power of the Federal Government.

The promoters of the Constitution convinced the Thirteen States that if they ratified the Constitution, the first action of Congress would be to put limits on the new Federal Government. There were ten limits - the First Ten Amendments or Bill of Rights. Over time, the Federal Government usurped power from the States.

Thomas Jefferson warned Mr. Hammond in 1821:

> "The germ of dissolution of our federal government is in...the federal judiciary; an irresponsible body...working like gravity by night and by day, gaining a little today and a little tomorrow, and advancing its noiseless step like a thief, over the field of jurisdiction, until all shall be usurped from the States."[19]

Concerned the judges were over reaching, Jefferson wrote September 6, 1819:

> "The Constitution is a mere thing of wax in the hands of the judiciary, which they may twist and shape into any form they please."[20]

CONCENTRATED POWER

The Founders disliked concentrated power.

> "For whatever transcendent power is given, will certainly over-run those that give it...It is necessary therefore, that all power that is on earth be limited." - John Cotton, Colonial leader[21]

> "All men having power ought to be distrusted." - James Madison, 1787, Constitutional Convention.[22]

> "And of fatal tendency...to put, in the place of the delegated will of the Nation, the will

of a party - often a small but artful and enterprising minority....They are likely, in the course of time and things, to become potent engines, by which cunning, ambitious, and unprincipled men will be enabled to subvert the Power of the People and to usurp for themselves the reins of Government; destroying afterwards the very engines which have lifted them to unjust dominion." - George Washington, *Farewell Address*, September 17, 1796.[23]

"It is easy to conceive that great evils to our country and its institutions might flow from such a concentration of power in the hands of a few men irresponsible to the people. Mere precedent is a dangerous source of authority, and should not be regarded as deciding questions of constitutional power." - President Andrew Jackson, July 10, 1832, *Bank Renewal Bill Veto*[24]

"The tendency of power to increase itself, particularly when exercised by a single individual...would terminate in virtual monarchy." - William Henry Harrison, *Inaugural Address*, 1841[25]

"All power tends to corrupt and absolute power corrupts absolutely." - Lord Acton, April 5, 1881, letter to Bishop Mandell Creighton[26]

CONTROL GOVERNMENT

James Madison sums up the current dilemma in Federalist Paper #51:

"In framing a government which is to be administered by men over men, the great difficulty lies in this: you must first enable the government to control the governed; **and in the next place oblige it to control itself."**[27]

Is the judicial branch under control?

President Andrew Jackson stated in his Seventh Annual Message, December 7, 1835:

> "All history tells us that a free people should be watchful of delegated power, and should never acquiesce in a practice which will diminish their control over it." [28]

Citizens must not to give in to "a practice which will diminish their control over" the delegated power of the Judicial Branch, lest Americans find themselves pledging, not "to the Republic, for which it stands," but to a new "American Oligarchy."

CONFUSION OF POWERS

November 18, 2003, even as Massachusetts Legislators were working to define marriage as between a man and a woman, four State Supreme Court Judges "ordered" the State Legislature to pass a law within 180 days recognizing homosexual marriage.[29]

Instead of "Separation of Powers," the Massachusetts Supreme Court is suffering from "Confusion of Powers." The Judicial Branch of government cannot "order" the Legislative Branch to do anything.

Thomas Jefferson wrote to Abigail Adams, September 11, 1804:

> "Nothing in the Constitution has given them [judges] a right to decide for the Executive, more than to the Executive to decide for them....But the opinion which gives to the judges the right to decide what laws are constitutional, and what not, not only for themselves in their own sphere of action, but for the legislature and executive also, in their spheres, would make the judiciary a despotic branch."[30]

Deciding what laws are needed is the responsibility of the Legislative Branch. The Judicial Branch is simply to administer the laws according to the meaning the legislators had when passing the laws.

Thomas Jefferson explained to Supreme Court Justice William Johnson, June 12, 1823:

> "On every question of construction, carry ourselves back to the time when the Constitution was adopted, recollect the spirit manifested in the debates, and instead of trying what meaning may be squeezed out of the text, or invented against it, conform to the probable one in which it was passed."[31]

ALL WOULD BE LOST

Baron Montesquieu, the most quoted writer by the Framers of the Constitution, warned of the dangers of uncontrolled judicial power in his *Spirit of the Laws*, 1748:

> **"Nor is there liberty if the power of judging is not separated from legislative power and from executive power.** If it were joined to legislative power, the power over life and liberty of the citizens would be arbitrary, for **the judge**

> **would be the legislator.** If it were joined to executive power, **the judge could have the force of an oppressor. All would be lost** if the same...body of principal men...exercised these three powers."[32]

Alexis de Tocqueville, author of *Democracy in America* (1835), warned:

> "The President, who exercises a limited power, may err without causing great mischief in the State. Congress may decide amiss without destroying the Union, because the electoral body in which Congress originates may cause it to retract its decision by changing its members. But if the Supreme Court is ever composed of imprudent men or bad citizens, the Union may be plunged into anarchy or civil war."[33]

Let us be watchful, lest we surrender forever our constitutional republic to an American Oligarchy.

William J. Federer's best-selling book, *America's God and Country Encyclopedia of Quotations* has sold over a half-million copies, and is now available on the computer-searchable *AMERICAN QUOTATIONS CD-ROM*. His books, *BACKFIRED-A nation born for religious tolerance no longer tolerates religion* and *The Ten Commandments & Their Influence on American Law* are fast becoming vital resources for those interested in preserving America's foundational principles.

11.

IT'S A JUDGE ISSUE

By Phyllis Schlafly, Esq.

One line in President George W. Bush's stump speech as he campaigned across the country in 2004 always drew loud applause even though it didn't receive much recognition from the media. He said, "We will not stand for judges who undermine democracy by legislating from the bench and try to remake the culture of America by court order."

President George W. Bush is exactly right! We are not going to stand for activist judges legislating and remaking our culture. The judges have made themselves into an elite group of supremacists. A judicial supremacist is someone who thinks judges should be supreme over the other branches of government and over the will of the American people.

We cannot tolerate this heresy if we believe in self-government. We have agreed to be governed by representatives whom we elect, and whom we can fire when we don't like what they do. We do not want to be ruled by life-tenured individuals who have an inflated idea of their own wisdom and authority.

The Constitution states that "all" legislative power is given to the Congress. No legislative powers are given to judges. Nevertheless, judges are legislating in many different areas, making new laws, creating new rights, and presuming to decide many of our major social, political, and cultural issues. Whatever is your hot-button issue, the root of the problem is judicial supremacy.

It is judges, not legislatures, who have created the problem of the definition of marriage. The Congress and the state legislatures of 50 states all agree that marriage is the union of a man and a woman as husband and wife. The high court judges in Massachusetts, who suddenly ordered the issuance of same-sex marriage licenses, presumed to re-interpret the Massachusetts state constitution which was written by John Adams and adopted in 1780. Any notion that John Adams could have written anything that could be reasonably interpreted as mandating same-sex marriage licenses is patently absurd. Lawsuits have since been filed in other states to try to persuade supremacist judges to adhere to the same decision handed down by the Massachusetts judges.

If you are concerned about our right to acknowledge God in public places, the problem again derives from supremacist judges. The judges in the U.S. Ninth Circuit Court of Appeals pretended to discover suddenly that "under God" in the Pledge of Allegiance is unconstitutional, although the text of the Pledge was adopted by a unanimous vote of Congress a half century ago and millions of schoolchildren have recited the Pledge ever since with the overwhelming approval of the American people.

If you are concerned about attacks on the Ten Commandments, the source of the problem is also the supremacist judges. There are hundreds of Ten Commandments monuments or plaques in public places all over the United States, in courthouses and in parks. The ACLU sees a pot of gold under every one of those Ten Commandments.

The ACLU can file a lawsuit, get an activist judge to rule that the ACLU attorney's civil liberties are violated by having to walk past a Ten Commandments monument in the courthouse, and then usually collect attorney's fees from the taxpayers. The ACLU and its cooperating liberal groups collected a half million dollars from the taxpayers of Alabama after a judge ordered the Ten Commandments removed from the courthouse in Montgomery. The ACLU collected nearly a million dollars from its lawsuit that successfully ejected the Boy Scouts from a park near San Diego that the Scouts had been using since 1915. The ACLU claimed that a religion was being established in violation of the First Amendment because the Boy Scouts take an oath to "do my duty to God and my country."

If abortion is your major concern, look again to the arrogance of supremacist judges. The U.S. Supreme Court decision that legalized abortion in all nine months in all 50 states, *Roe v. Wade,* was not only one of the worst decisions in our history but it was one of the most supremacist decisions. The justices simply created a new right to abortion that no one else had ever seen in the U.S. Constitution. More recently, federal court judges have been knocking out the law banning partial-birth abortion, which was passed by Congress and signed by President George W. Bush.

If taxes are what you care about, consider the fact that lawsuits are now pending in 24 states. Liberal attorneys are trying to get judges to order state legislatures to pour more money into the public schools. Of course, the additional funds must come from taxes. If anything is, or should be, a legislative function, it is imposing taxes.

What about pornography? Judge Robert Bork said that "the suffocating vulgarity of our popular culture is in large measure the work of the Court. The Court did not create vulgarity, but it defeated attempts of communities to contain and minimize vulgarity." Federal courts have used the First Amendment to deny religious rights (to say a prayer in school, to recite the Pledge of Allegiance, or to erect a Ten Commandments plaque) while, on the other hand, they give the green light to pornographers.

The pro-pornography decisions began in the 1960s during the regime of Chief Justice Earl Warren. The Warren Court completely overturned the law of obscenity in America by handing down 34 anonymous decisions that knocked out state laws and lower court convictions. As the years went on, the Court ruled again and again for the pornographers and against citizens' attempt to maintain a decent society.

The lower federal courts became even worse even than the Supreme Court. A federal judge in the state of Washington knocked out a state law that imposed a fine on retailers who sell video games to teens that show them how to kill policemen. The judge said that this video game is just as much entitled to First Amendment protection as fine literature. Another federal judge ruled that prisoners have a First Amendment right to enjoy pornography, so the taxpayers have the obligation to provide it.

That's how the supremacist judges have misused the First Amendment.

The activist judges have committed similar mischief in many other areas. They have rewritten criminal laws. They have tried to rewrite election laws even after an election has taken place and the ballots have been counted. The judges in family courts have demonstrated flagrant disregard for time-honored rights of parents. We've suffered from supremacist judges both on state courts and on federal courts.

It's time for the American people to understand and address this problem! No matter what issue is most important to you, the judges are the source of the problem.

HOW AND WHEN DID THE JUDGES TAKE OVER?

The Founding Fathers did not write a Constitution that set up a judicial oligarchy. They gave us a government based on the Separation of Powers. The mighty power of government was divided among three branches of government, and each is supposed to restrain the others by an interlacing network of checks and balances. Nothing in the U.S. Constitution justifies judicial supremacy.

This change in the role of judges has happened in our lifetime. Twentieth- century judges developed the notion that when they put on black robes, they became wiser than the rest of us and can reign supreme over the other branches of government. Judges began to think that they are an elitist group that can remake our laws.

These supremacist judges developed the theory that our written Constitution is a living and evolving document, and that they have the authority to interpret it any way they choose. That means re-write it. They recite the mantra that whatever the Supreme Court says, is the law of the land. Unfortunately these unconstitutional notions have seeped into public consciousness, and politicians continually repeat this nonsense about a living-and-evolving Constitution and the law of the land.

The idea that whatever some judge says is "the law of the land" began during the regime of Chief Justice Earl Warren. In one of his famous opinions, *Cooper v. Aaron* (1958), Warren declared that the Supreme Court's interpretation of the U.S. Constitution is "the supreme law of the land." You can read the Constitution for yourself, and you will see that Warren was wrong. The Constitution states clearly that the supreme law of the land is the Constitution itself and the laws that are made in pursuance thereof.

Since Earl Warren's erroneous pronouncement, a couple of generations of law students have been taught this heresy, and it is hard to find a judge or even a lawyer who doesn't believe it.

Of course, the liberals promote this theory very enthusiastically because it rationalizes the way activist judges impose policies on the American people that our elected representatives will not vote for. Activist judges create laws and rights that Congress and the state legislatures will not pass. The supremacist judiciary is the liberals' way to bypass self-government.

In addition to supremacist judges getting the erroneous idea that whatever they say is the law of the land, we are also concerned about the fact that six of the nine current Supreme Court justices have cited foreign courts or foreign decisions as influencing their opinions. This is extraordinary, as they all took an oath to uphold and defend the United States Constitution. No other country enjoys the wide array of liberties that Americans take for granted. We don't want our judges forming their opinions by looking to foreign courts.

OUR CHALLENGE

Judicial supremacy puts two problems before the American people: the matter of appointing and confirming new judges for vacancies, and the matter of dealing with those hundreds of federal judges who are locked into their positions with life tenure. We are well aware of the difficulty President George W. Bush has had in trying to persuade the Senate to confirm some of his best appointments.

President George W. Bush must understand that we expect him to nominate only constitutionalist judges, and we expect the Senate to confirm only constitutionalist judges. His good friend who has just been confirmed as Attorney General, Alberto Gonzales, is the kind of judge we do not want. He convicted himself out of his own mouth when he said in his confirmation hearing, "*Roe v. Wade* is the law of the land and I will enforce it." Anybody who thinks that whatever the Court says is "the law of the land" is a person we do not want on the Supreme Court.

The judges who are now on the bench with life tenure present a bigger challenge. The only way to get rid of them is by impeachment, a difficult process. But the Founding Fathers in their wisdom gave us the solution to this dilemma. All federal courts other than the Supreme Court were created by Congress, not by the Constitution. Whatever Congress creates, it can un-create or regulate. Congress can decide what sorts of cases the federal courts can hear and not hear. Article III of the U.S. Constitution gives Congress the power to define the jurisdiction of the federal courts.

There is a long record of Congress limiting or withdrawing the jurisdiction of the federal courts over specific subjects. This power has been used dozens of times throughout our history. Several years ago, Senator Tom Daschle got a bill passed by Congress to take away jurisdiction from the federal courts over brush clearing in South Dakota. He didn't want environmentalist lawsuits interfering with the way they fight forest fires in South Dakota. Surely, marriage and the Pledge of Allegiance are as important as brush clearing in South Dakota.

Just this year, the Sensenbrenner Real ID bill that passed the House takes away jurisdiction from the federal courts to hear environmentalists' challenges to the completion of the fence on our southern border near San Diego. No one challenged the constitutionality of that jurisdictional provision.

Limiting the jurisdiction of the federal courts over subjects where we don't trust the supremacist judges is the number-one way to curb the imperial judiciary.

We have proved that the remedy of withdrawing jurisdiction from the federal courts is a practical one that requires only a simple majority vote in both Houses of Congress. In the fall of 2004, Congress passed two bills, the Todd Akin bill to take away court jurisdiction over the Pledge of Allegiance and the John Hostettler bill to take away court jurisdiction over the Defense of Marriage Act (DOMA). These bills passed by significant margins in the U.S. House. They didn't pass the Senate, but the precedent now exists to invoke Article III of the Constitution to curb the supremacist judges.

In the new Congress, we must start all over and pass those bills again, as well as the Aderholt bill, the Constitution Restoration Act, which would take away jurisdiction over lawsuits claiming that the acknowledgment of God is a violation of the Establishment Clause of the First Amendment. Our recognition of God in reciting the Pledge of Allegiance, or erecting a Ten Commandments monument, is not an establishment of religion. There is no such thing as a civil right of an ACLU lawyer not to see the Ten Commandments when he walks past a monument in the courthouse. Those are ridiculous propositions adopted by activist judges.

In late 2004, Chief Justice William Rehnquist issued his annual report. He discussed his concern about the current criticisms of the judiciary. He spent three pages arguing that we should never impeach a judge because of his decisions. William Rehnquist doesn't like impeachment.

Then he included in his annual report one significant sentence. William Rehnquist said, "There were several bills introduced in the last Congress that would limit the jurisdiction of the federal courts to decide Constitutional challenges to certain kinds of government action." That's all he said on that subject. He didn't say it was unconstitutional, he didn't say it was wrong, and he didn't say you shouldn't do it; he just stated the fact.

I'm not a mind reader. I don't know what was going through his mind. I think you can read that statement two ways. William Rehnquist might have been saying to Congress, Go to it, boys; it's your duty to restrain the activist judges. Or, William Rehnquist might have been saying to the judges, Look out, my friends; you'd better shape up or you're going to lose some of your power.

At any rate, Chief Justice William Rehnquist's report implicitly confirms that Congress has the Article III power to limit jurisdiction on constitutional issues and take away from the federal courts the power to continue to do the sort of damage that they have been doing for the past several decades.

My new book, *The Supremacists: The Tyranny of Judges and How to Stop It,* is the layman's handbook for citizen action. It explains the problem of the activist judges in language that you don't have to be a lawyer to understand. It has all the necessary talking points about this issue and it answers the arguments you will hear. It enables you to tell your Member of Congress to hurry up and pass the legislation we need to put the judiciary back in its proper place in our constitutional

Separation of Powers. My book is unique in that it presents practical and constitutional remedies to curb the supremacist judges. All of these remedies can be passed by a majority vote in Congress, and none of them requires a constitutional amendment.

The crux of the issue of judicial supremacy is the preservation of self-government. Are we going to be governed by representatives whom we elect, and whom we can fire when they don't do what we want them to do? Or are we going to be ruled by supremacist judges who impose their own policies on us, overriding the other branches of government and the will of the American people?

The role that judges play in our system of government should be like that of baseball umpires. Umpires are essential to running a baseball game; someone has to call the balls and strikes and the close calls. But umpires are not permitted to change the rules of the game; the fans would not tolerate an umpire calling a batter out after two strikes.

The supremacist judges have been changing our nation's laws and culture, and as President George W. Bush said, we are not going to stand for it. The Constitution gives us the remedies for this judicial impudence. It's up to the American people to demand that Congress do its duty and use the constitutional remedies given us in the U.S. Constitution.

Phyllis Schlafly's latest book, ***The Supremacists-The Tyranny of Judges and How to Stop It***, is a highly recommended work which examines in-depth the issue of judicial activism.

12.

JUDICIAL ORDERED MURDER?

By James C. Dobson, Ph.D

—

Terri Schiavo slipped out of this life and into eternity on Thursday, March 31st, 2005.[1] This pitiful 41-year-old mentally disabled woman was condemned to death by an immoral Florida court judge named George Greer, who never came to visit her, yet ordered that she be dehydrated and starved to death at the insistence of her "husband," Michael.

Mr. Schiavo lived with another woman with whom he fathered two babies[2], and yet, he was designated as the "guardian" of Terri's welfare to the moment of death. Seven years after Terri's brain injury occurred, and five years after Michael successfully obtained a reputed million-dollar plus malpractice settlement[3] designated for his wife's care, he began saying he remembered that she didn't want to be sustained by a feeding tube.

His claim is nothing more than hearsay and there is no written record to substantiate it. But for Judge Greer, it was sufficient to grant his wish to have her put to death, despite the husband's enormous conflict of interest, related to his common law "marriage," divided loyalties and competing fiduciary responsibility.

To understand the enormity of this decision, it is important to recognize that Terri was not comatose before the killing began, was not on a respirator, and was not unaware of her circumstances. She smiled faintly, she followed people and objects with her eyes, and according to the registered nurse who had cared for her, she succeeded in saying a few words.

Nevertheless, Michael and the unjust judge made sure that Terri received the barest minimum of medical attention, no therapy such as assistance in learning to swallow, and, eventually, no food or water. Toward the end, the judge ordered that Terri not even be permitted to have ice chips placed in her mouth to moisten her parched tongue. She was confined to her room for five years with the shades drawn, could not be legally photographed or video taped, never received an MRI to determine the nature of her brain injury, and her parents were not even allowed to take her out in the warmth of the sun or to an outing at a mall.[4] And this is called justice.

Gary Bauer wrote this about Terri in a daily update distributed by his organization, American Values: "In the Gospel of Matthew, Chapter 25, verses 35 and 36, Jesus says, 'For I was hungry and you gave me food. I was thirsty and you gave me drink, I was a stranger and you welcomed me.' His disciples were puzzled and asked when they had done those things for Him. Christ responds (verse 40) - 'Truly, I say to you, as you did it to one of the least of these my brethren, you did it for me.'

Then Gary commented, "Surely, Terri Schiavo, abandoned by her husband, sentenced to death by our courts, regularly compared to a 'vegetable,' qualifies as 'the least of these.' Will someone give her a drink?"[5]

The answer was, "no." Judge Greer had police posted at the door to keep anyone from bringing relief to Terri, and an entire family was arrested for attempting to give her a sip of water.[6] Toward the end, Michael even refused to let the priest provide communion for Terri, and instructed the police to arrest him if he tried.[7] And shortly thereafter, Terri died. God forgive us!

Not even a dog or a cat in the pound, or a prisoner on death row, would be treated with such cruelty. In fact, on the very Sunday evening when House Majority Leader Tom DeLay and Senate Majority Leader Bill Frist were scrambling to pass a bill to save Terri, and President Bush flew back from Texas to Washington D.C. to sign the pending legislation, what was CBS television news doing? It aired a feature on the property rights of animals![8]

The media repeatedly told the American people that Terri was "brain dead" and that her brain had "turned to liquid".[9] Just before Terri's death, ABC's Good Morning America aired an interview between co-host Charlie Gibson and Dr. Jack Kevorkian, known as "Dr. Death", who is serving a 10-25 year prison sentence for helping people kill themselves.[10] With a straight face, Gibson asked Kevorkian to comment on the "circus" that surrounded the effort to save Terri.[11]

After the media had shamelessly made the people think that Terri was sustained by artificial means and was probably dying, ABC News conducted a poll to determine how folks felt about "letting" her die.

Have you wondered why the results were so lopsided in favor of death? Maybe I can explain it. The specific question asked by pollsters about whether or not it was appropriate to withhold food and water is as follows: "Schiavo suffered brain damage and has been on life support for 15 years. Doctors say she has no consciousness and her condition is irreversible. Do you support the decision to remove Terri's feeding tube?"[12]

Of course the majority of Americans answered affirmatively. Who would want to live unconscious, breathing with the aid of a respirator for 15 years? By distorting the facts given in the set-up question, the media got the results they were looking for. But, they were simply not accurate. Pollster John Zogby conducted a poll during the week of Terri's death and asked the following question:

"If a disabled person is not terminally ill, not in a coma, and not being kept alive on life support, and they have no written directive, should or should they not be denied food and water?"

These were the conditions Terri Schiavo was in prior to being sentenced to death by Judge Greer. To that question, 79 percent of those surveyed said the patient should not have food and water withheld![13] Have you seen that statistic quoted in your paper or on the evening news? Of course not-because it runs counter to the agenda of the mainstream press. Their silence is deafening.

This cooperative effort between the judiciary and the media to kill an innocent woman is one of the greatest miscarriages of justice in American history. It has implications for the 25,000 adults and 10,000 children in this country who are also fed and hydrated through a tube.[14] What are we going to do, kill them all?

Is every mentally disabled human being now fair game if they have an inconvenienced relative who wants to see him or her dead? Apparently, all they have to do is assert that starvation is what the victim wanted, and then find a wicked judge like George Greer who will order them subjected to slow execution. What a sad day this is for Terri and Schindler family, and for all of humanity! It is eerily similar to what the Nazis did in the 1930s. They began by "euthanizing" the mentally retarded, and from there, it was a small step to mass murder.

Terri's killing signifies conclusively that the judicial system in this country is far too powerful and is totally out of control. No agency of government can rival its reach. Not even the combined influence of the President, both Houses of the Congress and the Governor of Florida could override the wishes of a relatively low-ranking judge.

His decision was upheld by several federal court judges, and ultimately, by the U.S. Supreme Court that refused six times to hear Terri's case.[15] She was doomed by that time. How could Terri's parents have expected compassion from the Justices who have declared unconstitutional the ban on the horrible procedure known as partial birth abortion? Anyone who would sanction a law permitting the brains of healthy, unanaesthetized babies to be suctioned out is capable of any evil.

Unfortunately, this decision by the courts is symptomatic of a much wider slide by the courts into moral relativism. Consider, for example, another terrible decision handed down on March 14, 2005. Judge Richard Kramer of the San Francisco Superior Court summarily struck down California's law prohibiting same-sex marriage. The measure was deemed to be unconstitutional, he said, because "It appears that no rational purpose exists for limiting marriage in this state to opposite sex partners."[16] No rational purpose?

That takes us back to 2000, when, after a vigorous and highly emotional debate, fully sixty-one percent of Californians voted in a referendum to define marriage as being exclusively between one man and one woman; only thirty-nine percent disagreed.[17] Despite this overwhelming response by more than four million people, which became the law in the Golden State, Judge Kramer had the temerity to say that the will of the majority made no sense. He set himself up as the sole determiner of rationality. What utter arrogance! If the decision stands, it will be reflected in every department of government and in every California public school from kindergarten to high school.

We knew this judicial assault on the institution of marriage was coming, and it certainly won't be the last. Liberal judges throughout the nation are itching to sanction same-sex marriages by judicial decree, despite their awareness that the vast majority of Americans do not want the family to be redefined. There can be no doubt about that fact. Eighteen states have voted recently on the meaning of marriage, and all 18 have passed constitutional amendments defining marriage exclusively as being between one man and one woman. There have been no exceptions, not even in socially liberal Oregon and Hawaii. In all, 38 states have passed "defense of marriage acts."

Nevertheless, there in San Francisco sat an imperious judge who concluded that marriage-as it has existed for more than 5,000 years on every continent and in every culture on earth-is not rational and should be retooled. Although many fine men and women serve on the bench, this decision illustrates the heady abuse of power that is all too common among independent fiefdoms known as judges. They rule like royal monarchs. And sitting on the top of the pyramid is the U.S. Supreme Court, which threatens the liberty that was purchased with the blood of countless men and women who died to secure it.

How did this happen to us? How could such a great and freedom-loving people have allowed themselves to be dominated by a handful of unelected, unaccountable, arrogant and often godless judges, many of whom receive lifetime appointments and regularly circumvent the democratic process? It is a breath-taking and ominous development. Was this the desire of the Founding Fathers when they designed this great representative form of government? Hardly!

Thomas Jefferson warned repeatedly about the emergence of an out-of-control judiciary that would destroy the Constitution and, along with it, America's fundamental freedoms. He first became alarmed when, in 1803, the U. S. Supreme Court issued a landmark decision called *Marbury v. Madison*. It allowed the Justices to rule on the constitutionality of every legal issue, both inside and outside the government, giving themselves unrivaled imperial power.

The concept of "checks and balances" that was intended to keep one branch from eclipsing the other two was no longer in force-at least not with regard to the judiciary. Thereafter, the President, the Congress, and the will of millions of American people have been subservient to the rulings of five imperious justices, along with numerous lower court judges, who continue to issue their decrees beyond the reach of any authority.

When Jefferson recognized the full implications of the *Marbury* decision, he wrote this prophetic statement: "It is a very dangerous doctrine to consider the judges as the ultimate arbiters of all constitutional questions. It is one which would place us under the despotism of an oligarchy."[18]

BINGO! What we have today, 202 years later, is an oligarchy (rule by a small cadre of elites.) The courts simply strike down laws and policies they don't like, whether their opinions reflect the provisions of the Constitution or not. Furthermore, the activist judges and those who support them have turned the Constitution into what they call "a living, breathing document," in which its actual words no longer mean what they say. The Constitution "evolves," they tell us, to fit the biases of the court. Consequently, we no longer have a government "of the people, by the people and for the people," as Abraham Lincoln described it at Gettysburg. It is, instead-an oligarchy.

The *Marbury* decision in 1803 continued to agitate Jefferson for the next two decades. He wrote in 1819: "The Constitution...is a mere thing of wax in the hands of the judiciary which they may twist and shape into any form they please. It has long been my opinion, and I have never shrunk from its expression...that the germ of dissolution of our federal government is in the constitution of the federal Judiciary; working like gravity by night and by day, gaining a little today and a little tomorrow, and advancing its noiseless step like a thief, over the field of jurisdiction, until all shall be usurped."[19]

Jefferson issued one more warning in 1823, just three years before his death. This time, however, he was not simply predicting the rise of an imperious court; by then he had observed it first hand. Jefferson said, "At the establishment of our constitution, the judiciary bodies were supposed to be the most helpless and harmless members of the government. Experience, however, soon showed in what way they were to become the most dangerous..."[20]

Now, the misfortune that worried Jefferson has produced for us a culture of death that is steeped in moral relativism. We are victims in our day of the grab for power that should have been squelched two centuries ago. Since then, the Supreme Court Justices have simply overridden the will of the people, regularly and without apology. Every time they convene as a body it is like a mini-constitutional convention in which the meaning of the foundational document is changed without the consent of the governed. Henceforth, their pronouncements are the ultimate law of the land.

As we have seen, it was never intended to be that way. The Executive, the Legislative and the Judicial Branches of government are "co-equal" in the eyes of the law. We know that the President and Congress regularly limit each others power, but what about the judiciary? Many Americans do not know that Article 3, Section 1 of the Constitution clearly gives to Congress the responsibility to establish every court with the exception of the Supreme Court. These lower federal courts serve at the pleasure of the Congress, which can abolish or create them at will. For example, the troublesome Ninth Circuit Court of Appeals in San Francisco, which consistently issues off-the-wall rulings, (including the Pledge of Allegiance decision in 2002) could be abolished and then staffed by different judges immediately. But the Congress has not had the political gumption to take any such action. Consequently, the Courts arrogantly thumb their noses at the other co-equal authorities.

Look again at what happened in the Schiavo case. On March 18th, 2005, congressional Republicans subpoenaed Terri in an effort to protect her from the heinous orders of Judge Greer, who had demanded that her feeding tube removed that day.[21] Yet, Greer flouted the law, defiantly ignoring the congressional order! Three days later, in an extraordinary Palm Sunday weekend session, the House and Senate passed a bill, allowing for federal judicial review of Terri's case.[22] Yet, hours later, U.S. District Judge James Whittemore refused to order the reinsertion of the tube.[23]

After both the 11th Circuit and the U.S. Supreme Court refused to review the case, Judge Greer, a low-ranking County court probate judge, ignored new evidence that spoke to Terri's attempt to communicate a desire to live.[24] In the process, he not only defied the Congress and the President, but intimidated the Governor of Florida, Jeb Bush. The media defended Greer, of course, claiming the Congress had violated the "separation of powers."[25] They were entirely wrong. Our representatives were attempting to fulfill their constitutional obligations, but they lost their nerve when stared down.

So the unchecked judiciary plows ahead. In March of 2005, the Supreme Court struck down laws duly passed in 18 states permitting the execution of minors.[26] With that decision by five justices, the sentences of John Lee Malvo and other heinous killers were commuted. Malvo shot ten innocent people[27] standing peacefully on the streets just for the thrill of watching them die, yet he will not pay the ultimate price for his murderous spree.

Neither will Christopher Simmons, who broke into a house, bound and gagged an innocent woman with duct tape, beat her unmercifully, and then threw her body over the railing of a bridge. The autopsy revealed that she was still alive when Simmons dropped her to the river below.[28] And this was done for six dollars found in Shirley Ann Crook's purse. Does Simmons deserve to live? I think not. Please note that the same court that upholds the supposed Constitutional "right" to destroy innocent pre-born children has now prohibited the execution of cold-blooded murderers who are in their late teens.

While we can debate the wisdom of executing minors, (who, by the way, would have been at least 30 or 40 years old by the time their sentences were carried out,) the more important issue is how the law came to be struck down. It was not debated or decided by the American people or their representatives, where such issues should be deliberated and determined. It was nullified by judicial decree. The Oligarchy did it for us.

Even those who are opposed to the idea of capital punishment for minors should be gravely concerned about the criteria by which the Supreme Court arrived at its decision. In writing for the majority opinion, Justice Anthony Kennedy, whom I consider to be the most dangerous man in America, explained his rationale for the ruling, boldly claiming, "It is proper that we acknowledge the overwhelming weight of international public opinion against the juvenile death penalty."[29] This justification was written by a man who regularly ignores the weight of American public opinion in forcing his post-modern nonsense on our culture. Kennedy further promised that the Supreme Court of the United States would continue to look to "the laws of [selected] other countries and to international authorities" in re-interpreting the Constitution.[30]

Justice Kennedy should be impeached for taking such a position, along with O'Connor, Ginsberg, Souter, Breyer, and Stevens, who have recently made similar statements. It is outrageous that we, the people of the United States, not only find ourselves governed unwillingly by a judicial oligarchy, but we are manhandled and lectured by this tiny body of lawyers who increasingly base its rulings not on our Constitution, nor on legal precedent, nor even on international law-but on something they call "world opinion." The American people have neither chosen nor agree with this opinion. Kennedy and his liberal colleagues simply pick and choose the people in countries or continents that agree with them, usually from Europe and Canada, and ignore the rest, such as South America, Asia, and Africa. This is what we call "judicial tyranny!" and for good reason.

Justice Antonin Scalia, writing for the minority, referred to his colleagues on the Court as "black-robed masters."[31] A few weeks later, he went on to decry the manipulation of the Constitution by the other justices. He said, "Within the last 20 years, we have found...the right to abortion, which was so little rooted in the traditions of the American people that it was criminal for 200 years-[and] the right to homosexual sodomy, which was so little rooted in the traditions of the American people that it was criminal for 200 years."[32]

Justice Scalia continued, "So it is literally true . . . that the court has essentially liberated itself from the text of the Constitution, from the text and even from the traditions of the American people... and the Constitution is not a living organism, for Pete's sake. It's a legal document. And like all legal documents, it says some things and it doesn't say other things."[33]

Please tell me you understand the danger of this outrageous situation. To put ultimate power in the hands of those who promise to make up their rules as they go along-or to base them on treaties that were never ratified by Congress-is a recipe for disaster. Democracy itself hangs in the balance.

But the beat goes on. As we speak, the Supreme Court is debating whether or not to permit the Ten Commandments to be displayed in public buildings and elsewhere on public property. Of course, the nine justices sit every day in the Supreme Court Building that is adorned by three depictions of the Ten Commandments or of Moses.[34]

Our halls of government are positively brimming with references to our Judeo-Christian heritage. And don't forget the successive Sergeants at Arms, who since 1777 have opened each session of the Supreme Court by shouting, "God save this Court and the United States of America."[35] They will have to be silenced. Indeed, the entire nation will have to be transformed, it appears. And from here, religious liberty will hang precariously on every related decision.

Why? Because the American people demand it? No! It is because Justice Anthony Kennedy and the Oligarchy deem it so. Maybe they can find a rationale for trashing the remaining acknowledgments of the Creator somewhere in European public opinion. They certainly won't find it in this country. A CNN/USA Today/Gallup Poll released earlier this month found that 76 percent of respondents supported displaying the Ten Commandments, while only 21 percent were opposed.[36] But then, our opinions are of no consequence.

Thomas Jefferson, you saw it coming.

Judicial hostility to faith, and especially Christianity has never been greater than today. On George W. Bush's Inauguration Day, January 20, 2005, Judge Gary Lancaster of the U.S. District Court for Western Pennsylvania dismissed a federal case against hardcore pornographers that were distributing undeniably obscene sex videos depicting [pardon me for speaking graphically.] rape, mutilation, defecation, and the murder of women.

In so doing, he declared federal obscenity statutes unconstitutional, overriding three decades of Supreme Court precedent in the process. Judge Lancaster defended his decision by proclaiming: "After [the 2003 *Lawrence v. Texas* decision], however, upholding the public sense of morality is not even a legitimate state interest that can justify infringing one's liberty interest to engage in consensual sexual conduct in private"[37] [emphasis added].

This hardcore porn case is particularly troublesome. Judge Lancaster is essentially suggesting that America's laws cannot be based upon morality! Can you imagine such a ruling coming from a person who has sworn an oath to uphold the Constitution of the United States? Remember his name: Gary Lancaster. Never forget it! He is symbolic of what is wrong with America's judicial system. Heaven forbid that he should ever become a "black robed master" in the future.

Anti-religious rulings like the one made by Lancaster are coming in bunches now. Another occurred on March 28, 2005, when three members of the Colorado Supreme Court overturned the death-penalty verdict for cocaine addict, Robert Harlan.[38] Harlan was convicted and sentenced to die for kidnapping and raping a 25-year old waitress. He held her captive for two hours before killing her in cold-blood. The Court overturned the death penalty decision because, if you can believe this, five members of the jury had looked up Bible verses to help them understand the moral implications of capital punishment. In so doing, it was said, they violated the separation of church and state.[39] There was very little protest from the religious community in Colorado as the state moved yet another step closer to the concept of the law without reference to right and wrong.

What can we do to reverse this out of control court, especially on a federal level? First, we need legislators who have the moxie to do what is right for the country. With notable exceptions, many of them have been too timid to speak up. Congress needs to know we've had enough. Secondly, our country desperately needs principled judges who will interpret the Constitution as written, rather than creating their own version of it and imposing European socialism and "politically correct" thinking.

During his first term in office, President Bush tried repeatedly to nominate conservative, strict constructionist judges to a variety of vacant positions on Federal Courts of Appeals and District Courts throughout the country. However, he was thwarted at every turn by liberal senators, led by the recently "retired" Tom Daschle. The former Senator consistently led filibusters of nominees or engaged in otherwise obstructionist tactics to ensure that they would never receive a fair hearing. Today's liberals in the Senate need to understand that they will be held accountable at the ballot box if they try to prevent up or down votes on judicial nominees.

In a bold and principled move, the President has defied his liberal opponents in Congress by re-nominating twenty top-notch individuals and sending their names to the Senate for appointment to various judicial vacancies nationwide.[40] These judges are all committed to applying the Constitution of the United States in a conservative manner and interpreting it as it is written.

If these individuals, and many others like them, were to be appointed to the federal bench, we could make significant strides toward the restoration of religious speech to the public square, the enforcement of laws regulating obscenity, the protection of voluntary prayer in public schools, the defense of the institution of traditional marriage, and the protection of pre-born babies from the horrors of abortion. In short, the makeup of the federal judiciary in the coming years will play a key role in determining how these issues - and many others that we hold dear - will be decided, and in demonstrating what kind of people we are as a nation.

Again in 2005, however, Senate liberals are endeavoring to sabotage this process by blocking the confirmation of judges before they even have a chance to come up for a vote. In their minds, judges who will interpret the Constitution as written have no place on the federal judiciary. Senator Joe Biden made this clear during a recent Meet the Press interview. In discussing the impending retirement of Chief Justice William Rehnquist from the Supreme Court, host Tim Russert asked whether Senator Biden would support elevatng Antonin Scalia to the position of Chief Justice. This is an important point, because Senator Biden voted to confirm Scalia to the Court in 1987, saying at the time that it would be improper for the Senate to "deprive the president of the United States from being able to appoint [a] person or persons who have a particular point of view..."[41]

And yet now, that is exactly what Senator Biden and his cronies are advocating. He boldly told Mr. Russert that he would oppose elevating Antonin Scalia to Chief Justice "because of his methodology, the way he interprets the Constitution."[42] In other words, conservative, strict constructionists need not apply! So far, the liberals are using this same shameful reasoning in blocking the president's federal court nominees.

To counter these obstructionist tactics senators have been considering a change in Senate rules, dubbed the "constitutional option," whereby the requirement for cloture (a procedure by which 60 senators can vote to terminate a filibuster and allow a vote) could be done away with when it comes to judicial nominations.

Senator Robert Byrd, in a shocking display of arrogance, responded by suggesting that the majority was employing Hitler-esque tactics: "Hitler never abandoned the cloak of legality. He recognized the enormous psychological value of having the law on his side. Instead, he turned the law inside out and made illegality legal. And that is what the nuclear [constitutional] option seeks to do." [43] He further lamented his minority status, going so far as to suggest that "Minorities have an illustrious past, full of suffering, torture, smear and even death. Jesus Christ was killed by a majority..."[44]

What incredible hypocrisy! Senator Byrd is a former member of the Ku Klux Klan who filibustered the Civil Rights Act of 1964.[45] It takes a great deal of gall for him to lecture the majority - and the American people - on the struggles faced by minorities.

The shrill and desperate tone employed by Senator Byrd and others on the American Left is indicative of just how much is at stake in this battle. The nomination and confirmation of federal court judges represents a critical moment in the history of our nation, as well as a monumental opportunity for men and women of faith and others in the pro-family movement to stand up and make their voices heard.

In addition to contacting your leaders, I hope that you will keep this issue in your prayers. We desperately need divine intervention to preserve the nation that was birthed in prayer from the beginning. Otherwise, the federal judiciary will continue to hold incredible power in determining whether babies in the womb will live or die, whether children and families will be exposed to hardcore pornography, whether traditional marriage will be protected in law, and so many other important issues.

13.

INTERNATIONAL LAW?

By Alan E. Sears, Esq.

The U.S. Constitution, developed by some of the brightest and most able statesmen in history of this world, is the supreme secular law of the land. Its carefully drafted text—with its careful concept of checks and balances and a division of powers—resulted from the efforts of brave men to limit the reach and power of government and to protect the fist of liberty.

A cursory glance at the tremendous freedom and economic prosperity of America as compared to other nations—even many developed nations—should tell us that what the U.S. Constitution and its foundational principles have allowed are the envy of the world.

Even The Wall Street Journal took notice of this three years ago, reporting that in part due to their legal tradition the "U.S. and Britain have bigger stock markets and more shareholding citizens than Germany and France."

So if our constitutional tradition works so well why are we suddenly importing foreign, international law into the U.S. through judicial interpretations and application?

Foreign legal ideas from different legal traditions may be worth studying. But even if desirable they should only be adopted through proper channels of legislative deliberation and enactment.

More and more often our judicial elite seem to believe the Constitution's foundational principles can be bent to an agenda to make our law look more like that of other nations.

How being like other nations improves life in the U.S. is hard for many of us to see, but Justice Ruth Bader Ginsburg has openly advocated this position in her remarks to the American Constitution Society, when she derided our country's "Lone Ranger mentality."

Other justices say we can't ignore the rest of the world and they are correct. However, diplomacy is the job of the State Department not the judiciary.

If other nations want to adopt the legal infrastructure that makes America the economic destination of choice, great! But is it sensible to risk our progress for a gamble on judicial globalization? Judicial "transjudicialism" could very well make us like other nations in ways we won't like.

Foreign courts often cite U.S. courts when "life and liberty are at stake," which is the way it should be. Why should we, as the world's only superpower and as the leader of the free world bow to adopting foreign legal precedents to interpret—or reinterpret—our law?

Legal precedents have enough unforeseen results, and we have enough trouble with our courts interpreting our

Constitution. Why go seeking fresh legal problems abroad?

If courts can amend the Constitution with the wave of a magic wand by selectively incorporating foreign law to reach their desired results, then they have too much power.

God bless the memory of America's founders who rejected other traditions of law of their day to create this the best, most free and prosperous nation on this earth.

14.

JUST SAY NO TO JUDICIAL TYRANNY

By Don Feder

There's a movie - just released on video and DVD - called "Open Range." It's a morality tale set in the Old West. In one moving scene, Robert Duvall tells the townsfolk, "A man's got a right to protect his life and property. Ain't no rancher or his lawman gonna take that away!" Similarly, we could say, " A man or a woman's got a right to protect his faith, family, and freedom. Ain't no judge gonna take that away!"

For the past 40 years, judges have been unmaking the Constitution. Now, it's time for us to begin unmaking judges.

Judicial tyranny didn't start with the infamous Massachusetts decision in *Goodridge v. Department of Public Health.*

On Aug. 1, 2003, U.S. District Judge Myron Thompson ruled that Judge Roy Moore's Ten Commandments monument in the rotunda of the Alabama judicial building violated the

First Amendment's establishment clause. Lest we forget, the amendment reads in part, "Congress shall make no law respecting an establishment of religion, or prohibiting the free exercise thereof."

That must mean Roy Moore is Congress, and his monument to Mosaic Law is a state church.

In 2002, the U.S. 9th Circuit Appeals Court held the phrase "one nation under God" made it unconstitutional to say the Pledge of Allegiance in public schools. Poor Abraham Lincoln had no idea he was violating the establishment clause when he uttered those immortal words, "That this nation, under God, shall have a new birth of freedom," in dedicating a federal cemetery at Gettysburg, Pennsylvania.

In June 2003, in *Lawrence v. Texas*, the United States Supreme Court discovered a heretofore unimagined right to homosexual sodomy in the First Amendment - probably in the same non-existent clause that supposedly guarantees the "right" to abortion on demand.

Curiously, 14 years earlier, in *Bowers v. Hardwick*, the same court held there was no such right. It's amazing how much the inherent meaning of the Constitution changed in those 14 years.

Justice Sandra Day O'Connor voted one way in *Bowers v. Hardwick* and the other in *Lawrence v. Texas*. Which compels one to ask, "Madame Justice, what is it about the Constitution that you were confused about 14 years ago, but that you now understand?"

Of course, the Constitution didn't magically transform itself in those years, nor did Sandra Day O'Connor's ability to grasp the inherent meaning of the First Amendment. What changed is the culture. Liberal judges read the Constitution by the light of a cultural candle. The culture says sodomy is a right? Well, so must the Constitution! The culture ordains homosexual marriage? It must be in there somewhere.

Within days of *Lawrence v. Texas*, the Supreme Court ruled the 14th Amendment - which was intended to outlaw race-based discrimination - in fact mandates racial discrimination.

Which brings us, inevitably, tragically, to the infamous Massachusetts decision of last November, when (by a single vote) the state's highest court found a right to same-sex marriage in the Massachusetts constitution - a charter originally written at the time of the Revolutionary War. Who would have thought that John Adams - who said the U.S. Constitution was "written for a moral and a religious people, it is wholly inadequate for the governance of any other" - intended to put society's seal of approval on what then were called unnatural acts when he wrote the Mass. Constitution.

I could go on, but what's the point - other than to stress our enslavement by a gang of black-robed plantation masters. I can't wait for the day when some court, somewhere in this troubled land, rules that democracy is unconstitutional. As a matter of fact, they already have - without using those exact words.

Constitutionalists usually focus on three solutions to this crisis:

FIRST: Amend the Constitution.
SECOND: Appoint conservative judges
THIRD: Withdraw jurisdiction from the courts, under Article III, Section 2 of the U.S. Constitution.

Let me propose a FOURTH: - "Just say no to judicial tyranny."

How about simply ignoring the unlawful, unconstitutional edicts of black-robed Jacobins?

Andrew Jackson - who fought redcoats and duels for his wife's honor - was confronted with a similar situation during his tenure. Old Hickory declared: "Mr. Marshall has made his decision. Now, let him enforce it." We need to be equally defiant.

What enforcement powers does any court have? All rely on our acquiescence. In other words, we let them get away with it.

Take the crisis at hand. Say, Massachusetts Gov. Mitt Romney (reputed to be a Republican) issued a directive to the Massachusetts Department of Public Health to order city and town clerks not to issue marriage licenses to him and him, or her and her. What would the justices of the state's high court do? Hold their breaths until they turned blue? Kick and scream?

Let's be clear about one thing: What I am urging is not civil disobedience - which means to violate the lawful authority of the state. Ignoring the attempted usurpations of un-elected officials - social Bolsheviks — is the highest fidelity to the Constitution and rule of law.

I call this the Roy Moore principal. Last summer, the chief justice of the Alabama Supreme Court said to a gang of judicial activists, "You're telling me the First Amendment will not allow me to acknowledge God in a public place? Wrong. Unconstitutional. Not going to do it." In so doing, Moore fired the opening volley of the next American Revolution.

All that's lacking is the political will to stand up for the Constitution and the Judeo-Christian morality on which it is based. The will to stand up for original intent, to stand up for the grand vision of the Founding Fathers, to stand up to judicial Saddams and Osamas.

In so doing, we will have to combat an entrenched mindset. Most Americans honestly believe that judges are magicians and the Constitution (federal or state) is a magic hat from which these hyper-active Houdinis are allowed to pull the most grotesque and deformed mutant rabbits which all are expected to venerate.

But the day will come - mark my words - when the American people will have had enough, when the masses revolt.

And then we will pull down this Dark Tower of judicial tyranny with our bare hands.

15.

THE SOUL OF AMERICA

By Rev. Rick Scarborough

The soul of America is dying. What used to amaze us now only amuses us. Massachusetts continues its relentless assault on marriage, and while there is a modest outcry going up, the majority of Christians in America have once again decided to sit this one out. For forty years the assault on morality has continued unabated. Let's review some of the decisions that have been handed down by the courts, which have reshaped morality in America:

1) A ban on prayer in the public schools in 1962
2) A ban on Bible reading in the public schools in 1963
3) Abortion on demand in 1973
4) A ban on the posting of the Ten Commandments in public schools in 1980
5) The *Lawrence v. Texas* sodomy decision laying the foundation for same-sex marriage in 2003.

6) The partial birth abortion ban which our President signed into law was promptly deemed unconstitutional before it could take effect
7) Same-sex marriage granted equal status with traditional marriage in Massachusetts in 2004

Who's to blame for this slide toward Gomorrah? The Muslim world looks at the immorality of the West, and especially America, and calls us the Great Satan. Who's responsible for what has happened to our once great nation?

I submit to you the blame must be borne by the Church of the Lord Jesus Christ...and more specifically, the pastors of God's church. But they are not alone in this great day of moral decadence. The people of God have been willing co-conspirators, as we have bowed to the god of personal convenience and comfort.

> "They cling to deceit, they refuse to return. I have listened attentively but they do not say what is right. No one repents of his wickedness saying what have I done? Each pursues his own course like a horse charging into battle. Even the stork in the sky knows her appointed seasons and the dove, the swift and the thrush observe the time of migration. But my people do not know the requirement of the Lord."
>
> - Jeremiah 8:5-7

Pastors are more than willing to give the people what they want to hear as they have exchanged their role of prophet to that of psychologist, preaching an "I'm-OK-you're-OK" gospel.

Jeremiah 8:10-11 says:

> "From the least to the greatest all are greedy for gain; Prophets and priests alike, all practice deceit. They dress the wounds of my people as though they were not serious. 'Peace peace,' they say, when there is no peace."

And what is the great sin of the church? Pastor and people just sit and do nothing as this nation plunges toward the path of destruction. Listen to the prophet Jeremiah as he speaks on behalf of the Lord:

> "Why are we sitting here? Gather together!" Jer. 8:14

We foolishly wait for God to deliver us from the decadence we see all around, but while elitist Judges usurp powers they were never granted, exchanging their godless philosophies for the laws of God written into our nation's laws by God fearing men and women, we gather in our houses of worship day after day and month after month and piously sing "Kumbaya," waiting for our Lord to deliver us or snap his fingers and make it all go away. But it's not going away, and while we play church, men who hate God are systematically expunging Him from the Nation He created.

Think back with me:

> 1) When prayer was removed from the public schools, was it by a vote of the American people?
>
> 2) When Bible study was taken out of our public schools was it by a vote of the American people?
>
> 3) When it became legal for a woman to kill her own baby in her womb, was it by a vote of the American people?

4) When the Ten Commandments were stricken from public classrooms, was it by a vote of the American people?

5) When sodomy was declared to be a constitutionally protected right, was it by a vote of the American people?

6) When the partial birth abortion ban was declared unconstitutional, was it by a vote of the American people?

7) When that which God calls an abomination was declared to be Holy Matrimony, was it by a vote of the American people?

Judges who imposed their own personal agendas upon the nation, with no Constitutional authority whatsoever, mandated each of the above steps down the road to perdition upon the American people. With each pernicious ruling there was an outcry from the people, but the politicians, and especially the judges, simply ignored the people and persisted in their unabashed determination to change America. Tragically, the church, much like the popular song of a past generation, "Just kept wishing and hoping and planning and praying...." that it would all go away and somehow America would once again be like it was. The problem has been exacerbated by popular culture as the music, the movies, and the sitcoms all reflect the changing morality that the courts mandated upon the people.

Every civilization that has embarked on this path has died. America has been dying for a generation, and now the death pains are more violent and convulsive. When *Lawrence v. Texas* was handed down by the Supreme Court in June of 2003, declaring that the citizens of Texas could not pass a law restricting homosexual activities, Justice Antonin Scalia wrote a scathing dissent, in which he stated that for the first time in judicial history the Court had taken a side in the culture war. He rightly predicted the definition of marriage would soon be radically altered as this decision was carried out. Just like the illicit ruling against Alabama Chief Justice Roy Moore in the fall of 2003 resulted in the ACLU and other like-minded organizations fanning out across the country to remove every Ten Commandment monument from public display, homosexual activists began racing to city and county courthouses demanding that their once illegal activities be given the same status as Holy Matrimony. One has to ask oneself, where will this madness end?

Once again, the Scripture has a relevant and sobering response:

> "Are they ashamed of their loathsome conduct? No, they have no shame at all; they do not know how to blush, so they will fall among the fallen, they will be brought down when they are punished.
>
> I will take away their harvest, declares the Lord. There will be no grapes on the vine, no figs on the tree and their leaves will whither. What I have given them will be taken away."
>
> -Jeremiah 8:12-13

The most remarkable fact concerning the fall of American values and morality has been the foundation upon which it has been based. When prayer was removed it was based upon the myth that the Ffirst Amendment to the Constitution prohibited any religious expression to be made in the public square. So let's take a fresh look at the First Amendment:

> "Congress shall make no laws respecting an establishment of religion, or prohibiting the

free exercise thereof.

Now, let's examine this first of the Bill of Rights, guaranteed to the states. "Congress shall make no laws..." Not the courts...Congress. Our Constitution divided the powers of government between three branches: the Executive Branch, the Legislative Branch, and the Judicial Branch. All three have clearly defined roles, but generally speaking, the Legislative Branch makes the laws, the Judicial Branch makes sure they do not contradict the Constitution, and the Executive Branch sees that they are carried out and enforced.

When the Supreme Court in 1962 stated that prayer in schools was unconstitutional, they cited as their legal precedent, not the Constitution nor a previous ruling by a binding legal authority, but rather an obscure letter from Thomas Jefferson written to the Danbury Baptist Association. In the letter, Jefferson spoke of a "wall of separation" between the Church and the State, reassuring the Danbury Baptists that the newly adopted Constitution had erected a barrier preventing the Federal Government from ever institutionalizing the church. His letter wasn't even saying that states couldn't have state churches, which several states had adopted at the time of the founding of our country, only that there would never be a national church, like that of England or Spain.

The First Amendment states that, "Congress shall make no law..." If Congress can make no law, how then can the Court interpret a law which Congress cannot make? If the Court has no Constitutional authority to make a ruling, then their ruling is an illegal ruling. That makes the judges who make such a ruling tyrants, and the elected official and citizens who allow them to stand without challenge, complicit in their tyranny.

It's time for the men of God to call these actions what they are. We don't have activist judges in America, which implies something noble...a judge who takes his job seriously and acts on truth. We have black robed tyrants who believe they are above the law and appointed to help the uninformed masses make right decisions for their lives. And the citizens are not apathetic.... that implies that they are just lazy. When you see someone being brutalized and you can do something about it, but you do not...that's wickedness.

In the past 40 years we have witnessed the undermining of everything that was once sacred to Americans. When I grew up in Houston in the 50's, people slept by open windows with attic fans and open front doors. Kids played outside after dark, unattended without fear of being kidnapped and molested or worse. We gathered around black and white TV's and watched My Little Marjorie, My Three Sons, Ozzie and Harriet, The Andy Griffith Show and Leave It to Beaver. Later would come Bonanza and High Chaparral, all of which taught strong family values, courage, kindness, and commitment, with strong and wholesome parental figures. A foul word was unheard of and every broadcast day began with a pledge to uphold the standards of the nation and the playing of the National Anthem, and ended with a devotional and a prayer, donated by the networks.

In one generation we have witness this country slide from a Nation which...

Shared a moral vision based on the Judeo Christian Ethic...to a nation floundering in moral decay.

From life long marriages to the same partner as the general rule... to a divorce rate which exceeds 50%.

From homosexuality being criminalized.... to same-sex marriage being celebrated.

From courts where mercy and justice were meted out in fairness, and the Bible was used to invoke the fear of God in our testimonies by judges that were esteemed as men of character and integrity...to the removal of Alabama Chief Justice Roy Moore for his refusal to cease acknowledging God.

From entertainment that the whole family could enjoy together...to Sex In The City and Queer Eye For The Straight Guy.

From a nation where life was treasured and protected...to the aborting of 1/3 of the babies conceived, including partial birth abortion, which is full-term infanticide.

From political seasons which featured open and lively debate of the issues...to the politics of character assassination and media manipulation.

From public education, which produced the highest literacy rate in the world...to schools that are preoccupied with sex education, which is nothing more than the ***facilitation of fornication***. Good teachers are leaving public education in droves because they are called upon to parent at-risk kids, without morals or parental guidance. They're growing tired of risking their lives for pay that reflects that society does not value what they do. Many of our inner-city schools are falling down in the shadow of publicly funded mega-million dollar sports complexes where athletes who can barely read or write are rewarded with multimillion dollar contracts for playing games, a growing number of whom have criminal records.

From a nation known as the melting pot of many nations where everyone, despite their national origin, was an American, who ask not what their county could do for them, but what they could do for their country.... to a boiling pot of hyphenated Americans demanding their rights but refusing to own up to their personal responsibility.

To a very similar culture in Isaiah's day, the Lord God of Heaven asked the probing question:

> "Now you dwellers in Jerusalem and Judah...insert Washington and America....
>
> "Judge between me and my vineyard. What more could have been done for my vineyard than I have done for it?
>
> "Now you dwellers in Jerusalem and Judah...Washington and America...When I looked for good grapes why did it only yield bad? I will tell you what I am going to do to my vineyard: I will take away its hedge, and it will be destroyed.
>
> "I will break down its wall and it will be trampled. I will make it a wasteland."
>
> -Isaiah 5:3-5

Isaiah's nation had committed a series of transgressions, not unlike ours. In fact, I dedicated nine chapters in my book to a discussion of the nine documented sins of Isaiah's Judah. Isaiah 3 lists them. Let's look at a sampling:

> Verse 3: Mere children will rule over them...the King James Version uses the word, "babes". Young children hold no core values, but rather emulate the actions of others. They have no conviction and lack character development. ***A generation of politicians rather than statesmen.***

> Verse 6: A man will seize one of his brothers at his father's home and he will say, "You be our leader...." But in that day he will cry out, "...do not make me a leader of the people." *Apathy and personal comfort rule the day.*

> Verse 8-9: Jerusalem (Washington) stagers, Judah (America) is falling; their words and their deeds are against the Lord, defying his glorious presence. The look on their faces testifies against them; they parade their sin as Sodom, they do not hide it. Woe to them! They have brought disaster upon themselves. ***Gays out of the closet and marching down Main Street.***

The soul of America is dying. My good friend, Dr. Laurence White, Pastor of Our Savior Lutheran Church in Northwest Houston, has devoted much of his ministry to studying and documenting the role of the Church in the rise and fall of the Third Reich, under Adolph Hitler. The similarities between the failures of the American Church and Nazi Germany are frightening. Dr. White shows convincingly in his speeches how the soul of Germany died long before the nation was destroyed. Unfortunately, no one knows just when God finally says enough is enough to a nation, as He clearly did to Judah in Isaiah 5, but this truth is sure: God will not tolerate wickedness by a nation forever.

In Isaiah 3:10, God gives comfort to the righteous:

> "Tell the righteous it will be well with them for they will enjoy the fruit of their deeds."

What are your deeds? What seeds are you planting this morning? That is the crucial issue. I do not believe that it is ***too late*** for America...but I do believe it is ***late*** in America. I believe the Church, and by that I mean the true Church in America, holds the key to America's future. When I speak of church, I am not speaking of the Charismatics, nor the Baptists, nor the Catholics, nor any particular denomination, but those who hold the Bible as the Word of God, who have repented of their sins and been washed in the Blood of the Lamb and trust only Jesus for their salvation...that's the true Church. I believe that the Church holds the key to the future of America.

> Politicians in America will not preserve marriage.
> Politicians in America will not end abortion.
> Politicians in America will not reduce crime.
> Politicians in America will not improve education.
> Politicians in America will not reverse corruption.
> Politicians in America will not end immorality.

None of the great moral/political issues America faces can be corrected until we experience Revival in America, and that requires that Christians repent of their sins. Specific sin specifically named and specifically repented of by each of us. That brings personal revival, and that precedes national revival.

But national revival must also come if America is to be saved. That requires corporate action. The Church of the Living Loving Lord must rise up together and throw off the myth of ***Separation of Church and State.*** We must no longer sit by and watch the infidels run the nation into hell. We must pray without ceasing but we must become the answer to our own prayers as we stand for truth and righteousness in the public sector. We must register to vote and use our influence to get others registered to vote. We must get informed of the issues confronting this nation and then we must vote.... not as Republicans or Democrats, but as followers of Jesus Christ. We must join forces in unions with other like-minded God-fearing Americans and get over our fear of being political. Politics is the system we live in, and we should reclaim it and redeem it.

Charles Finney, more than 100 hundred years ago, stated correctly:

> "The Church must take right ground in regards to politics....
>
> "The time has come for Christians to vote for honest men and take consistent ground in politics or the Lord will curse them...
>
> "God cannot sustain this free and blessed country which we love and pray for, unless the church will take right ground. Politics are a part of religion in such a country as this and the Christians must do their duty to their country as a part of their duty to God. God will bless or curse this nation according to the course Christians take in politics."

16.

WHEN IN THE COURSE...

By Mathew D. Staver, Esq.

Aristotle once said that inherent in a free society is the ability of people to debate the question: "How ought we to order our life together?"[1] Today we hear a lot of rhetoric that the Bill of Rights is designed to protect the liberties of the minority against the majority. However, our constitutional makeup does not give the minority veto rights over the majority. Certainly the majority cannot trample constitutional rights, but the major political and social questions of our day have, by constitutional design, been given to the majority through the legislative process.

Continually taking away the right of the majority to shape their culture will ultimately result in rebellion. After all, the give and take of the political process provides that the majority voice have final say on major sociological issues. To take away the right of the people to debate the question leads to oligarchy (government of the few) and results in tyranny.

BASIS FOR GOVERNMENT

The signers of the Declaration of Independence clearly understood the purpose of government. They penned the following poignant words:

> "When in the course of human events it becomes necessary for one people to dissolve the political bands which have connected them with another, and to assume among the Power of the earth, the separate and equal station to which the Laws of Nature and of Nature's God entitle them, decent respect to the opinions of mankind requires that they should declare the causes which impel them to the separation.
>
> "We hold these truths to be self-evident that all men are created equal, that they are endowed by their Creator with certain unalienable Rights, that among these are Life, Liberty, and the pursuit of Happiness.
>
> "That to secure these rights, Governments are instituted among Men, deriving their just powers from the consent of the governed.
>
> "That whenever any Form of Government becomes destructive of these ends, it is the Right of the People to alter or abolish it, and to institute new Government, laying its foundation on such principles and organizing its powers in such form, as to them shall seem most likely to affect their Safety and Happiness...
>
> "But when a long train of abuses and usurpations, pursuing invariably the same Object, evinces a design to reduce them under absolute Despotism, it is their right, it is their

> duty, to throw off such Government, and to provide new Guards for their future security..."[2]

The founders clearly understood that government's purpose is to preserve life, liberty, and the pursuit of happiness. These liberties are God-given. Such liberties predate government and are inalienable,[3] meaning that government cannot (at least should not) take away these liberties. The sole purpose of government is to make sure these liberties are protected. Whenever any form of government fails to protect, or in the worst case, affirmatively destroys, these liberties, then it is the right and duty of the people to alter or abolish that system and to institute a new form of government.

SEPARATION OF POWERS

When contemplating a new form of government, the founders envisioned depositing governmental power into three separate branches. The founders clearly feared that if one branch of government accumulated too much power, it would overcome the other two branches of government, thus leading to tyranny. The human experience was itself sufficient reason for separating the powers of government. The founders knew quite well that power corrupts, and absolute power corrupts absolutely. George Washington in his farewell address observed the following:

> "A just estimate of that love of power, and proneness to abuse it which predominates in the human heart, is sufficient to satisfy us for the truth of this position. The necessity of reciprocal checks in the exercise of political power by dividing and distributing it into different depositories... has been [established]."[4]

Not only must government itself be checked and balanced, but government must also restrain human passion. When putting forth arguments to the people of New York as to why the colonies should adopt a constitution, Alexander Hamilton wrote:

> "Why has government been instituted at all? Because the passions of men will not conform to the dictates of reason and justice without constraint."[5]

The founders envisioned three separate branches of government which included the Executive, the Legislative and the Judiciary. The weakest branch of government was supposed to be the Judiciary, but today it has become the strongest branch. Indeed, not until 1935 did the United States Supreme Court find a permanent home in Washington, DC. Prior to its present location, it met in the basement of the Senate. Alexander Hamilton described the three branches of government as follows:

> "The executive not only dispenses the honors, but holds the sword of the community. The legislature not only commands the purse, but prescribes the rules by which the duties and rights of every citizen are to be regulated. The judiciary on the contrary has no influence over either the sword or the purse, no direction either of the strength or of the wealth of the society, and can take no active resolution whatsoever. It may be truly said to have neither Force nor Will, but merely judgment; and must ultimately depend upon the aid of the executive arm even for the efficacy of its judgments."[6]

As Alexander Hamilton noted, the executive carries the sword, the legislature holds the purse, and the judiciary is ultimately dependent upon the aid of the executive even for the efficacy of carrying out its judgments. In other words, the judiciary can issue an opinion, but that opinion has no power without the aid of the executive to enforce that opinion.

As originally envisioned, the judiciary was not only the weakest branch of government but was the least dangerous threat to political liberty. Again, Alexander Hamilton pointed out the following:

> "[T]he judiciary, from the nature of its functions, will always be the least dangerous to the political rights of the constitution; because it will least in capacity to annoy or injure them... [T]he judiciary is, beyond comparison, the weakest of the three departments of power... [T]he general liberty of the people can never be endangered from that quarter."[7]

Why did Alexander Hamilton believe that the judiciary could never threaten the liberties of the people? The judiciary was set up to decide cases and controversies – to solve disputes between parties. The judiciary could not execute its judgments, it could simply render them. The executive has the duty, and the discretion, to carry out a judicial decree. As originally established, the judiciary was only reactive, deciding cases and controversies that were brought to its attention. These cases or controversies ultimately resolve the disputes between the parties, and would not necessarily apply to the populace in general. The judiciary could not levy taxes or create new law. The judiciary was charged with the task of applying existing law to resolve a case or controversy.

James Madison understood how liberty could be undermined if too much power were exercised by the judiciary.

> "It is necessary that the supreme judiciary should have the confidence of the people. This will soon be lost if they are employed in the task

> of remonstrating against [opposing and striking down] popular measures of the legislature."[8]

Today it has become common place for the judiciary to strike down "popular measures of the legislature." In 1996, the United States Supreme Court struck down Colorado's Amendment 2 which provided an amendment to the state constitution that would prohibit giving special rights to homosexuals.[9] In 1995, a federal court found unconstitutional a voter approved California initiative withholding welfare benefits from illegal aliens,[10] and in 1996, another federal court found unconstitutional another California voter-approved initiative.[11]

The latter vote initiative abolished affirmative action, and therefore in essence stated that instead of preference based on skin color, the state would now treat its citizens equally. Amazingly, a federal court found that a voter approved amendment requiring that all people be treated equally regardless of skin color violated Equal Protection under the United States Constitution. A later court reversed this decision.[12] In a desegregation case, a federal court ordered that property taxes be increased to fund a desegregation program.[13] Though the United States Supreme Court later ruled that the federal court overstepped its authority,[14] the mere fact that a court even thought of the possibility of raising taxes is incomprehensible.

THE PROBLEM

Interestingly, the United States Supreme Court once declared that the "Federal Constitution does not give this Court the power to overturn the State's choice under the guise of constitutional interpretation because the Justices of this Court believe that they can provide better rules."[15] However, that is exactly what the justices of the Supreme Court and judges of other courts do every day. Therein lies the problem. In 1803,

Supreme Court Chief Justice John Marshall penned these now famous words; "It is, emphatically, the province and duty of the judicial department to say what the law is."[16] Sometime after the famous *Marbury v. Madison* decision, the Supreme Court again resurrected John Marshall's words in the famous case of *Cooper v. Aaron*, where the Court stated that the *Marbury decision* declared:

> "the basic principle that the federal judiciary is supreme in the exposition of the law of the Constitution, and that principle has ever since been respected by this Court and the Country as a permanent and indispensable feature of our constitutional system."[17]

There are several problems inherent in the judicial branch. First, the federal judiciary is appointed, not elected. Once appointed, they are essentially appointed for life unless subsequently impeached. The federal judiciary is an unelected body precisely because it is supposed to be independent of, and not necessarily swayed by, popular political opinion.

Generally this would work fine if the judiciary would exercise self restraint, and interpret, rather than create law. However, if the judicial branch has the ultimate responsibility of interpreting the meaning of the Constitution, then the judiciary will always have a trump card on the other two branches of government. If the branch which interprets the law has final word over the branch that creates the law, then the branch that creates the law is essentially irrelevant because no matter what is created, the judiciary can interpret it differently. Since the judiciary has evolved to this power platform over time, it has gradually taken away the opportunity from the people to debate the social issues of our day.

All the major social and political questions of our time are now decided by the judiciary, not the people en masse. For example, a single state court judge ruled that prohibiting same-sex marriage is unconstitutional under the State of Hawaii's Constitution.[18] The judge accepted testimony that there was no difference between homosexual and heterosexual marriage, and consequently there was no reason under Hawaii's equal protection clause of the state constitution to deny a marriage license to homosexuals.

As noted above, notwithstanding the fact that 53% of the Colorado voters adopted Amendment 2 which prohibited special treatment based upon sexual orientation, the United States Supreme Court found the state constitutional amendment to be contrary to the federal Constitution.[19] Justice Antonin Scalia in dissent criticized the Court for assuming a political role.

> "Today's opinion has no foundation in American constitutional law, and barely pretends to. The people of Colorado have adopted an entirely reasonable provision which does not even disfavor homosexuals in any substantive sense, but merely denies them preferential treatment. Amendment 2 is designed to prevent piecemeal deterioration of the sexual morality favored by a majority of Coloradans, and is not only an appropriate means to that legitimate end, but a means that Americans have employed before. Striking it down is an act, not of judicial judgement, but of political will."[20]

Justice Antonin Scalia did not think it was any "business of the courts (as opposed to the political branches) to take sides in this culture war."[21] However, the Court did take sides.

POSSIBLE REMEDIES FOR CURING JUDICIAL TYRANNY

A full detailed description of these solutions can be found in my book *Faith & Freedom*:

- Congressional Limitation of Jurisdiction

  Some have suggested that the legislature should limit the jurisdictional power of the federal courts using Article III, Section 2, Clause 2 of the United States Constitution.

- Term Limits for Federal Judges

  Another suggested remedy is to place term limits on judges much like term limits for the legislature.

- Supermajority to Overturn Statutes

  Professor Richard Duncan of the University of Nebraska College of Law has suggested amending the Constitution to require 7 votes of the Justices to declare state or federal legislation unconstitutional.

- Impeachment

  Whatever Congress deems to be an impeachable offense is an impeachable offense regardless of whether the activity violates any civil or criminal statute.

- Congressional Check on Supreme Court

  Judge Robert Bork has suggested that a constitutional amendment be passed making any federal or state court decision subject to being over-ruled by a majority vote of each house of Congress.

- Executive Refusal to Enforce Court Decisions

A final way to consider reigning in judicial power is for the executive branch not to enforce court decisions. This is also called the doctrine of nonacquiescence.

When the liberties of the people are given one day and taken away the next by five unelected judges,[22] then our liberties are indeed fragile, depending more on the whim of a few individuals than upon immutable constitutional principles. Something must be done to prevent judicial tyranny.

The judiciary must be thwarted in its effort to swallow up the other two branches of government. If the trend toward judicial supremacy over the other two branches continues, then there is no question that our Republican form of government has been exchanged for an oligarchy. The result is nothing less than tyranny.

Mathew D. Staver examines these issues in further detail in his acclaimed book, *Faith and Freedom-A Complete Handbook for Defending Your Religious Rights* .

17.

THE POWER OF EACH STATE

By Herbert W. Titus, Esq.

Adapted from a speech given September 2000
at the New Hampshire Center
for Constitutional Studies Conference

When I was a student at Harvard I took a Constitutional Law class and we never read the Constitution. We only read the opinions of the Supreme Court about the Constitution. As we sketch out a blueprint for state action to recover constitutional liberty and law for America, we are actually going to look at the document and read what it says.

The 10th Amendment reads, "The powers not delegated to the United States by the Constitution, nor prohibited by it to the states, are reserved to the states respectively, or to the people."

Now I have talked to many people about the 10th Amendment and most do not ask the next question, "What are those powers not delegated to the United States nor prohibited to the states but reserved to the states or to the people?"

Now I do not have the space to expound on very many of those powers so I am going to speak on one power that has been forgotten in all the literature I have read, which is the power of interposition. Yet, at the very heart of liberty in America is the exercise of lower civil magistrates to interpose between the people and a tyrannical government. Indeed, if you read the Declaration of Independence it was the lower civil magistrates of the colonial assemblies that risked their lives, fortunes, and sacred honor to interpose themselves between the people and a tyrannical king and lawless Parliament. If you look at the last paragraph of the Declaration, the Charter of the United States, you will see that they were the representatives of the United States of America and they declared the independence of the States. There was never a time in the history of the colonies that they were one national government. There was no such thing as one nation. It was a nation of free and independent states because it was the officers of the state that interposed between the people and the tyrannical king and lawless Parliament.

So it is today. The states are established by the United States Constitution to interpose, or put themselves, between their people and a tyrannical government that has taken over the nation in Washington, DC. Today there are four practical action opportunities for the states of the United States to interpose between the people whose liberties and lawful opportunities are being stolen by a tyrannical government that has taken over in Washington, D.C. (1) political interposition, (2) legal interposition, (3) economical interposition, and (4) Constitutional interposition.

When you look at how the Constitution was ratified, it was by the people, state by state, not by the people as a whole, because the people of the United States do not act as a whole, they act state by state. Thus, the Constitution retained the charter principle that this was a union of free and independent, sovereign states, and consequently the officials of each state had a duty to protect the liberties of the people of the states they represented. One way they would protect the liberties of the people was that the proposed Constitution would not become the Constitution of the United States unless it was ratified by at least 9 state conventions composed of representatives elected by the people of those original states. They did this while retaining the power of the states to interpose between the people of the states and this new government should this government not obey the new written constitution.

POLITICAL INTERPOSITION

In presidential elections there is only one authority that determines how the president is to be elected. Article 2, Section 1, paragraph 2 states, "Each State shall appoint, in such Manner as the Legislature thereof may direct, a Number of Electors, equal to the whole number of Senators and Representatives to which the State may be entitled in the Congress. But no Senator or Representative, or Person holding an Office of Trust or profit under the United States, shall be appointed an Elector."

Did you know, for example, that the state legislature of New Hampshire could decide that the presidential electors of this state would be appointed by the state legislature? There is nothing in the Constitution that commands that the President be popularly elected! Did you know that the Congress today completely governs the manner by which the President is elected in America through a Federal Election Commission that subsidizes the President with your money? I know that most of you have not checked that box on your tax return form! Do you know that it does not matter? They still take your money! That box is only there to give Congress guidance as to how much of your money will be appropriated to subsidize the presidential elections. Perhaps some of you read just recently in the Wall Street Journal where one of the new members of the Federal Election Commission stated "Did you enjoy the Democratic and Republican National Conventions? You should have! You paid for them!"

Not only that but they give special licensing privileges to some candidates and not to others. What we would see in the October debates is "Tweedle Dee" and "Tweedle Dum" because the FEC is composed of three Democrats and three Republicans. It is deliberately designed that way by Congress to shape the political debate. So it will be either a Democrat or a Republican, and it is getting hard to tell the difference. This is a licensed "duopoly!" Isn't it interesting that the government is chasing Microsoft when they ought to be chasing the Democratic and Republican Parties that have monopolized the elections?

Yet, Article 2, Section 1, paragraph 2 says that it is the state legislatures that have the authority to determine the manner by which presidents are elected. Congress has no authority to limit campaign contributions to a presidential candidate. Congress has no authority to prohibit soft money, hard money, or stolen money. They have no authority and it is time for the state legislatures to step in and say, "We will do our constitutional duty. We will determine the manner by which the President is elected according to Article 2, Section 1, paragraph 2!" That is political interposition and it is time for the state legislatures to take their constitutional duty seriously and determine the manner in which the president is elected.

Now if you don't believe this then look at Article 2, Section 1, paragraph 4 and you will see what Congress' role is. "The Congress may determine the time of choosing the Electors, and the Day on which they shall give their votes; which day shall be the same throughout the United States."

That is all the Congress has authority to do, to determine the time. The place where the electors meet to elect the President is determined in the 12th Amendment. Contrast that language with Article 1, Section 4 which states, "The times, places and manner of holding elections for Senators and Representatives, shall be prescribed in each state by the legislature thereof; but the Congress may at any time by Law make or alter such regulations, except as to the places of choosing Senators."

Notice that the state legislatures have authority to set the time, places and manner of holding elections for the House and the Senate. But there is an escape clause. The Congress does have authority with regard to the time place and manner with respect to the members of the House and Senate but by the constitutional text itself they only have the authority to determine the day on which the electors and the Electoral College meet.

Now, back to Article 2, Section 1. Not one member of the House and not one member of the Senate can be one of those Electors. They are disqualified. Why? If you read the Federalist Papers you would know that they did not want the President to be dependent upon the Congress. They wanted the President to be responsive to the State Legislatures and the States. It was designed deliberately to enhance the power of the States, to ensure that the one elected to the highest office in the land would not be a tyrant but would be responsive to the interests of the people state by state.

LEGAL INTERPOSITION

Recently, the United States Supreme Court struck down the partial birth abortion statute enacted by the Nebraska State Legislature and in the process the other statutes passed by over 35 other states. In addition, the Supreme Court also struck down a Texas case that people could no longer pray at a football game. Now those from Texas will know that these are fighting words when you can't pray at a football game!

If George W. Bush were a Constitutional governor he would have told the Supreme Court, "We will not obey that lawless order!" If the governor of Nebraska were doing his constitutional duty he would have told the Supreme Court, "We will enforce the law prohibiting partial birth abortion in this state! I don't care what the Supreme Court has said!" But neither the governor of Texas nor the governor of Nebraska has read Article 6 of the Constitution. See today, state officials would have you believe that the only one who has a Constitutional duty is the Court. In fact they believe that the Court is Supreme! Now Article 6 does not say that this Supreme Court is the supreme law of the land! To the contrary it says, "This Constitution, and all the Laws of the United States which shall be made in pursuance thereof; and all treaties made, or which shall be made, under the authority of the United States, shall be the supreme Law of the land." A Court opinion is not the constitution! It is just a Court opinion. Sir William Blackstone put it this way, "Court opinions are evidence of Law, not law themselves." Today most Court opinions are bad evidence of law because they don't pay attention to the law! They don't read the Constitution, they just read their own opinion.

Let's look at the second paragraph of Article 6. "The Senators and Representatives before mentioned, and the Members of the several State Legislatures, and all executive and judicial officers, both of the United States and of the several States, shall be bound by Oath or affirmation, to support this Constitution;" **not** the opinions of the Supreme Court about what the Constitution means. Every state officer, whether they are a governor, state legislator, or attorney general, or local prosecutor, or police officer, or sheriff, is bound by Article 6 to support this Constitution. If the United States Supreme Court renders a decision contrary to the Constitution, what are these officials by their oath of office bound to do? Disobey! Disobey! To enforce the court's opinion would require the President to send out the National Guard. Now can you imagine the President sending out the Guard to a Texas football game?

The power of the state to interpose on behalf of its people in the name of this Constitution is a power that has been neglected **not** because it isn't in the 10th Amendment of the Constitution, but because state leaders would rather have you not know that they have that duty. Life is much easier to say: "the Supreme Court has spoken. We must obey."

We have not seen a constitutional governor for some time in our nation, although former Alabama Governor Fob James took a bold stand when he said that if a federal court tells Judge Roy Moore to take Ten Commandments off the wall of his court room, "I'll be at the door of the Court House." That is the type of governor that this Constitution is speaking of. That is the type of governor we must insist upon. That's the kind of governor that would interpose and do his constitutional duty on behalf of his state against a tyrannical Supreme Court. After all, one thing about Courts is that they cannot enforce their own opinion. That is why Alexander Hamilton called them the least dangerous branch. The only one who can enforce a court opinion is the one who has executive power. If a governor who has executive power in a state says, "I will not execute that Supreme Court opinion," then it is going to require the President to send out the troops.

We have not seen a President since Abraham Lincoln who exercised this Constitutional duty. Article 2, Section 3 says that the President "...shall take care that the laws be faithfully executed..." Now if a state governor would refuse to obey a Supreme Court opinion, it would require the President to decide what the Law is. He would have to determine whether or not the Supreme Court opinion was lawful. If he sent out the National Guard we would know that it was only by force and not by law what that decree was for.

ECONOMIC INTERPOSITION

We have heard much talk about the 16th Amendment. There is no question that it has been used to rob the people of what is rightfully theirs. Many times, instead of asking what kind of economic power they have, the State officials hide behind the 16th Amendment and say, "Well, it is because the Federal Government takes all the taxes and sends them to Washington that we just don't have any power any more because we cannot raise enough money from the people."

I worked on a case by filing an amicus brief challenging the constitutionality of the Clean Air Act on the grounds that it was an unlawful delegation of Congressional power. If you look at the statute to find out what the rules are in regards to clean air, you cannot find them in the statute even though Article 1, Section 1 vests all legislative power in the Congress and the very essence of legislative power is to pass the rules. Instead the EPA passes the rules. But did you know that they don't enforce them? Did you know that when th EPA passed the rules on ozone and particulate matter in the air that they don't enforce them? Do you know who does? The states! The states enforce the federal standards for clean air that were not even enacted by Congress.

Now by what constitutional authority does the state enforce federal law? The answer is none, zero, nada! How do we know that? Because we, unlike most governors, have read Article 2, Section 2. The President "...shall have power, by and with the advice and consent of the Senate, to make treaties, provided that two thirds of the Senators present concur; and he shall nominate, and by and with the advice and consent of the Senate, shall appoint ambassadors, other public ministers and consuls, judges of the Supreme Court, and all other officers of the United States, whose appointments are not herein otherwise provided for, and which shall be established by Law..." Now did the President appoint the Governor of New Hampshire? No! The people of the state of New Hampshire elected him. So is the Governor of New Hampshire a federal officer? No! Yet, the Clean Air Act requires him to enforce the clean air standards passed by the EPA.

Now why would Congress do that? Because it is regulation on the cheap. It is cheaper that way. It is called unfunded mandates. They mandate the state officials to enforce the federal law because they don't want to take the money they have and spend that money to enforce the rules. Do you want to know another reason the Congress does not want to spend the money? Because they do not want to make the hard choices. When the EPA hands down a new rule about ozone or particulate matter, it is up to the Governor to decide which industries have to be shut down. He has to make the tough choices. You know what these governors should do? Make the Federal officers enforce it. Then Congress might say, "If you want your highway funds..." But if 50 governors said we won't enforce it, then what?

You know the governors meet periodically. Have you ever watched what they talk about? They become a lobbying organization. Like all the rest, they go to Washington to see how much they can get of your money instead of doing their constitutional duty by saying, "Look, Article 2, Section 1 of the Constitution of the United States vests all executive power in the President. He has only the authority to appoint other federal officers and that has to be done with and by the advice and consent of the Senate. We are not one of those officers. We cannot enforce this law and we won't enforce this law."

That is what two sheriffs did when they passed the Brady Bill. The sheriffs in Montana and Arizona did this and were taken to Court and the United States Supreme Court agreed with them. But the United States Supreme Court would not have had the opportunity to agree with them if they had acted like all the other sheriffs and never challenged it.

What would happen if the school board said, "We will not take your money!"? I have read recent studies that educational quality does not turn on how much money they spend. As a matter of fact I have seen that the more money they spend the worse the education they have. We need to get away from this notion that if you spend more money you get more quality. In fact, do you know where all that money goes? It goes to the people who do not teach! Now we have discovered that teachers teach because they cannot do, and administrators don't teach because they cannot teach!

So Congress has essentially enslaved the states just as much as the Court has usurped state power.

The Federal Communications Commission has hijacked the presidential election process. It is time not only for political interposition, not only for legal interposition, not only for economic interposition, but it is also time for Constitutional interposition.

CONSTITUTIONAL INTERPOSITION

You know the greatest danger for our liberty is not in Washington D.C., but in New York City. If you have been following the newspapers recently they have just had a conference on Global Government. It was the United Nations. I have a copy of the United Nation's Charter. I suggest you read it, but not before going to bed! We are told that the Charter is a treaty. It is not. It was never designed as a treaty. It was designed as a Constitution for world government from the beginning.

Like the United States Constitution, it has provision whereby it may be amended without it ever being submitted to the United States Senate for ratification. It has its own internal amendment process, and just like the United States Constitution may be amended without the unanimous consent of the member nations.

Some people say, "Yes, but we have veto power in the Security Council." But veto power is not constitutionally sufficient. If a new member is to be added to the United Nations, it should only be if the Senate ratifies it, *if it was a treaty*. But it was never designed to be a treaty! Indeed, all you have to do is read the first words of the Charter, "We the people of the United Nations." Look at the Preamble to the United States Constitution. What does it say? "We the People of the United States..." If the UN Charter was a treaty it should say, "We the government officials of the various member nations..." They are the ones who have authority to make treaties. Why did they say "We the People of the United Nations"? Simply because they were displacing the Constitution of the United States with a new Constitutional document. But unlike the Constitution of the United States, it has never been submitted to the People of the United States for ratification.

I read President Bill Clinton's speech that he gave at this Council on Global Government and he was giving kudos to Kofi Annan, that wonderful United Nations bureaucrat who is the only one who came up through the ranks to become Secretary General. This is what Bill Clinton said, "This man is sent from heaven." There is only one I know who has been sent from heaven. There is only one who is Prince of Peace. The United Nations would bring peace by outlawing war. They outlaw war by ridding us of our national boundaries. Then everything becomes a police action.

Is that really what they are about? In a human development report in 2000 Kofi Annan said, "The United Nations is composed of member nations but it exists for the benefit of the peoples of the world and no national boundaries will stand in the way of our reaching the peoples of the world!" That's Kofi Annan. That's the United Nations and the way it is designed.

Some say, "Well, they have not yet taxed us!" Oh yes they have. Article 1, Section 7 of the United States Constitution says, "All bills for raising revenue shall originate in the House of Representatives..." Do you know where the bill originates that raises revenue for the United Nations? In the General Assembly! That's why they bill us! It would be the same as if the EPA said, "This is the amount of money we need. Now you owe it to us, Congress!" You see we are already being *taxed without representation*. It already violates that principle upon which the Revolution was founded, "no taxation without Representation!" We must resist the illegitimate and unlawful United Nations that would usurp the power of the people to constitute the government as this nation had been founded.

What shall we do then? May I propose that cities, counties, and states pass laws declaring that they are a United Nations free zone? There is a way to combating an illegitimate intrusion upon the national sovereignty of the nation and the sovereignty of the 50 states. It is time that the people rise up and remind our government officials that we constitute the government—THEY DON'T! It is time for action in this arena. We continue to be betrayed by the President of the United States and his minions in the Senate who are afraid to stand on principle.

PRAYERFUL INTERCESSION

If you are someone who prays, and if you don't you ought, may I ask you to pray the prayer based upon Proverbs 21:1, "The heart of a king is a channel of water in God's hands. He moves it whichever way that He wishes." Indeed, if we are to see action as I have outlined to you, in having the state officials interpose and once again bring the presidential elections back home where it belongs, out of the clutches of the FEC; if we are to see state officials exercise the legal authority they have to defend the Constitution against unconstitutional opinions of the Supreme Court of the United States; if we are going to see state officials who are willing to exercise the economic power they have even though they might risk losing some of those federal funds; and if we are to see the People of the United States rise up and say, "We are the ones who constitute our government, we will not be a part of an unconstitutional United Nations" - we need to pray. For what I have outlined for you is impossible; but with God all things are possible, for He is the One who moves the hearts of kings."

I was once involved with a Christian Law school that had to go before the American Bar Association to be accredited. I can assure you that the American Bar Association was not happy that the Bible has reentered a law school classroom. This law school I was associated with was of all places Oral Roberts University. We got one vote from a committee and 22 against us in 1981. We had another opportunity to get a second review and there was 21 against us. In August the American Bar Association accredited the Law school. Why? Because God moves the hearts of even an accrediting authority of the American Bar Association. How do I know this? Because we took them to court. Guess what; God gave us an activist judge who said to the American Bar Association, "if you do not accredit that Law School, I will!"

Now the American Bar Association could have appealed and taken it to a higher court. Instead they folded. The second committee where we only got one vote, voted unanimously. The chairman of that committee spoke on our behalf and voted for us. Two weeks later I got a letter with a newspaper article in which that man who voted and spoke for us said, "the biggest mistake the American Bar Association has ever done is accredit the law school at ORU. "The heart of a king is like a channel of water in His hands, He moves it whichever way He wishes."

So if we are to see a blueprint of restoration where the states take their constitutional duty and right of interposition, we need to be on our knees praying that even though those state governors who do not want to do it would be moved by God to do what they do not want to do. You see God is not out of the nation-building business. He still moves kings and governors and presidents and judges. We just need to take a stand. In order to take this stand, we need to know what the Constitution says.

CONCLUSION

Jesus Christ, who is my political hero, demonstrated that when He encountered the devil in the wilderness. When He was challenged by the devil to turn the stone into bread, and He had the *power* to do so for He was the Son of God, He showed He did not have the *authority* to do so for He said this; "Man does not live by bread alone but by every word that proceeds out of the mouth of God." Satan picked up on that in the next temptation when he said, "Jump off the pinnacle of this Temple." And then he quoted Scripture, "for the angels will take care of you." Remember what Jesus said? You live by every word of God. He responded by that word, "You shall not tempt the Lord your God." Then Satan showed Him all the kingdoms of this world. He said, there you are. They are yours for the taking if you will "bow down and worship me." Jesus said, "Thou shalt worship the Lord your God and Him alone."

Remember each time that Jesus responded He said "**It is written! It is written! It is written**!" If we are to serve in this nation, then we not only have to know the written Word of God, we also need to know the written word of this Constitution! If we neglect that written word, then how can we hold our state officials to what is written?

Even Chief Justice Marshall, if you read the case of *Marbury v. Madison*, said that the reason why the Court would strike down a Congressional statute and have the power to do so was because the Constitution is written. It is written for the purpose of establishing the rule of law by which no government official can transcend. Then he said this, "The Constitution is an instrument for the government of the Court as well as an instrument for the government of Congress." He did not believe that the Court was above the written Constitution because he had read in Article 6 that this Constitution is the Supreme law of the land. Not a court opinion! Not your opinion or my opinion but the Constitution as it is written.

I challenge you, I exhort you, I encourage you that as God calls you as citizens of this great land, that you step out in faith trusting that as you stand for the written covenant of this great nation; and as you call upon your local and state officials to interpose and defend the liberties of the people against this tyranny we face in this nation, may you do your part. When you meet your Maker He will say, "Well done thou good and faithful servant."

18.

THE FINAL MOMENTS OF CRISIS

By Ambassador Alan Keyes
Adapted from a speech given
April 3, 2004 in Dallas, TX

In this address, I am going to start where I would ordinarily end. Usually, one builds up as a conclusion to the question of why people have come to hear a talk, and what they ought to intend to do after they finish hearing and grasping a message. But I want to start there today, because everything that I have to share with you now is oriented towards getting us to comprehend one fundamental fact: and that is the simple truth that we can no longer take for granted in this nation very basic, very foundational assumptions. Common ground, common sense, and understandings about our freedoms and how we may exercise them are now eroded. We are now not merely in the midst of a crisis that will determine the future of our liberty and our nation – we are actually approaching the final moments of that crisis.

Decisions are confronting us right now, today, in different parts of our country with respect to institutions absolutely fundamental, not just to freedom, but to civilization itself. Decisions are being taken, even as we speak, that will determine in this generation the fate of all the generations to come in our nation and in our world. Because given the dominant role of America around the globe, one has to assume that, just as we were the champion against all manner of evil in the 20th century, should we sacrifice all that is essential to sustaining the moral foundations of our country, we will transform the great power of this nation from a force for good, into a global force for evil in the 21st century.

We just don't get it. I don't believe for one instant that America ends up as some mediocrity in history. We are either going to be a commanding power for great good, as we have been, or a commanding power for great evil, as we must become if we do not succeed in mobilizing those communities who mean to stand for the truth, and against those who have declared war upon God in our public life.

And so, the question, my friends, is clear: what are we going to do? People are always lamenting the fact that basic beliefs and basic institutions and basic rights are being assaulted and destroyed, that clear wickedness and corrosive absurdities are now being put forward in our law, that fundamental institutions are being thrown aside, and yet we sit on our hands and act like there's nothing we can do.

And that is particularly true, by the way, of people who profess to be believers in Judeo-Christian law, in the Christian faith, and in the American way of life. I still think it is the case, and it especially seems to be when you look at the polls, and the ballot initiatives, and the elections, and so forth, that folks who believe in the right things to keep this nation in God's ways are still the overwhelming majority of Americans.

It's true. You look at the will of the people now on this whole issue of homosexual marriage; people across the country are solidly against it. They are solidly against taking the Ten Commandments out of our public life, they were solidly against taking prayer out of public schools, they were solidly against taking Bible instruction out of our classrooms, they have been solidly against every step that represented the divorce between this nation and its Godly heritage.

So given that we define this as a government of the people, by the people, for the people, if the people are solidly against it, why does it happen? You do have to wonder. Maybe it's because we're just nasty, bad, lazy, ignorant people, and we don't care as much as we profess to; we have opinions, but we won't act on them; we have beliefs, but we don't do anything to put them into practice, because we no longer have the faith, or the sense or the courage to do it. Do you think that's right?

Well, before we go accepting that thesis, I think we have to examine a little bit the situation in which we find ourselves. It's a situation that gives evidence of the insidious nature of the wickedness we're faced with in America right now. Because, you see, I don't think it's because people are just lazy and shiftless and lacking in courage. There may be some who are, but I don't think that's the essential reason we are in this crisis. No.

I think in fact we live in a time when the decent characteristics of our people, who are actually quite good and Godly, have been exploited and manipulated in order to undermine their willingness to act in defense of that which is virtuous and faithful. It's fascinating, isn't it?

And the situation of Chief Justice Roy Moore in Alabama is a perfect case in point. I remember when he was being persecuted, first by the federal judge ordering him to take the Ten Commandments monument out of the state judicial building, then by folks in his own state on that Supreme Court in Alabama, removing him from office. I would encounter people who were friends of mine, who professed to be conservatives, moral conservatives, and they would just say, "Well, I believe in the Ten Commandments, but he should obey the law! He's breaking the law; Roy Moore is a law-breaker – we can't have that!"

Now, wait a minute. I was always taught that before you criticize folks and start calling them names, you need to be very, very clear and careful that you're telling the world the truth, and saying something useful and necessary for it to know. So first thing: obedience to law is very important to the success of our country. Always has been. One of the reasons why self-government and government of the people, government through elected representatives, government based upon the authority of the people, has worked in America so well when it has so often failed in other parts of the world is because, by and large, Americans will obey the law. Americans believe in the rule of law, because they, the American people themselves, through their elected representatives, ultimately make the laws. And they will generally obey the judges who sit on the bench, because the judges represent the authority and the majesty of the law. All this is not a bad thing.

This is not something we want to do away with, because it is fundamental to the success of our country.

But here's the insidious part. If you're going to enforce "the law," you better make sure you've got a constitutional law on the books to enforce! Some decades back, we let folks go into court making specious arguments claiming, "Well, it is unconstitutional, it violates the First Amendment of the Constitution, which established separation of church and state, it violates that separation of church and state for there to be. . . ." and then there was a long list of things they've gone after, right?

It started with any kind of interaction between the government and education that involves religion, and continued with getting prayer out of the public schools, and then Bible study and everything else. It has moved forward to remove the prayers from the games that were associated with public education, and invocations and benedictions, and on and on, until finally it becomes the basis for scouring the school hallways and the classrooms and the competitions of every vestige, not just of organized acknowledgment of God, not just of reference to His authority over human affairs, but even of personal beliefs, which have been under assault in many school systems around the country - all under the rubric of this alleged doctrine of "separation of church and state."

But that's not the only thing. A lot of folks in our country right now are fighting in the effort to save marriage. We want to see that institution strengthened and preserved. It is now under direct assault. It is under attack in a manner that makes mock of the very idea of marriage, and that would extend the privileges and unique status of marriage in such a way as to destroy its very meaning.

Many who are fighting the battle for marriage understand that *Lawrence v. Texas* and other recent court decisions are based on the same notion used against prayer in school, and against Judge Moore - that it is somehow illegitimate to apply the moral convictions and consequences of faith to law and politics. "You can't do this! You can't say that!" "The fact that this religion or that one holds that homosexuality is a sin doesn't mean you can legislate against it!" - that's what we are told. "The fact that marriage is outlined in the Scriptures as between a man and a woman doesn't mean that you can have that understanding of marriage as the foundation in your law," that's what they are telling us. Why? Ultimately, for the same reason that prayer and God are out of our schools, and Judge Moore is alleged to be a "law-breaker"

– because of the so-called doctrine of separation of church and state.

And there might be those who say, "Well, that's only assuming that marriage is religiously based." Well, I've got news for you. It is!

The understanding of marriage in this country is directly derived from our biblical heritage and tradition. Directly derived! This was explicitly acknowledged by the Supreme Court back in the 19th century, when they were dealing with the issue of polygamy, and in fact nothing has changed. The truth of the matter is that when secularist judges assault our rights to see reflected in our public life and in our laws the consequences of our faith, they assault all those institutions that are drawn from, derived from, and justified by that faith.

Let me be plain. If we do not win the battle for our right to publicly acknowledge God, then we shall lose the battle to defend every institution based upon the Word of God!

And don't fool yourselves. Some people think, "Well, we're going to go down this road a ways, but then we'll rest. There might be civil unions, some homosexual marriage, that kind of thing – but overall, things will stabilize." But we need to deal with simple common sense things nobody seems to want to look at, partly because they are kind of unpleasant, and one doesn't want to spend too much time concentrating, as a believer, on what sinful people do. But we need to in this case, so I hope you won't mind if I mention the fact that, in reading I've done over the years about homosexual couples, do you know one of the things they take pains to do when they decide that they would like to have a family, have children? They take pains to make sure that in whatever means they use to conceive a child, they mask the identity of the other biological parent. So, if it's a lesbian couple, they don't want to know who the man was who "genetically contributed" to the conception of the child; if it's a male homosexual couple, they don't want to know who the woman was who was involved. They want to find some way to mask that - especially from the child. They think that's going to interfere with their "parenting rights" under this so-called "two mommies," "two daddies" sort of arrangement.

Now, you see, here's where we lose the common sense of it. Last time I looked, there was this commandment, and it said, "Honor thy father and thy mother."

Somebody's going to have to explain to me how one can honor a father or a mother you don't, and can't, even know. It gets worse when we think it through. Because, if you don't know who your mom and dad are, you also don't know who your brother is or who your sister is. And that means that not only have we abandoned the commandment that says "honor thy father and mother," we've also crossed the line, and no matter what you argue, the necessary, factual, practical implication is that incest becomes more and more likely to take place, because people won't know who their brothers and sisters are.

We think that we're dealing with just one issue here. We are actually dealing with all the sins where God's authority has established institutions that are meant to preserve the integrity of that nature which He instills in us. We're not thinking it through. If there's some confusion about this, this applies to other things, as well, the rampant promiscuity and other sin and vice that goes on in our world now, but it also applies here.

And we are also dealing with it, of course, at another level, because the whole thrust of the movement that is clamoring for homosexual marriage and societal acceptance of homosexuality is based on what? Well, the idea that somehow homosexuality is an ineluctable element or expression of human biology. I remember going to a women's conference quite some years ago in Nairobi. They talked about human sexuality as if there were many genders, right? There aren't just two. I think in one document they had five. Well, excuse me if I can't remember what they are, but there they were!

What does that imply? I've watched this with church denominations and others who've gone astray, as the Episcopalians have done in some areas. What are they doing? Do they know? I wonder. They will leave aside their rejection of Christ's understanding of marriage. Christ actually took some pains to define marriage, and the phrase that He used was, "And the two become one flesh." Isn't that right? When do the two become one flesh? In the child, of course. In the child! The two become one flesh in the child who is conceived. Now our scientific knowledge knows that that is infinitely true, that two become one flesh, that elements of both mother and father become the basis for the being and identity of that child in a biological sense. Christ understood this. He knew that marriage was, in fact, a fleshly institution, and that its definition involved procreation.

"Male and female, made He them." If in principle there can be no procreation, there can in principle be no marriage. And I know there are going to be concerns, "Well, what about couples who are infertile?" "What about couples beyond child-bearing years?" These are not in principle. They are what we would logically term incidental conditions. These are factual, accidental inabilities, not an inability in principle. When two males attempt to mate, that is in principle a situation in which procreation is impossible, and in which marriage cannot exist.

Accept and embrace that idea of marriage, and you have rejected Christ's understanding, Christ's definition of marriage. Why call yourself a Christian after that? I don't know. You also have the fact that we are Christian people based on what? Based on our belief that Jesus Christ is the Savior, and that that belief was established on the truth of the Holy Scripture. Search all the way back to the Old Testament, what do we find? Well, as I recall, right there in the beginning when God created us, it says very clearly, "Male and female He created them. In the image and likeness of God created He them." Who can dispute that maleness and femaleness are not incidental, not accidents, but are both essential to our nature?

As understood in that scriptural sense, that first thought, and second, that male and female we are Created, that's the vision in our nature, not only tells us something about us; if we search that scripture seriously, it tells us something about God.

Don't we get it yet that in our nature there is a reflection of God, and that that phrase is not used of us until after Eve is created? Why not? Because it is only after Eve is created that man is complete, that he is perfected in the image and likeness of God. The sexual distinction therefore introduces us to something that we would need to explore and understand about who and how God is. Reject the sexual distinction, and you have rejected that mystery. It's not just behavioral, it's theological.

Deeply grounded, therefore, is the institution of marriage, deeply grounded is this understanding of human sexuality in the religious heritage of our people. Reject that heritage, declare that there is a wall of separation that keeps that heritage from having any legitimate influence on our law, and you cannot defend the understanding of our human nature, you cannot defend the institutions that define our ordered liberty. Because ultimately, these rely upon God's Word and authority.

So, I say to you quite clearly: this is not just a battle about whether or not Roy Moore can put the Ten Commandments in the state Supreme Court building in Alabama. It's a battle about whether we are going to keep the institution of marriage, whether we're going to respect the innocence of our children, whether we'll respect the incest taboo, whether we'll respect any of the injunctions written down in the Bible that require that we acknowledge God's authority in the way that we conduct our affairs.

But then we come up against that hard point: "If it is true, and there is a wall of separation between church and state, then it doesn't matter what you just said. It doesn't matter at all."

How do we get past this? Well, see, there's an easy way to get past it. If someone tells you that the Constitution says X, what's the first thing you ought to do? Read it!

The wonderful thing about having a written Constitution, which makes it far superior to a Constitution passed on by some oral tradition, is that you don't have to rely on what judges and lawyers tell you. You don't have to rely on what I'm telling you, either! Aren't you glad we don't have to rely on what others tell us in America, because the laws are actually written down, for all of us to read and understand?

And what do you find in the Constitution of the United States? When people approach me about Justice Moore, and they say, "He's a lawbreaker, he doesn't respect the law, the federal judge is ordering the law," I say, "What law? Where is it? Show it to me. What law is it that requires this separation of church and state?"

If they try to tell me a federal law, I go to the Constitution and say, "Wait a minute. Right here, right here, in the First

Amendment it says, 'Congress shall make no law respecting an establishment of religion!'" So, if there's a law on the books that deals with the subject of religious establishment, how religion in the states is related, if there is such a law on the federal books, that law is obviously unconstitutional.

But there isn't one. Well, let's try it again. They'll say, "Well, it's in the Constitution," and then, you know, this is the trick of it. They will take us in the Constitution to that very phrase of the First Amendment, and they'll say, "There it is! That's the prohibition. You can't have any kind of mingling of church and state. 'Congress shall make no law.'"

Leaving aside the fact that we were talking about Chief Justice Moore, who is no part of Congress, leaving aside little common sense things like that, **what the phrase actually says, though, is not a prohibition against religious establishment. It is a prohibition against federal congressional action dealing with the subject.**

When are we going to get this through our heads? For the last forty, and fifty, and sixty years, the lawyers and the judges who have pretended that there is some reference to separation in the Constitution have lied to us!

And we must no longer act as the victims of this lie! It is by means of this lie that they have made our reverence for law the enemy of our reverence for God! They have put us in a position where we sit idly by while laws are put on the books, which a day is soon coming we cannot in Christian conscience obey.

When are we going to wake up to what they're doing here? We have taken our citizenship and the comfortable relationship between our faith and our freedom so cavalierly that now we'll sit on our hands while it's destroyed?

Will somebody answer me what a Christian is going to do when they place a law in the books directly requiring that you honor what God does not, that you accept as good what God says is wrong, that you embrace as right what God says is sinful? What will you do? How will you answer that challenge?!! It will then not just be some challenge to your tolerance; it will be a deep challenge to your faith!

And that is where we're headed right now. In California, they had a law that was going to require that in order to adopt a child in California, you had to affirm homosexuality.

If they succeed in legitimizing what the Scripture says is sinful, then it will become unlawful, you understand, to preach that homosexuality is a sin.

Don't you understand what we are getting into here? And the force of law will then be brought down upon our heads, and we will go from a country in which being a Christian was comfortable to a country where if you in fact act as a Christian believer, you will be punished and persecuted even as we were in the beginning.

Now, I would say maybe that we'd better prepare for that persecution, but we better go back to those thoughts of the Scripture where Christ makes it clear that this is part of our Christian vocation. But I also believe that we should not sit back and simply expect this fate as inevitable! Not when we know that this whole structure of persecution will be based upon a lie!

In fact, the Constitution of the United States, far from requiring separation of church and state, was written so as to make sure that the federal government **could not** impose upon the states any uniform regime of religion – including an "enlightened' eradication of public religion – in this country.

It said, quite clearly, not that there can be no religious establishment, not that there be no God in politics, not that there could be no reference to religion in any of our laws. No, it didn't say that at all. It simply said that anything that had to do with these questions had to be decided by, and was left in the hands of, the states and the people of the states, free from interference by the federal government.

Now, you tell me something. How have we gotten from a Constitution that guarantees the right of the states to deal with this issue according to the state constitutional choices of their people, to a situation where a federal judge sitting on a bench can serve dictates that the Ten Commandments must be ripped out of the heart of the people of Alabama, and they can do nothing about it?

See, I don't believe we are there. I believe we are only going to be there if we passively let ourselves be placed in this position. For, where the Constitution recognizes the rights, it also provides the remedy. And there in Article 3, Section 2, of the U.S. Constitution there is a clear remedy. This remedy is meant, by the way, for just these situations where the federal judges overstep their boundaries, and encroach upon the prerogatives of the people and the states, as well as the other co-equal branches of federal government – the legislative and executive branches – and the Congress has the right to make exception to their jurisdiction, to take an area and remove it from the jurisdiction of the federal courts.

And what better area as a candidate for the immediate exercise of this authority than that area which the First Amendment, according to its terms, leaves in the hands of the states and the people respectively?

Understand that what we are dealing with here – if left uncorrected, if left unchecked – threatens the very moral foundations of every institution we hold dear. That what we are dealing with here is based upon an insidious lie. That we, in fact, have the constitutional and lawful right, even the duty, to stand up and demand that Congress defend this fundamental liberty of our people.

And unless we do, we shall see imposed throughout this land, in every state, in every locality, in every school, in every public place, throughout our public life, a uniform regime of atheism that will drive not only from the public square but from our laws every vestige of influence that comes from our faith and our religious heritage.

I can't believe you're going to let this happen. I can't believe that Christian people, born into a country that was founded on principles that respect the fundamental tenets of our faith, including the sovereignty of Almighty God, will let this happen. "All men are created equal," not made equal by law, not made equal by the president, not made equal by judicial fiat, but made equal by the will and authority of the Creator, God!

As God, and His authority, was invoked when this nation was founded on the basis of our rights, so we shall only keep those rights if we hold on to the right to appeal for God's authority when they are violated!

But, you see, we watched Justice Roy Moore being removed for what? Because, if you had seen, he refused to give up as a public official his right to acknowledge God! You must see, my friends, in Justice Moore's situation, not just the situation of one man, or one public official, you must see your situation! For, every time you pick up the ballot, you exercise the most vital public office in this country! And if we are being told that we cannot hold such offices if we hold to those beliefs which are the consequence of our faith, then, like Roy Moore, we shall be removed from that office. We shall be set in conflict with ourselves: our duty to God made the enemy of those duties they seek to impose upon us by the force of law.

Is this what self-government is supposed to be? Quite the contrary.

The Founders protected this fundamental right of religious liberty first, because they felt and understood that it was the most important. They knew that a people that appeals to God for their rights and for their understanding of their nature and their worth must always be free to acknowledge God, and to reverence God in the conduct of its public affairs. Give up that right, and you give up your liberty. It's really as simple as that.

Are any of you going to start wondering? The ACLU, all these people, they come and they're complaining that free exercise somehow interferes with somebody's religious freedom. These folks aren't advocates for freedom. They are assaulting that fundamental right which makes freedom possible. They are assaulting that fundamental right of appeal to God, which makes the courage of a free people possible. They are assaulting that which has been the basis in every generation of this nation's life, for folks to rally 'round when their rights were trampled upon, for folks to rally 'round when injustice was being done, for folks to stand against those forces, even armed with the mighty powers of the law and the state, when those forces abused them in a way contrary to the laws of God.

I ask you, are we still such a people?

I don't know. But I do know this: once we have taken God's name from every wall, removed His laws from every courthouse, removed the sound of hearts prayerfully lifted up to Him from every school and every public place, once we have taken the Bible verses off the Liberty Bell, and scoured the Ten Commandments from the walls of the Supreme Court, I do know this; we shall no longer be a people living in the midst of that foundation for our courage which made our freedom possible.

There are those of us who remember, as an echo of our upbringing, the truth. Freedom shall be gone, and there shall be those only who have lived in a wasteland of atheism, made to feel ashamed of their faith, ashamed to act upon it as citizens. That truth which made us free will be forgotten, and so, I fear, will be the courage to defend that freedom.

Is this the legacy we intend to leave for our future generations? Shall we be the first that leave the foundations of liberty not stronger, but so weakened after us that they have been destroyed?

This is the question, and I put it, especially, not just to citizens at large, I put it especially to citizens who are believers. I put it especially to citizens who acknowledge in their heart the sovereignty and authority of God. Christ tells us to be good Samaritans. We're not supposed to pass by, unaffected, those who have been robbed and left bloodied and beaten in a ditch.

Don't we Christians see that our country is the victim of just such a theft, that the great principle of God's authority which is the foundation for our claim to liberty was a treasure, and that, lo, these past decades, we have been robbed of it?

And now, with the destruction of our vital institutions, the body politic of our freedom lies bleeding from a thousand wounds that soon shall be fatal to our character and our liberty. When are we going to get down off our high horse, stop saying we love America, and start acting as if we love our country? Not with the love of the flesh and not with the love of emotion and materialism, but with the Christian love that Christ recommends.

And that is a love which will not stand idly by when our nation is robbed of truth, but will stand forward with courage to defend that truth and to defend in its name our right to acknowledge the Author of all truth, Almighty God.

This is the challenge for all of us, and I hope we'll answer that challenge because, you see, we are in the process of holding rallies, calling people together, but each one is just the seed of another. We must go forward, we must spread this word into our churches and into our neighborhoods, and into houses of our friends, and into our workplace, building toward that day when, by the thousands and hundreds of thousands, Americans will converge on Washington, D.C., and raise up the banner of our true religious liberty to demand of the Congress that they take action to end this tyranny of the federal judiciary which assaults the moral life of our people and intends to destroy their freedom!

I believe that we must in faith take on this challenge with the courage shown by those in the past, like Washington, who went down upon his knees to pray to God in the darkest days of the Revolutionary War, knowing that if he persevered, however long the odds, with God's help, he could prevail.

Don't we still believe this? Because, if we do, then regardless of the odds, and regardless of the numbers, and regardless of the vilification that may be brought against us, we must move forward in faith and in a true spirit of Christian love. We must act to give a witness of that revival of this nation's faithful spirit that will signal for the future the restoration of its true and righteous liberty. Then we shall defend the family, then we shall restore the true understanding of marriage, then we shall rediscover the basis of family life and procreation and sexual discipline. Then we shall see all these shadows that now haunt our land, including that scourge of abortion, which reaches into the womb to destroy the very life of our innocent future, then shall they all be defeated, they shall all be overthrown, but they shall be overthrown because we have restored in the heart of America our God upon His throne.

If we are willing to move forward with courage, and come what may, to pursue this great objective as the goal of our Christian patriotism, our Christian citizenship, our Christian dedication to public life, then and then alone will we have acted to secure the blessings of liberty to ourselves and our posterity. And only then will we have ensured that this great nation which has so enjoyed those blessings will live on to share them as we have, not just with all Americans, but with all those people from every race and color and clime, whom together we represent, holding aloft that hope which this nation can still offer if it returns to God, a hope not for itself, but for all of human kind.

19.

TO IMPEACH OR NOT TO IMPEACH?

By Mark I. Sutherland

I believe that the Bible contains the answers to every problem we face, and as we look at the ongoing problem of judges who are causing havoc in our nation we are required as Christians to look at God's Word and see what He would instruct us to do with out-of-control judges.

According to Exodus 18:16, the duty of judges is to "make them know the statutes of God and His laws" rather than create new laws based on the opinion of the day. In Genesis 18:21 the godly requirements for a judge are given. They are to be "capable men...who fear God, trustworthy men who hate dishonest gain." In Deuteronomy 1:16 & 17 these judges are given instruction on how they are to act. They are instructed to "judge fairly" and to "not show partiality" and to remember that the source of all "judgment belongs to God."

In Deuteronomy 16 further instructions are given on the expected behavior of a judge. They are instructed in verse 19 to "not pervert justice" and in verse 20, "Follow justice and justice alone." Verse 20 then makes a promise to us if our judges follow these guidelines: that "you may live and possess the land the Lord your God is giving you."

Isaiah 33:22 again reminds us that God is the one in charge and we are answerable to him (this is also the verse the founding fathers used to create our three branches of government, combined with their views of church leadership). Isaiah 33:22 reads, "For the Lord is our judge, the Lord is our lawgiver, the Lord is our king; it is he who will save us." This verse describes the separation of powers we find in our government. Additionally the structure of church government in our nation at the time of the writing of the Constitution shows that biblical values were integral in influencing our nation.

In the southern colonies, Episcopalianism was the dominant denomination of Christianity. Under this system of church government we find a single head that makes all decisions. From this denomination the concept of the executive branch was developed. In the central colonies the predominant denomination was Presbyterianism. The Presbyterian system was headed by a group of elders who represented the interests of the church members. From this denomination the concept of the judicial branch was developed. In the northern colonies the Congregationalist were the dominant denomination, and their form of church government was purely democratic. From this denomination the legislative branch was developed. These separate designs of government were given certain powers and duties.

Our Founding Fathers agreed, in the Declaration of Independence, that government should be limited to securing our God-given rights and that all officials needed to be ruled by an inner constraint. They knew that man was capable of terrible things and that power corrupted men. They knew from personal experience that Jeremiah 17:9 was absolutely true when it stated, "The heart is deceitful above all things and desperately wicked; who can know it?" Part of the Declaration of Independence, the very organic foundation of our nation, stated, "But when a long train of abuses and usurpations, pursuing invariably the same Object, evinces a design to reduce them under absolute Despotism, it is their right, it is their duty, to throw off such Government, and to provide new Guards for the future security."

Our founding fathers recognized that when a government becomes abusive, and violates the God-given standards of how a government should operate, that the people have a right to do something about it. In the case of judges who violate the biblical and constitutional limits of their office, our founding fathers gave us numerous ways to deal with them, including de-funding, restricting, and firing.

They feared an over-reaching judicial system, and repeatedly warned of its dangers. Thomas Jefferson wrote, "You seem…to consider the judges as the ultimate arbiters of all constitutional questions; a very dangerous doctrine indeed, and one which would place us under the despotism of an oligarchy." The founders did not consider judges to be the final say. In fact, Alexander Hamilton explained that "the judiciary is, beyond comparison, the weakest of the three departments of power." The current situation we find ourselves in, with judges creating, declaring, and enforcing their own decisions, is the absolute opposite of what our Founding Fathers, in applying biblical principles, envisioned for our nation.

So what can we do if we see a judge operate in an ungodly fashion and violate the moral values and convictions of the people that judge is supposed to serve? Here's a novel concept: we fire him! Novel today, but commonplace at the beginning of our nation. Our founding fathers felt that if a judge could not restrain himself to applying the law and could not maintain a moral record of decisions, then the last place he needed to be was on the bench. So in the U.S. Constitution they gave us the tool of impeachment, or the power of the "pink-slip," over judges.

Our founding fathers set up a system of government to make all three branches accountable to the people. The last thing they wanted was tyranny from the bench, like they had experienced at the hands of the English judges. In the Constitution of the United States the founding fathers put such a value on impeachment that they mentioned it six times.

But the question today is "what is an impeachable offense?" In the last few years many seemingly educated people have declared that in order for you to impeach someone they have to have committed a criminal offense. For the answer we once again turn to our founding fathers.

Our founding fathers answered this question with their actions. Did they impeach murderers or thieves? No. Not once. They left those crimes to the police and the criminal court system. The crimes of the judicial branch that resulted in impeachment were rudeness to witnesses, cussing in court, drunkenness in private, and striking down laws put in place by the legislative branch. Impeachment was designed to be a bridle in the hands of the legislature to keep the judicial branch accountable to the people, so that tyranny could never occur here in the United States.

It is time to make our judges accountable to the people once again. It is time to start impeaching those judges among us who decide to make law from the bench. It is time to impeach those judges who throw out jury decisions, it is time to impeach those judges who throw out legislative decisions, and it time to throw out those judges who declare themselves to be the absolute and definite authority on what is constitutional.

It is in cases like this where our elected representatives need to step in and protect our values, our rights and our morals as a society.

Together we can make a difference, and ensure that radical social agendas that violate God's laws and standards are not imposed on us by tyrannical judges who violate the limits of their granted powers.

20.

WHAT DO I DO NOW?

By Mark I. Sutherland

So what now? You've read the articles from men who are fighting hard on the front lines to restore the religious freedoms that are being destroyed by an illegally operating judicial branch. But now, what do you do? What can you do? Can one person make any difference?

The answer is absolutely yes. In our system of government we have the privilege, and responsibility, of selecting those who serve us in government. And those we elect to represent us are supposed to be accountable to us and to the values we hold dear. If a judge is legislating from the bench, and destroying our freedoms, those we elect are responsible to defend our freedoms. They are there to fight for us, and protect our God-given rights and freedoms. But unless they hear from us, they will not do anything.

For years now, I have been driven to do everything I can to wake up our nation to the danger that is fast approaching. But unless you, now that you know the details of the problem, take action and force those who represent you to defend our rights, all will be lost. We will lose our nation unless those who value freedom and liberty take a stand and, as the founding fathers did, risk life, liberty and property to ensure our children's children are free.

But what if we take this stand? What if we call our elected representation at the local, state, and federal levels? What if we visit their offices, and get copies of books like this into other citizens' hands so that our army increases in size? What if we do all this, and they still do nothing? What can we do? Can we do anything??

We can vote! We can vote smart! We can make sure others vote and vote smart also.

The only thing that an ungodly politician fears is your vote. The ungodly seek power, and an educated, motivated electorate will force ungodly politicians to take action in support of moral issues. If they do not, it is our duty to replace them with those that will.

And what of the godly politicians? Those we know should know better, but still seem to do nothing. They need to hear from us that the issues that are of deep concern to them, are the issues of deep concern to us. They need to know that if they were to take action, and step out into areas, like restricting judges, that we will support them. Imagine thousands of moral politicians, taking serious action in support of moral issues, because they know those who elected them support them.

We are the answer to the problems our nation faces.

- We are the answer to the education system in our nation
- We are the answer to families struggling to make ends meet

- We are the answer to every societal problem
- We are the answer to the environmental problems we face
- We are the answer to the threat of terrorism in our nation

And as moral Americans, one of our fundamental duties is to make sure that those who lead our nation have the moral character and biblical knowledge to make just, righteous, and godly decisions. They will make decisions that affect every aspect of our lives – decisions that either protect our God-given rights and freedoms or destroy the very liberties that God gives to all mankind.

But does my vote matter? Who is it going to affect if I don't show up at the polls? These are questions that we have all asked. However, we can just look back a few years and see that every vote does matter. In 2002, in one of the Colorado Congressional races, over 170,000 votes were cast. <u>The victor won by only 121 votes</u>! And in South Dakota that same year, <u>the U.S. Senate race was decided by 524 votes</u> out of the more than 337,000 votes cast. This only pales in comparison when we look back at 2000 and remember that <u>our current president was placed in office because of only 537 votes</u>. Your vote matters, not only because it could be the deciding vote, but also because, in our nation, this is government of the people, by the people, and for the people. We must take our duty to vote seriously.

We must also strongly consider running for office ourselves. We need moral men and women, who understand the principles of limited government, serving on our school boards, our county councils, our state legislatures, and in our federal government. The problem has been that for 50 years we have been ignorant of the truth, and have been misled by people who wish to remold our great nation into a hedonistic, socialist society.

I strongly recommend you pick up additional resources that are available to you out there. Just a few of my recommendations are:

1. *Freedom Tide,* by Chad Connelly
2. *America's Providential History,* by Stephen McDowell and Mark Beliles
3. *Original Intent,* by David Barton
4. *The Supremacists,* by Phyllis Schlafly
5. *So Help Me God,* by Chief Justice Roy Moore

You can get these books in local bookstores, or on the Joyce Meyer Ministries website at www.joycemeyer.org. The Supremacists is available www.eagleforum.org.

You can also take advantage of the resources available at the following websites:

www.standupandbecounted.org
www.marksutherland.net
www.morallaw.org
www.renewamerica.us
www.visionamerica.org
www.conservativeusa.org
www.americanpriorities.org
www.christianlaw.org
www.lc.org
www.heritage.org
www.telladf.org
www.eagleforum.org

I also encourage you to read the Declaration of Independence and the U.S. Constitution, found at the end of this book. These documents do not take long to read, and we must know what they say in order to know what principles govern us. If more people had known these documents, and had known what the FirstAmendment really says, then 50 years of living under the lie of "separation of church and state" may not have happened.

We must become educated once again, so when we are lied to in the future, we have enough knowledge to see it for what it is. The truth is powerful; it will set our nation free again. But we must know what that truth is, and know how to apply it to our society as a whole.

Thank you for reading this book, and taking the time to become part of the solution. Together we will make a difference; together we will restore this nation into a beacon of liberty and freedom, as it was designed to be from the beginning.

Signing of the Declaration of Independence
Original Painting by John Trumbull

DECLARATION OF INDEPENDENCE

Second Continental Congress, July 4, 1776

When in the Course of human events it becomes necessary for one people to dissolve the political bands which have connected them with another and to assume among the powers of the earth, the separate and equal station to which the Laws of Nature and of Nature's God entitle them, a decent respect to the opinions of mankind requires that they should declare the causes which impel them to the separation.

We hold these truths to be self-evident, that all men are created equal, that they are endowed by their Creator with certain unalienable Rights, that among these are Life, Liberty and the pursuit of Happiness. —That to secure these rights, Governments are instituted among Men, deriving their just powers from the consent of the governed,

—That whenever any Form of Government becomes destructive of these ends, it is the Right of the People to alter or to abolish it, and to institute new Government, laying its foundation on such principles and organizing its powers in such form, as to them shall seem most likely to effect their Safety and Happiness.

Prudence, indeed, will dictate that Governments long established should not be changed for light and transient causes; and accordingly all experience hath shewn that mankind are more disposed to suffer, while evils are sufferable than to right themselves by abolishing the forms to which they are accustomed.

But when a long train of abuses and usurpations, pursuing invariably the same Object evinces a design to reduce them under absolute Despotism, it is their right, it is their duty, to throw off such Government, and to provide new Guards for their future security.

—Such has been the patient sufferance of these Colonies; and such is now the necessity which constrains them to alter their former Systems of Government.

The history of the present King of Great Britain is a history of repeated injuries and usurpations, all having in direct object the establishment of an absolute Tyranny over these States.

To prove this, let Facts be submitted to a candid world.

He has refuted his Assent to Laws, the most wholesome and necessary for the public good.

He has forbidden his Governors to pass Laws of immediate and pressing importance, unless suspended in their operation till his Assent should be obtained; and when so suspended, he has utterly neglected to attend to them.

He has refused to pass other Laws for the accommodation of large districts of people, unless those people would relinquish the right of Representation in the Legislature, a right inestimable to them and formidable to tyrants only.

He has called together legislative bodies at places unusual, uncomfortable, and distant from the depository of their Public Records, for the sole purpose of fatiguing them into compliance with his measures.

He has dissolved Representative Houses repeatedly, for opposing with manly firmness his invasions on the rights of the people.

He has refused for a long time, after such dissolutions, to cause others to be elected, whereby the Legislative Powers, incapable of Annihilation, have returned to the People at large for their exercise; the State remaining in the mean time exposed to all the dangers of invasion from without, and convulsions within.

He has endeavoured to prevent the population of these States; for that purpose obstructing the Laws for Naturalization of Foreigners; refusing to pass others to encourage their migrations hither, and raising the conditions of new Appropriations of Lands.

He has obstructed the Administration of Justice by refusing his Assent to Laws for establishing Judiciary Powers.

He has made Judges dependent on his Will alone for the tenure of their offices, and the amount and payment of their salaries.

He has erected a multitude of New Offices, and sent hither swarms of Officers to harass our people and eat out their substance.

He has kept among us, in times of peace, Standing Armies without the Consent of our legislatures.

He has affected to render the Military independent of and superior to the Civil Power.

He has combined with others to subject us to a jurisdiction foreign to our constitution, and unacknowledged by our laws; giving his Assent to their Acts of pretended Legislation:

For quartering large bodies of armed troops among us:

For protecting them, by a mock Trial from punishment for any Murders which they should commit on the Inhabitants of these States:

For cutting off our Trade with all parts of the world:

For imposing Taxes on us without our Consent:

For depriving us in many cases, of the benefit of Trial by Jury:

For transporting us beyond Seas to be tried for pretended offences:

For abolishing the free System of English Laws in a neighbouring Province, establishing therein an Arbitrary government, and enlarging its Boundaries so as to render it at once an example and fit instrument for introducing the same absolute rule into these Colonies

For taking away our Charters, abolishing our most valuable Laws and altering fundamentally the Forms of our Governments:

For suspending our own Legislatures, and declaring themselves invested with power to legislate for us in all cases whatsoever.

He has abdicated Government here, by declaring us out of his Protection and waging War against us.

He has plundered our seas, ravaged our Coasts burnt our towns, and destroyed the lives of our people.

He is at this time transporting large Armies of foreign Mercenaries to compleat the works of death, desolation, and tyranny, already begun with circumstances of Cruelty & Perfidy scarcely paralleled in the most barbarous ages, and totally unworthy the Head of a civilized nation.

He has constrained our fellow Citizens taken Captive on the high Seas to bear Arms against their Country, to become the executioners of their friends and Brethren, or to fall themselves by their Hands.

He has excited domestic insurrections amongst us, and has endeavoured to bring on the inhabitants of our frontiers, the merciless Indian Savages whose known rule of warfare, is an undistinguished destruction of all ages, sexes and conditions.

In every stage of these Oppressions We have Petitioned for Redress in the most humble terms: Our repeated Petitions have been answered only by repeated injury. A Prince, whose character is thus marked by every act which may define a Tyrant, is unfit to be the ruler of a free people.

Nor have We been wanting in attentions to our British brethren. We have warned them from time to time of attempts by their legislature to extend an unwarrantable jurisdiction over us.

We have reminded them of the circumstances of our emigration and settlement here.

We have appealed to their native justice and magnanimity, and we have conjured them by the ties of our kindred. to disavow these usurpations, which would inevitably interrupt our connections and correspondence.

They too have been deaf to the voice of justice and of consanguinity.

We must, therefore, acquiesce in the necessity, which denounces our Separation, and hold them, as we hold the rest of mankind, Enemies in War, in Peace Friends.

We, therefore, the Representatives of the United States of America, in General Congress, Assembled, appealing to the Supreme Judge of the world for the rectitude of our intentions, do, in the Name, and by Authority of the good People of these Colonies, solemnly publish and declare, That these United Colonies are, and of Right ought to be Free and Independent States, that they are Absolved from all Allegiance to the British Crown, and that all political connection between them and the State of Great Britain, is and ought to be totally dissolved;

and That as Free and Independent States, they have full Power to levy War, conclude Peace, contract Alliances, establish Commerce, and to do all other Acts and Things which Independent States may of right do.

—And for the support of this Declaration, with a firm reliance on the protection of Divine Providence, we mutually pledge to each other our Lives, our Fortunes and our sacred Honor.

NEW HAMPSHIRE:
Josiah Bartlett, William Whipple, Matthew Thornton

MASSACHUSETTS:
John Hancock, Samuel Adams, John Adams, Robert Treat Paine, Elbridge Gerry

RHODE ISLAND:
Stephen Hopkins, William Ellery

CONNECTICUT:
Roger Sherman, Samuel Huntington, William Williams, Oliver Wolcott

NEW YORK:
William Floyd, Philip Livingston, Francis Lewis, Lewis Morris

NEW JERSEY:
Richard Stockton, John Witherspoon, Francis Hopkinson, John Hart, Abraham Clark

PENNSYLVANIA:
Robert Morris, Benjamin Rush, Benjamin Franklin, John Morton, George Clymer, James Smith, George Taylor, James Wilson, George Ross

DELAWARE:
Caesar Rodney, George Read, Thomas McKean

MARYLAND:
Samuel Chase, William Paca, Thomas Stone, Charles Carroll of Carrollton

VIRGINIA:
George Wythe, Richard Henry Lee, Thomas Jefferson, Benjamin Harrison, Thomas Nelson, Jr., Francis Lightfoot

Lee, Carter Braxton

NORTH CAROLINA:
William Hooper, Joseph Hewes, John Penn

SOUTH CAROLINA:
Edward Rutledge, Thomas Heyward, Jr., Thomas Lynch, Jr., Arthur Middleton

GEORGIA:
Button Gwinnett, Lyman Hall, George Walton

CONSTITUTION OF THE UNITED STATES

We the people of the United States, in order to form a more perfect union, establish justice, insure domestic tranquility, provide for the defense, promote the general welfare, and secure the blessings of liberty to ourselves and our posterity, do ordain and establish this Constitution for the United States of America.

ARTICLE I

SECTION 1

All legislative Powers herein granted shall be vested in a Congress of the United States, which shall consist of a Senate and House of Representatives.

SECTION 2

The House of Representatives shall be composed of Members chosen every second Year by the People of the several States, and the Electors in each State shall have the Qualifications requisite for Electors of the most numerous Branch of the State Legislature.

No Person shall be a Representative who shall not have attained to the Age of twenty five Years, and been seven Years a Citizen of the United States, and who shall not, when elected, be an Inhabitant of that State in which he shall be chosen.

[Representatives and direct Taxes shall be apportioned among the several States which may be included within this Union, according to their respective Numbers, which shall be determined by adding to the whole Number of free Persons, including those bound to Service for a Term of Years, and excluding Indians not taxed, three fifths of all other Persons.]*
*(Changed by section two of the Fourteenth Amendment.)

The actual Enumeration shall be made within three Years after the first Meeting of the Congress of the United States, and within every subsequent Term of ten Years, in such Manner as they shall by Law direct.

The Number of Representatives shall not exceed one for every thirty Thousand, but each State shall have at Least one Representative; and until such enumeration shall be made, the State of New Hampshire shall be entitled to choose three, Massachusetts eight, Rhode-Island and Providence Plantations one, Connecticut five, New-York six, New Jersey four, Pennsylvania eight, Delaware one, Maryland six, Virginia ten, North Carolina five, South Carolina five, and Georgia three.

When vacancies happen in the Representation from any State, the Executive Authority thereof shall issue Writs of Election to fill such Vacancies.

The House of Representatives shall choose their Speaker and other Officers; and shall have the sole Power of Impeachment.

SECTION 3

The Senate of the United States shall be composed of two Senators from each State, [chosen by the Legislature thereof,]* for six Years; and each Senator shall have one Vote.

Immediately after they shall be assembled in Consequence of the first Election, they shall be divided as equally as may be into three Classes. The Seats of the Senators of the first Class shall be vacated at the Expiration of the second Year, of the second Class at the Expiration of the fourth Year, and of the third Class at the Expiration of the sixth Year, so that one third may be chosen every second Year; [and if Vacancies happen by Resignation, or otherwise, during the Recess of the Legislature of any State, the Executive thereof may make temporary Appointments until the next Meeting of the Legislature, which shall then fill such Vacancies.]* *(Changed by the Seventeenth Amendment.)

No Person shall be a Senator who shall not have attained to the Age of thirty Years, and been nine Years a Citizen of the United States, and who shall not, when elected, be an Inhabitant of that State for which he shall be chosen.

The Vice President of the United States shall be President of the Senate, but shall have no Vote, unless they be equally divided.

The Senate shall choose their other Officers, and also a President pro tempore, in the Absence of the Vice President, or when he shall exercise the Office of President of the United States.

The Senate shall have the sole Power to try all Impeachments. When sitting for that Purpose, they shall be on Oath or Affirmation. When the President of the United States is tried, the Chief Justice shall preside: And no Person shall be convicted without the Concurrence of two thirds of the Members present.

Judgment in Cases of Impeachment shall not extend further than to removal from Office, and disqualification to hold and enjoy any Office of honor, Trust or Profit under the

United States: but the Party convicted shall nevertheless be liable and subject to Indictment, Trial, Judgment and Punishment, according to Law.

SECTION 4

The Times, Places and Manner of holding Elections for Senators and Representatives, shall be prescribed in each State by the Legislature thereof; but the Congress may at any time by Law make or alter such Regulations, except as to the Places of choosing Senators.

The Congress shall assemble at least once in every Year, and such Meeting shall be [on the first Monday in December,]* unless they shall by Law appoint a different Day. *(Changed by section two of the Twentieth Amendment.)

SECTION 5

Each House shall be the Judge of the Elections, Returns and Qualifications of its own Members, and a Majority of each shall constitute a Quorum to do Business; but a smaller Number may adjourn from day to day, and may be authorized to compel the Attendance of absent Members, in such Manner, and under such Penalties as each House may provide.

Each House may determine the Rules of its Proceedings, punish its Members for disorderly Behaviour, and, with the Concurrence of two thirds, expel a Member.

Each House shall keep a Journal of its Proceedings, and from time to time publish the same, excepting such Parts as may in their Judgment require Secrecy; and the Yeas and Nays of the Members of either House on any question shall, at the Desire of one fifth of those Present, be entered on the Journal.

Neither House, during the Session of Congress, shall, without the Consent of the other, adjourn for more than three days, nor to any other Place than that in which the two Houses shall be sitting.

SECTION 6

The Senators and Representatives shall receive a Compensation for their Services, to be ascertained by Law, and paid out of the Treasury of the United States. They shall in all Cases, except Treason, Felony and Breach of the Peace, be privileged from Arrest during their Attendance at the Session of their respective Houses, and in going to and returning from the same; and for any Speech or Debate in either House, they shall not be questioned in any other Place.

No Senator or Representative shall, during the Time for which he was elected, be appointed to any civil Office under the Authority of the United States, which shall have been created, or the Emoluments whereof shall have been increased during such time; and no Person holding any Office under the United States, shall be a Member of either House during his Continuance in Office.

SECTION 7

All Bills for raising Revenue shall originate in the House of Representatives; but the Senate may propose or concur with Amendments as on other Bills.

Every Bill which shall have passed the House of Representatives and the Senate, shall, before it become a Law, be presented to the President of the United States;

If he approves he shall sign it, but if not he shall return it, with his Objections to that House in which it shall have originated, who shall enter the Objections at large on their Journal, and proceed to reconsider it.

If after such Reconsideration two thirds of that House shall agree to pass the Bill, it shall be sent, together with the Objections, to the other House, by which it shall likewise be reconsidered, and if approved by two thirds of that House, it shall become a Law.

But in all such Cases the Votes of both Houses shall be determined by yeas and Nays, and the Names of the Persons voting for and against the Bill shall be entered on the Journal of each House respectively.

If any Bill shall not be returned by the President within ten Days (Sundays excepted) after it shall have been presented to him, the Same shall be a Law, in like Manner as if he had signed it, unless the Congress by their Adjournment prevent its Return, in which Case it shall not be a Law.

Every Order, Resolution, or Vote to which the Concurrence of the Senate and House of Representatives may be necessary (except on a question of Adjournment) shall be presented to the President of the United States; and before the Same shall take Effect, shall be approved by him, or being disapproved by him, shall be repassed by two thirds of the Senate and House of Representatives, according to the Rules and Limitations prescribed in the Case of a Bill.

SECTION 8

The Congress shall have Power To lay and collect Taxes, Duties, Imposts and Excises, to pay the Debts and provide for the Defence and general Welfare of the United States; but all Duties, Imposts and Excises shall be uniform throughout the United States;

To borrow Money on the credit of the United States;

To regulate Commerce with foreign Nations, and among the several States, and with the Indian Tribes;

To establish an uniform Rule of Naturalization, and uniform Laws on the subject of Bankruptcies throughout the United States;

To coin Money, regulate the Value thereof, and of foreign Coin, and fix the Standard of Weights and Measures;

To provide for the Punishment of counterfeiting the Securities and current Coin of the United States;

To establish Post Offices and post Roads;

To promote the Progress of Science and useful Arts, by securing for limited Times to Authors and Inventors the exclusive Right to their respective Writings and Discoveries;

To constitute Tribunals inferior to the supreme Court;

To define and punish Piracies and Felonies committed on the high Seas, and Offences against the Law of Nations;

To declare War, grant Letters of Marque and Reprisal, and make Rules concerning Captures on Land and Water;

To raise and support Armies, but no Appropriation of Money to that Use shall be for a longer Term than two Years;

To provide and maintain a Navy;

To make Rules for the Government and Regulation of the land and naval Forces;

To provide for calling forth the Militia to execute the Laws of the Union, suppress Insurrections and repel Invasions;

To provide for organizing, arming, and disciplining, the Militia, and for governing such Part of them as may be employed in the Service of the United States, reserving to the States respectively, the Appointment of the Officers, and the Authority of training the Militia according to the discipline prescribed by Congress;

To exercise exclusive Legislation in all Cases whatsoever, over such District (not exceeding ten Miles square) as may, by Cession of particular States, and the Acceptance of Congress, become the Seat of the Government of the United States, and to exercise like Authority over all Places purchased by the Consent of the Legislature of the State in which the Same shall be, for the Erection of Forts, Magazines, Arsenals, dock-Yards, and other needful Buildings;—And

To make all Laws which shall be necessary and proper for carrying into Execution the foregoing Powers, and all other Powers vested by this Constitution in the Government of the United States, or in any Department or Officer thereof.

SECTION 9

The Migration or Importation of such Persons as any of the States now existing shall think proper to admit, shall not be prohibited by the Congress prior to the Year one thousand eight hundred and eight, but a Tax or duty may be imposed on such Importation, not exceeding ten dollars for each Person.

The Privilege of the Writ of Habeas Corpus shall not be suspended, unless when in Cases of Rebellion or Invasion the public Safety may require it.

No Bill of Attainder or ex post facto Law shall be passed.

No Capitation, or other direct, Tax shall be laid, unless in Proportion to the Census or Enumeration herein before directed to be taken.* *(See the Sixteenth Amendment.)

No Tax or Duty shall be laid on Articles exported from any State.

No Preference shall be given by any Regulation of Commerce or Revenue to the Ports of one State over those of another: nor shall Vessels bound to, or from, one State, be obliged to enter, clear, or pay Duties in another.

No Money shall be drawn from the Treasury, but in Consequence of Appropriations made by Law; and a regular Statement and Account of the Receipts and Expenditures of all public Money shall be published from time to time.

No Title of Nobility shall be granted by the United States: And no Person holding any Office of Profit or Trust under them, shall, without the Consent of the Congress, accept of any present, Emolument, Office, or Title, of any kind whatever, from any King, Prince, or foreign State.

SECTION 10

No State shall enter into any Treaty, Alliance, or Confederation; grant Letters of Marque and Reprisal; coin Money; emit Bills of Credit; make any Thing but gold and silver Coin a Tender in Payment of Debts; pass any Bill of Attainder, ex post facto Law, or Law impairing the Obligation of Contracts, or grant any Title of Nobility.

No State shall, without the Consent of the Congress, lay any Imposts or Duties on Imports or Exports, except what may be absolutely necessary for executing it's inspection Laws: and the net Produce of all Duties and Imposts, laid by any State on Imports or Exports, shall be for the Use of the Treasury of the United States; and all such Laws shall be subject to the Revision and Control of the Congress.

No State shall, without the Consent of Congress, lay any Duty of Tonnage, keep Troops, or Ships of War in time of

Peace, enter into any Agreement or Compact with another State, or with a foreign Power, or engage in War, unless actually invaded, or in such imminent Danger as will not admit of delay.

ARTICLE II

SECTION 1

The executive Power shall be vested in a President of the United States of America. He shall hold his Office during the Term of four Years, and, together with the Vice President, chosen for the same Term, be elected, as follows

Each State shall appoint, in such Manner as the Legislature thereof may direct, a Number of Electors, equal to the whole Number of Senators and Representatives to which the State may be entitled in the Congress: but no Senator or Representative, or Person holding an Office of Trust or Profit under the United States, shall be appointed an Elector.

[The Electors shall meet in their respective States, and vote by Ballot for two Persons, of whom one at least shall not be an Inhabitant of the same State with themselves. And they shall make a List of all the Persons voted for, and of the Number of Votes for each; which List they shall sign and certify, and transmit sealed to the Seat of the Government of the United States, directed to the President of the Senate. The President of the Senate shall, in the Presence of the Senate and House of Representatives, open all the Certificates, and the Votes shall then be counted. The Person having the greatest Number of Votes shall be the President, if such Number be a Majority of the whole Number of Electors appointed; and if there be more than one who have such Majority, and have an equal Number of Votes, then the House of Representatives shall immediately choose by Ballot one of them for President; and if no Person have a Majority, then from the five highest on the List the said House shall in like Manner choose the President. But in choosing the President, the Votes shall be taken by States, the Representation from each State having one Vote; A quorum for this Purpose shall consist of a Member or Members from two thirds of the States, and a Majority of all the States shall be necessary to a Choice. In every Case, after the Choice of the President, the Person having the greatest Number of Votes of the Electors shall be the Vice President. But if there should remain two or more who have equal Votes, the Senate shall choose from them by Ballot the Vice President.]* *(Changed by the Twelfth Amendment.)

The Congress may determine the Time of choosing the Electors, and the Day on which they shall give their Votes; which Day shall be the same throughout the United States.

No Person except a natural born Citizen, or a Citizen of the United States, at the time of the Adoption of this Constitution, shall be eligible to the Office of President; neither shall any Person be eligible to that Office who shall not have attained to the Age of thirty five Years, and been fourteen Years a Resident within the United States.

[In Case of the Removal of the President from Office, or of his Death, Resignation, or Inability to discharge the Powers and Duties of the said Office, *(See Note 9)* the Same shall devolve on the Vice President, and the Congress may by Law provide for the Case of Removal, Death, Resignation or Inability, both of the President and Vice President, declaring what Officer shall then act as President, and such Officer shall act accordingly, until the Disability be removed, or a President shall be elected.]* *(Changed by the Twenty-Fifth Amendment.)

The President shall, at stated Times, receive for his Services, a Compensation, which shall neither be increased nor diminished during the Period for which he shall have been elected, and he shall not receive within that Period any other Emolument from the United States, or any of them.

Before he enter on the Execution of his Office, he shall take the following Oath or Affirmation: — "I do solemnly swear (or affirm) that I will faithfully execute the Office of President of the United States, and will to the best of my Ability, preserve, protect and defend the Constitution of the United States."

SECTION 2

The President shall be Commander in Chief of the Army and Navy of the United States, and of the Militia of the several States, when called into the actual Service of the United States; he may require the Opinion, in writing, of the principal Officer in each of the executive Departments, upon any Subject relating to the Duties of their respective Offices, and he shall have Power to grant Reprieves and Pardons for Offences against the United States, except in Cases of Impeachment.

He shall have Power, by and with the Advice and Consent of the Senate, to make Treaties, provided two thirds of the Senators present concur; and he shall nominate, and by and with the Advice and Consent of the Senate, shall appoint Ambassadors, other public Ministers and Consuls, Judges of the supreme Court, and all other Officers of the United States, whose Appointments are not herein otherwise provided for, and which shall be established by Law: but the Congress may by Law vest the Appointment of such inferior Officers, as they think proper, in the President alone, in the Courts of Law, or in the Heads of Departments.

The President shall have Power to fill up all Vacancies that may happen during the Recess of the Senate, by granting Commissions which shall expire at the End of their next Session.

SECTION 3

He shall from time to time give to the Congress Information of the State of the Union, and recommend to their Consideration such Measures as he shall judge necessary and expedient; he may, on extraordinary Occasions, convene both Houses, or either of them, and in Case of Disagreement between them, with Respect to the Time of Adjournment, he may adjourn them to such Time as he shall think proper; he shall receive Ambassadors and other public Ministers; he shall take Care that the Laws be faithfully executed, and shall Commission all the Officers of the United States.

SECTION 4

The President, Vice President and all civil Officers of the United States, shall be removed from Office on Impeachment for, and Conviction of, Treason, Bribery, or other high Crimes and Misdemeanors.

ARTICLE III

SECTION 1

The judicial Power of the United States, shall be vested in one supreme Court, and in such inferior Courts as the Congress may from time to time ordain and establish. The Judges, both of the supreme and inferior Courts, shall hold their Offices during good Behaviour, and shall, at stated Times, receive for their Services, a Compensation, which shall not be diminished during their Continuance in Office.

SECTION 2

The judicial Power shall extend to all Cases, in Law and Equity, arising under this Constitution, the Laws of the United States, and Treaties made, or which shall be made, under their Authority;—to all Cases affecting Ambassadors, other public Ministers and Consuls;—to all Cases of admiralty and maritime Jurisdiction;—to Controversies to which the United States shall be a Party;—to Controversies between two or more States;—[between a State and Citizens of another State;]*—between Citizens of different States, —between Citizens of the same State claiming Lands under Grants of different States, and between a State, or the Citizens thereof, and foreign States, Citizens or Subjects. *(Changed by the Eleventh Amendment.)

In all Cases affecting Ambassadors, other public Ministers and Consuls, and those in which a State shall be Party, the supreme Court shall have original Jurisdiction. In all the other Cases before mentioned, the supreme Court shall have appellate Jurisdiction, both as to Law and Fact, with such Exceptions, and under such Regulations as the Congress shall make.

The Trial of all Crimes, except in Cases of Impeachment, shall be by Jury; and such Trial shall be held in the State where the said Crimes shall have been committed; but when not committed within any State, the Trial shall be at such Place or Places as the Congress may by Law have directed.

SECTION 3

Treason against the United States, shall consist only in levying War against them, or in adhering to their Enemies, giving them Aid and Comfort. No Person shall be convicted of Treason unless on the Testimony of two Witnesses to the same overt Act, or on Confession in open Court.

The Congress shall have Power to declare the Punishment of Treason, but no Attainder of Treason shall work Corruption of Blood, or Forfeiture except during the Life of the Person attainted.

ARTICLE IV

SECTION 1

Full Faith and Credit shall be given in each State to the public Acts, Records, and judicial Proceedings of every other State. And the Congress may by general Laws prescribe the Manner in which such Acts, Records and Proceedings shall be proved, and the Effect thereof.

SECTION 2

The Citizens of each State shall be entitled to all Privileges and Immunities of Citizens in the several States.

A Person charged in any State with Treason, Felony, or other Crime, who shall flee from Justice, and be found in another State, shall on Demand of the executive Authority of the State from which he fled, be delivered up, to be removed to the State having Jurisdiction of the Crime.

[No Person held to Service or Labor in one State, under the Laws thereof, escaping into another, shall, in Consequence of any Law or Regulation therein, be discharged from such Service or Labor, but shall be delivered up on Claim of the Party to whom such Service or Labor may be due.]* *(Changed by the Thirteenth Amendment.*)*

SECTION 3

New States may be admitted by the Congress into this Union; but no new State shall be formed or erected within the Jurisdiction of any other State; nor any State be formed by the Junction of two or more States, or Parts of States, without the Consent of the Legislatures of the States concerned as well as of the Congress.

The Congress shall have Power to dispose of and make all needful Rules and Regulations respecting the Territory or other Property belonging to the United States; and nothing in this Constitution shall be so construed as to Prejudice any Claims of the United States, or of any particular State.

SECTION 4

The United States shall guarantee to every State in this Union a Republican Form of Government, and shall protect each of them against Invasion; and on Application of the

Legislature, or of the Executive (when the Legislature cannot be convened) against domestic Violence.

ARTICLE V

The Congress, whenever two thirds of both Houses shall deem it necessary, shall propose Amendments to this Constitution, or, on the Application of the Legislatures of two thirds of the several States, shall call a Convention for proposing Amendments, which, in either Case, shall be valid to all Intents and Purposes, as Part of this Constitution, when ratified by the Legislatures of three fourths of the several States, or by Conventions in three fourths thereof, as the one or the other Mode of Ratification may be proposed by the Congress; Provided that no Amendment which may be made prior to the Year One thousand eight hundred and eight shall in any Manner affect the first and fourth Clauses in the Ninth Section of the first Article; and that no State, without its Consent, shall be deprived of its equal Suffrage in the Senate.

ARTICLE VI

All Debts contracted and Engagements entered into, before the Adoption of this Constitution, shall be as valid against the United States under this Constitution, as under the Confederation.

This Constitution, and the Laws of the United States which shall be made in Pursuance thereof; and all Treaties made, or which shall be made, under the Authority of the United States, shall be the supreme Law of the Land; and the Judges in every State shall be bound thereby, any Thing in the Constitution or Laws of any State to the Contrary notwithstanding.

The Senators and Representatives before mentioned, and the Members of the several State Legislatures, and all executive and judicial Officers, both of the United States and of the several States, shall be bound by Oath or Affirmation, to support this Constitution; but no religious Test shall ever be required as a Qualification to any Office or public Trust under the United States.

ARTICLE VII

The Ratification of the Conventions of nine States, shall be sufficient for the Establishment of this Constitution between the States so ratifying the Same.

Done in Convention by the Unanimous Consent of the States present the Seventeenth Day of September in the Year of our Lord one thousand seven hundred and Eighty seven and of the Independence of the United States of America the Twelfth. In witness whereof We have hereunto subscribed our Names,

George Washington - President
and deputy from Virginia

DELAWARE
Geo: Read — Gunning Bedford Jr.
John Dickinson — Richard Bassett
Jacob Broom

MARYLAND
James McHenry — Daniel of St. Thomas Jenifer
Daniel Carroll.

VIRGINIA
John Blair — James Madison Jr.

NORTH CAROLINA
WM Blount — Richard Dobbs Spaight
Hugh Williamson

SOUTH CAROLINA
J. Rutledge Charles Cotesworth Pinckney
Charles Pinckney Pierce Butler.

GEORGIA
William Few Abraham Baldwin

NEW HAMPSHIRE
John Langdon Nicholas Gilman

MASSACHUSETTS
Nathaniel Gorham Rufus King

CONNECTICUT
William Samuel Johnson Roger Sherman

NEW YORK
Alexander Hamilton

NEW JERSEY
William Livingston David Brearley
William Paterson. Jonathan Dayton

PENNSYLVANIA
Benjamin Franklin Thomas Mifflin
Robert Morris George Clymer
Thomas FitzSimons Jared Ingersoll
James Wilson Gouverneur Morris

AMENDMENTS TO THE CONSTITUTION OF THE UNITED STATES

*CONGRESS OF THE UNITED STATES

*(On September 25, 1789, Congress transmitted to the State Legislatures twelve proposed amendments, two of which, having to do with Congressional representation and Congressional pay, were not adopted. The remaining ten amendments became the Bill of Rights.)

Begun and held at the City of New-York, on Wednesday March 4, 1789

The Convention of a Number of the States, having at the time of their adopting the Constitution, expressed a desire, in order to prevent misconstruction or abuse of it's powers, that further declaratory and restrictive clauses should be added: And as extending the ground of public confidence in the Government, will best ensure the beneficent ends of its institution:

RESOLVED by the Senate and House of Representatives of the United States of America, in Congress assembled, two thirds of both Houses concurring, that the following Articles be proposed to the Legislatures of the several States, as Amendments to the Constitution of the United States, all or any of which Articles, when ratified by three fourths of the said Legislatures, to be valid to all intents and purposes, as part of the said Constitution; viz..

ARTICLES in addition to, and Amendment of the Constitution of the United States of America, proposed by Congress, and ratified by the Legislatures of the several States, pursuant to the fifth Article of the original Constitution....

FREDERICK A. MUHLENBERG, Speaker of the House of Rep.

JOHN ADAMS, Vice-President of the United States, And President of the Senate.

ATTEST, JOHN BECKLEY, Clerk of the House of Rep.

SAM. A. OTIS, Secretary of the Senate.

THE BILL OF RIGHTS

The first ten Amendments, known as the Bill of Rights, were ratified effective December 15, 1791.

AMENDMENT I

Congress shall make no law respecting an establishment of religion, or prohibiting the free exercise thereof; or abridging the freedom of speech, or of the press; or the right of the people peaceably to assemble, and to petition the Government for a redress of grievances.

AMENDMENT II

A well-regulated militia, being necessary to the security of a free state, the right of the people to keep and bear arms, shall not be infringed.

AMENDMENT III

No soldier shall, in time of peace be quartered in any house, without the consent of the owner, not in time of war, but in a manner prescribed by law.

AMENDMENT IV

The right of the people to be secure in their persons, houses, papers, and effects, against unreasonable searches and seizures, shall not be violated, and no warrants shall issue, but upon probable cause, supported by oath or affirmation and particularly describing the place to be searched, and the persons or things to be seized.

AMENDMENT V

No person shall be held to answer for a capital, or otherwise infamous crime, unless on a presentment of indictment of a grand jury, except in cases arising in the land or naval forces or in the militia, when in actual service in time of war or public danger; nor shall any person be subject for the same offense to be twice put in jeopardy of life or limb; nor shall be compelled in any criminal case to be a witness against himself, nor be deprived of life, liberty, or property, without due process of law; nor shall private property be taken for public use, without just compensation.

AMENDMENT VI

In all criminal prosecutions, the accused shall enjoy the right to a speedy and public trial, by an impartial jury or the state and district wherein the crime shall have been committed, which district shall have been previously ascertained by law, and to be informed of the nature and cause of the accusation; to be confronted with the witnesses against him; to have compulsory process for obtaining witnesses in his favor, and to have the assistance of counsel for his defense.

AMENDMENT VII

In suits at law, where the value in controversy shall exceed twenty dollars, the right of trial by jury shall be preserved, and no fact tried by a jury shall be otherwise re-examined in any court of the United States, than according to the rules of law.

AMENDMENT VIII

Excessive bail shall not be required, nor excessive fines imposed, nor cruel and unusual punishments inflicted.

AMENDMENT IX

The enumeration in the Constitution, of certain rights, shall not be construed to deny or disparage others retained by the people.

AMENDMENT X

The powers not delegated to the United States by the Constitution, nor prohibited by it to the states, are reserved to the states respectively, or to the people.

AMENDMENTS XI - XXVII

AMENDMENT XI
Ratified January 8, 1798

The judicial power of the United States shall not be construed to extend to any suit in law or equity, commenced or prosecuted against one of the United States by citizens of another states, or by citizens or subjects of any foreign state.

AMENDMENT XII
Ratified September 25, 1804

The electors shall meet in their respective states, and vote by ballot for President and Vice President, one of whom, at least, shall not be an inhabitant of the same state with themselves; they shall name in their ballots the person voted for as President, and in distinct ballots the person voted for as

Vice-President, and they shall make distinct lists of all persons voted for as President, and of all persons voted for as Vice-President, and of the number of votes for each, which lists they shall sign and certify, and transmit sealed to the seat of the government of the United States, directed to the President of the Senate;

— the President of the Senate shall, in the presence of the Senate and House of Representatives, open all the certificates and the votes shall then be counted;

— The person having the greatest number of votes for President, shall be the President, if such number be a majority of the whole number of Electors appointed; and if no person have such majority, then from the persons having the highest numbers not exceeding three on the list of those voted for as President, the House of Representatives shall choose immediately, by ballot, the President.

But in choosing the President, the votes shall be taken by states, the representation from each state having one vote; a quorum for this purpose shall consist of a member or members from two-thirds of the states, and a majority of all the states shall be necessary to a choice.

[And if the House of Representatives shall not choose a President whenever the right of choice shall devolve upon them, before the fourth day of March next following, then the Vice-President shall act as President, as in case of the death or other constitutional disability of the President. —]*

The person having the greatest number of votes as Vice-President, shall be the Vice-President, if such number be a majority of the whole number of Electors appointed, and if no person have a majority, then from the two highest numbers on the list, the Senate shall choose the Vice-President; a quorum for the purpose shall consist of two-thirds of the whole number of Senators, and a majority of the whole number shall be necessary to a choice.

But no person constitutionally ineligible to the office of President shall be eligible to that of Vice-President of the United States. *(Superseded by section three of the Twentieth Amendment.)

AMENDMENT XIII
Ratified December 18, 1865

SECTION 1

Neither slavery nor involuntary servitude, except as a punishment for crime whereof the party shall have been duly convicted, shall exist within the United States, or any place subject to their jurisdiction.

SECTION 2

Congress shall have the power to enforce this article by appropriate legislation.

AMENDMENT XIV
Ratified July 9, 1868

SECTION 1

All persons born or naturalized in the United States, and subject to the jurisdiction thereof, are citizens of the United States and of the state wherein they reside. No State shall make or enforce any law which shall abridge the privileges or immunities of citizens of the United States; nor shall any State deprive any person of life, liberty, or property, without due process of law; nor deny to any person within its jurisdiction the equal protection of the laws.

SECTION 2

Representatives shall be apportioned among the several States according to their respective numbers, counting the whole number of persons in each State, excluding Indians not taxed. But when the right to vote at any election for the choice of electors for President and Vice-President of the United States, Representatives in Congress, the Executive and Judicial officers of a State, or the members of the Legislature thereof, is denied to any of the male inhabitants of such State, being twenty-one years of age,* and citizens of the United States, or in any way abridged, except for participation in rebellion, or other crime, the basis of representation therein shall be reduced in the proportion which the number of such male citizens shall bear to the whole number of male citizens twenty-one years of age in such State. *(Superseded by Section one of the Twenty-Sixth Amendment.)

SECTION 3

No person shall be a Senator or Representative in Congress, or elector of President and Vice-President, or hold any office, civil or military, under the United States, or under any State, who, having previously taken an oath, as a member of Congress, or as an officer of the United States, or as a member of any State legislature, or as an executive or judicial officer of any State, to support the Constitution of the United States, shall have engaged in insurrection or rebellion against the same, or given aid or comfort to the enemies thereof. But Congress may by a vote of two-thirds of each House, remove such disability.

SECTION 4

The validity of the public debt of the United States, authorized by law, including debts incurred for payment of pensions and bounties for services in suppressing insurrection or rebellion, shall not be questioned. But neither the United States nor any State shall assume or pay any debt or obligation incurred in aid of insurrection or rebellion against the United States, or any claim for the loss or emancipation of any slave; but all such debts, obligations and claims shall be held illegal and void.

SECTION 5

The Congress shall have the power to enforce, by appropriate legislation, the provisions of this article.

AMENDMENT XV
Ratified February 3, 1870

SECTION 1
The right of the citizens of the United States to vote shall not be denied or abridged by the United States or by any state on account of race, color, or previous condition of servitude.

SECTION 2
The Congress shall have power to enforce this article by appropriate legislation.

AMENDMENT XVI
Ratified February 3, 1913

The Congress shall have power to lay and collect taxes on incomes, from whatever source derived, without apportionment among the several states, and without regard to any census or enumeration.

AMENDMENT XVII
Ratified April 8, 1913

The Senate of the United States shall be composed of two Senators from each State, elected by the people thereof, for six years; and each Senator shall have one vote. The electors in each State shall have the qualifications requisite for electors of the most numerous branch of the State legislatures.

When vacancies happen in the representation of any State in the Senate, the executive authority of such State shall issue writs of election to fill such vacancies: Provided, That the legislature of any State may empower the executive thereof to make temporary appointments until the people fill the vacancies by election as the legislature may direct.

This amendment shall not be so construed as to affect the election or term of any Senator chosen before it becomes valid as part of the Constitution.

AMENDMENT XVIII

Ratified January 16, 1919

Repealed December 5, 1933 (21st Amendment)

SECTION 1

After one year from the ratification of this article the manufacture, sale, or transportation of intoxicating liquors within, the importation thereof into, or the exportation thereof from the United States and all territory subject to the jurisdiction thereof for beverage purposes is hereby prohibited.

SECTION 2

The Congress and the several States shall have concurrent power to enforce this article by appropriate legislation.

SECTION 3

This article shall be inoperative unless it shall have been ratified as an amendment to the Constitution by the legislatures of the several States, as provided in the Constitution, within seven years from the date of the submission hereof to the States by the Congress.

AMENDMENT XIX

Ratified August 18, 1920

The right of citizens of the United States to vote shall not be denied or abridged by the United States or by any State on account of sex.

Congress shall have power to enforce this article by appropriate legislation.

AMENDMENT XX
Ratified January 23, 1933

SECTION 1

The terms of the President and the Vice President shall end at noon on the 20th day of January, and the terms of Senators and Representatives at noon on the 3rd day of January, of the years in which such terms would have ended if this article had not been ratified; and the terms of their successors shall then begin.

SECTION 2

The Congress shall assemble at least once in every year, and such meeting shall begin at noon on the 3rd day of January, unless they shall by law appoint a different day.

SECTION 3

If, at the time fixed for the beginning of the term of the President, the President elect shall have died, the Vice President elect shall become President. If a President shall not have been chosen before the time fixed for the beginning of his term, or if the President elect shall have failed to qualify, then the Vice President elect shall act as President until a President shall have qualified; and the Congress may by law provide for the case wherein neither a President elect nor a Vice President shall have qualified, declaring who shall then act as President, or the manner in which one who is to act shall be selected, and such person shall act accordingly until a President or Vice President shall have qualified.

SECTION 4

The Congress may by law provide for the case of the death of any of the persons from whom the House of Representatives may choose a President whenever the right of choice shall have devolved upon them, and for the case of the death of any of the persons from whom the Senate may choose a Vice President whenever the right of choice shall have devolved upon them.

SECTION 5

Sections 1 and 2 shall take effect on the 15th day of October following the ratification of this article.

SECTION 6

This article shall be inoperative unless it shall have been ratified as an amendment to the Constitution by the legislatures of three-fourths of the several States within seven years from the date of its submission.

AMENDMENT XXI
Ratified December 5, 1933

SECTION 1

The eighteenth article of amendment to the Constitution of the United States is hereby repealed.

SECTION 2

The transportation or importation into any State, Territory, or Possession of the United States for delivery or use therein of intoxicating liquors, in violation of the laws thereof, is hereby prohibited.

SECTION 3

This article shall be inoperative unless it shall have been ratified as an amendment to the Constitution by conventions in the several States, as provided in the Constitution, within seven years from the date of the submission hereof to the States by the Congress.

AMENDMENT XXII
Ratified February 27, 1951

SECTION 1

No person shall be elected to the office of the President more than twice, and no person who has held the office of President, or acted as President, for more than two years of a term to which some other person was elected President shall be elected to the office of President more than once. But this Article shall not apply to any person holding the office of President when this Article was proposed by Congress, and shall not prevent any person who may be holding the office of President, or acting as President, during the term within which this Article becomes operative from holding the office of President or acting as President during the remainder of such term.

SECTION 2

This article shall be inoperative unless it shall have been ratified as an amendment to the Constitution by the legislatures of three-fourths of the several States within seven years from the date of its submission to the States by the Congress.

AMENDMENT XXIII
Ratified March 29, 1961

SECTION 1

The District constituting the seat of Government of the United States shall appoint in such manner as Congress may direct:

A number of electors of President and Vice President equal to the whole number of Senators and Representatives in Congress to which the District would be entitled if it were a State, but in no event more than the least populous State; they shall be in addition to those appointed by the states, but they shall be considered, for the purposes of the election of

President and Vice President, to be electors appointed by a State; and they shall meet in the District and perform such duties as provided by the twelfth article of amendment.

SECTION 2

The Congress shall have power to enforce this article by appropriate legislation.

AMENDMENT XXIV
Ratified January 23, 1964

SECTION 1

The right of citizens of the United States to vote in any primary or other election for President or Vice President, for electors for President or Vice President, or for Senator or Representative in Congress, shall not be denied or abridged by the United States or any State by reason of failure to pay poll tax or other tax.

SECTION 2

The Congress shall have power to enforce this article by appropriate legislation.

AMENDMENT XXV
Ratified February 10, 1967

SECTION 1

In case of the removal of the President from office or of his death or resignation, the Vice President shall become President.

SECTION 2

Whenever there is a vacancy in the office of the Vice President, the President shall nominate a Vice President who shall take office upon confirmation by a majority vote of both Houses of Congress.

SECTION 3

Whenever the President transmits to the President pro tempore of the Senate and the Speaker of the House of Representatives his written declaration that he is unable to discharge the powers and duties of his office, and until he transmits to them a written declaration to the contrary, such powers and duties shall be discharged by the Vice President as Acting President.

SECTION 4

Whenever the Vice President and a majority of either the principal officers of the executive departments or of such other body as Congress may by law provide, transmit to the President pro tempore of the Senate and the Speaker of the House of Representatives their written declaration that the President is unable to discharge the powers and duties of his office, the Vice President shall immediately assume the powers and duties of the office as Acting President.

Thereafter, when the President transmits to the President pro tempore of the Senate and the Speaker of the House of Representatives his written declaration that no inability exists, he shall resume the powers and duties of his office unless the Vice President and a majority of either the principal officers of the executive department or of such other body as Congress may by law provide, transmit within four days to the President pro tempore of the Senate and the Speaker of the House of Representatives their written declaration that the President is unable to discharge the powers and duties of his office. Thereupon Congress shall decide the issue, assembling within forty-eight hours for that purpose if not in session. If the Congress, within twenty-one days after receipt of the latter written declaration, or, if Congress is not in session, within twenty-one days after Congress is required to assemble, determines by two-thirds vote of both Houses that the President is unable to discharge the powers and duties of his office, the Vice President shall continue to discharge the same as Acting President; otherwise, the President shall resume the powers and duties of his office.

AMENDMENT XXVI
Ratified July 1, 1971

SECTION 1

The right of citizens of the United States, who are eighteen years of age or older, to vote shall not be denied or abridged by the United States or by any State on account of age.

SECTION 2

The Congress shall have power to enforce this article by appropriate legislation.

AMENDMENT XXVII
Although submitted in 1789, finally ratified May 7, 1992

No law, varying the compensation for the services of the Senators and Representatives, shall take effect, until an election of representatives shall have intervened.

ABOUT THE AUTHORS

MARK I. SUTHERLAND was born in Irvine, Scotland in 1975. The son of a minister, Mark grew up being taught that everyone is created equal. When he immigrated to the United States in 1989 he discovered an entire nation that believed the same. He soon fell in love with the principles that made America great and with the American people who accepted him as one of their own.

Mark moved directly to St. Louis, MO when he came to the United States. He worked for many years in local radio, as a DJ, a talk show host and even as a personality on the Steve and DC Morning Show. In 1997, Mark was a key part of developing the Rage Against Destruction anti-violence school program, and served as the media/government relations director from 1999-2002 as the program worked across the nation with over 1/4 million students.

In late 2002, Mark started working as a political and constitutional analyst, and in late 2004 he formed the National Policy Center. Mark currently works as the public relations director for Joyce Meyer Ministries, and he also continues his work with political organizations, state politicians and members of Congress across the United States. His work has allowed him to work alongside Chief Justice Roy Moore, Ambassador Alan Keyes and many other American patriots. He is married with three children.

Mark's entire life is devoted to serving his fellow Americans, and his goal is to leave a better country for his children, grandchildren and great-grandchildren.

Former Alabama Chief Justice Roy Moore: "Mark Sutherland has exhibited an exceptional intellectual ability to understand the necessity for courts to act in accordance with a rule of law on moral issues. He is a man of integrity and exceptional intellectual ability who has used his talents for the improvement of others."

The Honorable Howard Phillips - Chairman of the Conservative Caucus: "His solid constitutional knowledge, and his belief that government is the servant of the people, will be an incredible asset to those he represents. He is a good friend, and an American patriot."

Congressman Walter Jones - North Carolina: "In these challenging times where morality is being assaulted on every side, we need more people like Mark Sutherland"

Steve Shannon - Host of The Steve & DC Show: "I've watched as Mark Sutherland has become a devoted husband/ father, morally grounded conservative, and passionate proud American. He inspires his friends and acquaintances by example. He is a true leader."

JAMES C. DOBSON, Ph.D., is founder and chairman of the board of Focus on the Family, a nonprofit organization that produces his internationally syndicated radio programs heard daily on more than 3,000 radio facilities in North America and in 15 languages on approximately 3,300 facilities in over 116 other countries. His commentaries are heard by more than 200 million people every day, including a program translation carried on China National Radio (Channel 1) in the People's Republic of China. He is seen on 80 television stations daily in the U.S.

For 14 years Dr. Dobson was an Associate Clinical Professor of Pediatrics at the University of Southern California

School of Medicine, and served for 17 years on the Attending Staff of Children's Hospital of Los Angeles in the Division of Child Development and Medical Genetics. He has an earned Ph.D. from the University of Southern California (1967) in the field of child development. He is a clinical member of the American Association for Marriage and Family Therapy, a licensed psychologist in California, and is listed in *Who's Who in Medicine and Healthcare.*

His film series, "Focus on the Family," has been seen by over 70 million people. His second film series, "Turn Your Heart Toward Home," was released in 1986. A third seven-part series, "Life on The Edge," designed to help late teens bridge the gap between adolescence and young adulthood, was released in 1994. In 2002, he produced an eleven-part series based on his best-selling book, "Bringing up Boys."

Dr. Dobson's first book, *Dare to Discipline,* has sold more than 3 million copies and was selected as one of 50 books to be rebound and placed in the White House Library. It is revised and updated as *The New Dare to Discipline.* His subsequent books for the family are also best-sellers: *The New Hide or Seek, What Wives Wish Their Husbands Knew About Women, The New Strong-Willed Child, Preparing for Adolescence, Straight Talk to Men, Emotions: Can You Trust Them?, Love Must Be Tough, Parenting Isn't for Cowards, Love for a Lifetime, Children at Risk, When God Doesn't Make Sense, Life on the Edge, Home With a Heart, Coming Home, In the Arms of God, NightLight: A Devotional for Couples, Bringing Up Boys, NightLight for Parents, Marriage Under Fire.*

BENJAMIN D. DUPRE' was born and raised in New York. Benjamin received his law degree in 1998, graduating cum laude from Regent University School of Law.

From 2001-2003, Benjamin worked for former Alabama Supreme Court Chief Justice Roy Moore, resigning after Moore was suspended from office. Benjamin currently lives in Montgomery with his wife Jerusha, and works as an attorney for the Foundation for Moral Law.

DON FEDER was a *Boston Herald* editorial writer and syndicated columnist from June 1983 to June 2002. He currently serves as the Communications Director for Vision America.

For 19 years, his column appeared in *The Herald*, New England's second-largest newspaper. On February 28, 2002, the paper published his 2,000th column. Don Feder's latest books are *Who is Afraid of the Religious Right* and *A Jewish Conservative looks at Pagan America.*

WILLIAM J. FEDERER is a nationally known speaker, best-selling author and former U.S. Congressional Candidate whose books are used by members of Congress, judges, teachers, journalists and citizens across the United States.

His book *America's God and Country Encyclopedia of Quotations* has sold over a half-million copies. Other works include: *The Ten Commandments & their Influence on American Law, Three Secular Reasons America Should Be Under God, The Interesting History of Income Tax, American Quotations CD ROM, Library of Classics CD ROM, There Really is a Santa Claus-The History of Saint Nicholas & Christmas Holiday Traditions, George Washington Carver-His Life & Faith in His Own Words, Saint Patrick, American Minute-Notable Events of American Significance Remembered on the Date They Occurred,* and *BACKFIRED-A nation born for religious tolerance no longer tolerates religion.*

His daily 'American Minute' commentary is featured on radio stations and web sites nationwide. He is the president of Amerisearch, Inc., and founder of American Priorities, a non-profit educational foundation.

DAVID C. GIBBS, III, works with Gibbs Law Firm and the Christian Law Association defending rights of churches and Christians nationwide. His daily radio program, *The Legal Alert,* is heard on 1,050 stations. He has appeared on Larry King Live, Prime Time America, Open Line and was the attorney for Terri Schiavo's family in the alarming case of her being starved to death.

ALAN KEYES spent 11 years with the U.S. State Department. He served in the U.S. Foreign Service and on the staff of the National Security Council before becoming Ronald Reagan's ambassador to the United Nations Economic and Social Council, where he represented the interests of the United States in the U.N. General Assembly (1983-85). In 1985, he was appointed Assistant Secretary of State for International Organizations (1985-88).

Ambassador Keyes has a Ph.D. in government from Harvard and wrote his dissertation on constitutional theory. He is the author of *Masters of the Dream: The Strength and Betrayal of Black America* (1995); and *Our Character, Our Future: Reclaiming America's Moral Destiny* (1996).

EDWIN MEESE, former U.S. Attorney General, was among President Ronald Reagan's most important advisors. As Chairman of the Domestic Policy Council and the National Drug Policy Board, and as a member of the National Security Council, he played a key role in the development and execution of domestic and foreign policy.

During the 1970s, Mr. Meese was Director of the Center for Criminal Justice Policy and Management and Professor of

Law at the University of San Diego. He earlier served as Chief of Staff for then-Governor Reagan and was a local prosecutor in California. Mr. Meese is a Distinguished Visiting Fellow at the Hoover Institution, Stanford University, and a Distinguished Senior Fellow at the Institute of United States Studies, University of London. He earned his B.A. from Yale University and his J.D. from the University of California, Berkeley

DAVE MEYER is a veteran of the United States Army and held a career in engineering prior to joining his wife, Joyce Meyer, in full-time ministry. He is the vice-president of Joyce Meyer Ministries and has been married to Joyce for over thirty-six years.

With a deep conviction to pass on the understanding of our rich Christian heritage to the next generation, Dave passionately shares his knowledge of our unique blessing of liberty and is actively involved in community, social, and political action.

ROY S. MOORE graduated from the U.S. Military Academy at West Point with a bachelor of science degree in 1969 and completed his *Juris Doctor* degree from the University of Alabama School of Law in 1977. Roy Moore became a judge of the Sixteenth Judicial Circuit of Alabama in 1992, and served until his election as chief justice of the Alabama Supreme Court in 2000. The former Chief Justice lectures throughout the country, teaching about America's history and our right to acknowledge God, and is chairman of the Foundation for Moral Law, Inc., in Montgomery, Alabama.

HOWARD PHILLIPS is a former Presidential candidate. Phillips left the Republican Party in 1974 after some two decades of service to the GOP as precinct worker, election warden, campaign manager, Congressional aide, Boston Republican Chairman, and assistant to the Chairman of the Republican National Committee. During the Nixon Administration, Phillips headed two Federal agencies, ending his Executive Branch career as Director of the U.S. Office of Economic Opportunity in the Executive Office of the President.

Since 1974, Phillips has been Chairman of The Conservative Caucus, a non-partisan, nationwide grass-roots public policy advocacy group which has been in the thick of battles, in opposition to the Panama Canal and Carter-Brezhnev SALT II treaties in the 1970s, in support of SDI and major tax reductions during the 1980s, and in the vanguard of efforts to terminate Federal subsidies to ideological activist groups under the banner of "defunding the left."

DR. RICK SCARBOROUGH holds a Master of Divinity Degree from Southwestern Baptist Theological Seminary and a Doctor of Ministry Degree from Louisiana Baptist Theological Seminary. He holds a Bachelor of Arts Degree from Houston Baptist University, with a double major in Political Science and Speech.

In 1998, he founded Vision America, a ministry dedicated to "informing and mobilizing Pastors and their congregations to become salt and light, becoming pro-active in restoring Judeo-Christian values in America." Dr. Scarborough regularly speaks in churches, at rallies, political conventions and before civic clubs.

PHYLLIS SCHLAFLY, Esq., B.A., M.A., J.D., the president of Eagle Forum, is one of the most effective grassroots political leaders in American history. An attorney and mother of six, she is the author of 20 books, a nationally syndicated column, and a daily radio commentary broadcast on over four hundred stations nation-wide. Her latest book, *The Supremacists-The Tyranny of Judges and How to Stop It,* is a highly recommended work which examines in depth the issue of judicial activism.

She is a member of the Bar in Missouri, Illinois, Washington, DC, and the U.S. Supreme Court.

ALAN E. SEARS, Esq., is the President and General Counsel for the Alliance Defense Fund.

Previously, he held numerous positions with the United States Government including the Department of Justice, under Attorneys General William French Smith and Ed Meese III, as an Assistant United States Attorney and Chief of Criminal Section; as Director of the Attorney General's commission on Pornography; and the Department of Interior under Secretary Donald Hodel as an Associate Solicitor, with other not-for-profit public interest legal organizations, and in the private practice of law.

MATHEW D. STAVER is President and General Counsel of Liberty Counsel, Vice President of Law and Policy and a member of the Board of Trustees for Liberty University.

Staver has argued in numerous state and federal courts across the country. He has appeared on numerous briefs before the United State Supreme Court and has argued before the Court in the free speech picketing case of *Madsen v. Women's Health*

Center. He represented voters from Seminole and Martin Counties during the 2000 election cases. Most recently he argued in defense of the Ten Commandments in front of the U.S. Supreme Court in March 2005.

HERBERT W. TITUS, Esq., has taught constitutional law, and other subjects for nearly thirty years at five different American Bar Association-approved law schools. Today he is engaged in a general practice with a concentration in constitutional strategy, litigation, and appeals.

Mr. Titus has written numerous articles, book chapters and constitutional studies and analyses. He is the author of *God, Man & Law: The Biblical Principles,* a widely acclaimed text on American law. Mr. Titus also served as lead counsel to former Chief Justice Roy Moore during his fight to acknowledge God in Alabama.

ACKNOWLEDGMENTS
from Mark Sutherland

GOD - All thanks and honor goes to God, both for His blessing and inspiration as this book took shape, and for His gift of freedom and liberty. Without Him, this book would not have been possible.

AMY - Next, my wife. It is true what they say, that behind every man is an incredible woman. Without her support as I travel the country and work to restore our nation I don't believe I could do what I do. The Bible was right when it said, "He who finds a wife, finds a good thing."

MUM AND DAD - I owe a huge thank you to my parents. They raised me to believe biblical principles and godly standards, and when we immigrated to the United States I found a country in which those principles were in the very foundations. I also am eternally grateful for their obedience to God when He asked them to move to the United States from England. Without their obedience I would not be here today.

DAVE AND JOYCE MEYER - Thank you for taking a chance on a young immigrant who wanted to change the world. The doors that I have been able to walk through due to your trust and support are incredible. I can never repay the debt I owe you.

CHIEF JUSTICE ROY MOORE - The time over the past few years that you have invested in me has equipped me to be effective in this work. Your knowledge of law, history, and

God has been an ongoing inspiration to me. Thank you for taking the time and thank you for being my friend.

DOUG PHILLIPS - Your faithfulness in investing in young men around our nation, and teaching them true constitutional and biblical principles is having more impact than you will ever know. You challenged me, made me think, and impacted my heart. Thank you.

The list goes on and on of those who have inspired me, worked along side me, and to whom our country owes a debt of gratitude: J. Thomas Smith, Howard Phillips, Alan Keyes, Rev. Rob Schenck, Rev. Rick Scarborough, Rich Hobson, Ben DuPre', Jessica Quinn, Chad Connelly, Sam Jernigan, Dr. Mel Glenn, Sen. John Loudon, Don Feder, Bill Federer, Phyllis Schlafly, Herb Titus, Ron Calzone, Tracy Ammons, Steve Shannon, Lanier Swann, DC Chymes, Michael Peroutka, Rep. Mark Wright, Peter Lloyd, Katie Loovis, Bill Wichterman, Tim Goeglein, John Phillips, Dan Meyer, Phillip Jauregui and many others.

And lastly, thank you to all the contributors to this book. Your willingness to partner with me, and to work together to turn our nation around, speaks volumes of your character and commitment. Together we can do anything.

ENDNOTES

—

CHAPTER 2: THOU SHALT HAVE NO GOD BEFORE US - BENJAMIN D. DUPRE', ESQ.

1. ***Declaration of Independence (1776).***
2. ***Ibid.***
3. *Ibid.*
4. ***Ibid.***
5. Trial Transcript for *Glassroth v. Moore*, 229 F. Supp. 2d 1290 (M.D. Ala. 2002), Vol. I, p. 4.
6. *Ibid.* at p. 11.
7. *Ibid.* at 11-12.
8. Trial Transcript, *supra* at note 5, Vol. III, p. 34.
9. *Ibid.* at 38.
10. J. Madison, *Memorial and Remonstrance* (1785). *Constitution of Virginia, Bill of Rights* (June 12, 1776), reprinted in *Sources of Our Liberties* 313 (Perry rev. ed., Amer. Bar Found. ed. 1978).
11. Trial Transcript, *supra* at note 5, Vol. VII, p. 62.
12. *Ibid.* at 63.
13. *Ibid.* at 73.
14. *Ibid.*
15. *Glassroth v. Moore*, 229 F. Supp. 2d 1290, 1293 (M.D. Ala. 2002).
16. *Ibid.* at 1310 (emphasis in original).
17. *Ibid.* at 1312 (emphasis in original).
18. *Ibid.* at 1318.
19. *Ibid.* at 1313, fn. 5.
20. J. Locke, *Second Treatise of Civil Government*, Chap. XVIII, Sec. 199.
21. *Ibid.* at Sec. 201.
22. 4 United States Code Sec. 4, and annotations thereto, codifying that the Pledge of Allegiance to the flag would include the phrase "one nation under God." 36 United States Code Sec. 302, codifying "In God We Trust" as the National Motto of the United States.

23. W. J. Federer, *America's God and Country, Encyclopedia of Quotations* 530 (1996), quoting President Ronald Reagan at an Ecumenical Prayer Breakfast in Dallas, Texas, on the occasion of the enactment of the Equal Access Act of 1984.
24. J. Locke, *supra* at note 20, at Sec. 202.
25. *See* Genesis 3:5 (KJV).
26. Federer, *supra* at note 23, at 654, quoting George Washington's October 3, 1789 *National Day of Thanksgiving Proclamation.*

CHAPTER 3: THE POWER OF OUR TRUE HISTORY - DAVE MEYER
1. Barton, David, *Original Intent: The Courts, the Constitution and Religion,* p. 227, (2004).
2. Barton, David, *Original Intent: The Courts, the Constitution and Religion,* p. 229, (2004).
3. Barton, David, *Original Intent: The Courts, the Constitution and Religion,* p. 230, (2004).

CHAPTER 9: REDEFINING THE RULES - MARK I. SUTHERLAND
1. *Virginia Declaration of Rights of 1776*
2. *Congress of the United States of America.* September 25, 1789, recommending a *National Day of Public Thanksgiving and Prayer. Annals of Congress of the United States – First Congress* (Washington, D.C.: Gales & Seaton, 1834-56), Vol. I, p. 914.
3. *Congress of the Confederation.* 1787, under the Articles of the Confederation, approved a *Treaty with the Kaskaskia Indians,* which was extended under President Thomas Jefferson, December 3, 1803; also in the *Treaty with the Wyandotte Indians,* extended by Jefferson, 1806; and the *Treaty with the Cherokee Indians,* extended by Jefferson, 1807.
4. *Ibid.* July 13. 1787, Articles of the Confederation, approved *THE NORTHWEST ORDINANCE OF 1787, Section 13, 14; Article I, III.* This ordinance was signed into law under the US Constitution by George Washington, August 4, 1789.
5. *Congress of the United States of America.* June 8, 1789, James Madison introducing the initial version of the First Amendment. *Annals of Congress of the United States – First Congress* (Washington, D.C.: Gales & Seaton, 1834-56), Vol. I, p. 434.
6. *Ibid.* August 15, 1789, Samuel Livermore of New Hampshire proposed wording of the First Amendment. pp. 729, 731.

7. John Fitzgerald Kennedy. January 20, 1961, Friday, in his Inaugural Address. *Inaugural Addresses of the Presidents of the United States – From George Washington 1789 to Richard Milhous Nixon 1969* (Washington, D.C.: United States Government Printing Office; 91st Congress, 1st Session, House Document 91-142, 1969).
8. Douglas W. Phillips, Esq. "Do Laws And Standards Evolve?" *Impact No. 303, September 1998.*
9. *Glassroth v. Moore,* 335 F.3d 1282 (11th Cir. 2003).
10. *U.S. Constitution. Articles I, II, & III.*
11. *Ibid.*
12. *Debates and Proceedings,* p. 645, 7th Congress, 2nd Session, March 3, 1803.
13. *Ibid,* p. 272, 8th Congress, 1st Session, March 13, 1804 and pp. 1237-1240, March 26, 1804.
14. *Proceedings and Debates,* 58th Congress, 3rd Session, Vol. XXXIX, pp. 1281-1283, January 24, 1905.
15. *Ibid,* 69th Congress, 1st Session, Vol. LXVII, Part 6, pp. 6585-6589, March 30, 1926
16. Edmund Burke. January 9, 1795, in a letter to William Smith
17. Continental Congress. July 2, 1776, *Declaration of Independence,* Philadelphia, PA.

CHAPTER 7: THE RULE OF LAW -
CHIEF JUSTICE ROY MOORE

1. "Loyalty to the Constitution," Constitution Corner, United States Military Academy, West Point, New York.
2. Ibid.
3. U.S. Constitution, art. 6, para. 2.
4. See United States v. Calley, 48 C.M.R. 19, 22 USCMA 534 (1973).
5. "Loyalty to the Constitution," Constitution Corner, USMA.
6. New Encyclopedia Britannica, 15th ed., vol. 7 (Chicago, 1992), 673.
7. Henry de Bracton, On the Laws and Customs of England, vol. 2, ed. Samuel Thorne (Cambridge, Mass.: Belknap Press of Harvard University Press, 1968), 33.
8. Ibid.
9. Samuel Rutherford, Lex Rex, or The Law and the Prince: A Dispute for the Just Prerogative of King and People, reprint of original 1644 ed. (Virginia: Sprinkle Publ., 1982).
10. Encyclopedia Britannica, 15th ed., vol. 10, Robert McHenry (1992).
11. Declaration of Independence.
12. Benjamin Franklin, America's God and Country, 246.

13. Jonathan Mayhew, A Discourse Concerning Unlimited Submission and Non-Resistance to the Higher Powers, available at: http://www.lawandliberty.org/mayhew.htm) (emphasis added).
14. Ibid.
15. "Congress shall make no law respecting an establishment of religion or prohibiting the free exercise thereof . . . .," U.S. Constitution, amend. 1.
16. Roy S. Moore, Alabama chief justice, statement, around July 4, 2003 (emphasis in original).
17. "Moving Day-Monument's move is victory for rule of law," Birmingham News, August 28, 2003.
18. Ibid.
19. Moore v. Judicial Inquiry Commission, transcript, no. 33, vol. 4 (2003), 156.
20. Associate justices, Alabama Supreme Court, brief in support of motion to dismiss McGinley v. Houston, 282 F. Supp. 2d 1304 (M.D. Ala. 2003), 2. Available at http://news.lp.findlaw.com/hdocs/docs/religion/mcginhstn82603oppbrf.pdf (emphasis added).
21. Champ Lyons Jr., "His Monument, My Oath, and the Rule of Law," May 12, 2004, 8, 10.
22. Ibid., 13.
23. Ibid., 24.
24. James Madison, The Federalist No. 51, ed. George W. Carey and James McClellan (2001), 268-69.
25. Thomas Jefferson, "Resolutions Relative to the Alien and Sedition Acts," reprinted in The Founders Constitution 1, ed. P. Kurland and R. Lerner (1987), 293.
26. U.S. Constitution, art. 6, para. 2.
27. James Madison, The Federalist No. 45, eds. George W. Carey and James McClellan (2001), 241.
28. Marbury v. Madison, 5 U.S. 137, 163 (1803).
29. Ibid., 165.
30. Ibid., 180 (emphasis in original).
31. Cooper v. Aaron, 358 U.S. 1, 18 (1958).
32. Marbury v. Madison, 5 U.S. 179-80 (emphasis added).
33. Attorney General Bill Pryor, official statement, August 21, 2003.
34. Abraham Lincoln, first inaugural address, March 4, 1861, reprinted in The Essential Abraham Lincoln, ed. John G. Hunt (New York: Gramercy Books, 1993), 218-19.
35. Thomas Jefferson, letter to Judge Spencer Roane, September 6, 1819, reprinted in Writings, 1426.
36. 410 U.S. 113 (1973).
37. 539 U.S. 558 (2003).
38. 478 U.S. 186 (1986).

CHAPTER 10: AMERICAN OLIGARCHY - WILLIAM J. FEDERER

1. Thomas Jefferson, September 28, 1820, in a letter to William Jarvis. Thomas Jefferson, *Jefferson's Letters,* Wilson Whitman, ed., (Eau Claire, WI: E.M. Hale & Co., 1900), p. 338. Gary DeMar, *God and Government-A Biblical and Historical Study* (Atlanta, GA: American Vision Press, 1982), p. 166.

2. Friday, September 17, 1999 Planned Parenthood gains injunction against abortion law Follows Senate action overriding Gov. Mel Carnahan veto By GERRY TRITZ News Tribune The state Senate enacted a "partial-birth abortion" ban against Gov. Mel Carnahan's wishes on Thursday, making him the seventh Missouri governor since statehood in 1821 to have a veto overturned. The new law took effect Thursday evening, but failed to last through noon today. U.S. District Judge Scott Wright issued a 10-day stay against enforcing the new law after Planned Parenthood filed a constitutional challenge this morning. http://newstribune.com/stories/091799/sta_0917990040.asp http://report.kff.org/archive/repro/2000/06/kr000630.1.htm

3. Judge Blocks Partial-Birth Abortion Ban By KEVIN O'HANLON Associated Press LINCOLN, Neb. (AP) - November 5, 2003 at 11:54:35 PST A federal judge blocked implementation of a federal ban on certain late-term abortions Wednesday less than an hour after President George W. Bush signed the ban into law. U.S. District Judge Richard Kopf issued a temporary restraining order citing concerns that the law did not contain an exception for preserving the health of the woman seeking the abortion.

4. http://www.crlp.org/st_law_pba.html

5. Thomas Jefferson, September 28, 1820, in a letter to William Jarvis. Thomas Jefferson, *Jefferson's Letters,* Wilson Whitman, ed., (Eau Claire, WI: E.M. Hale & Co., 1900), p. 338. Gary DeMar, *God and Government-A Biblical and Historical Study* (Atlanta, GA: American Vision Press, 1982), p. 166.

6. Harrison, William Henry. March 4, 1841, Thursday, in his Inaugural Address. James D. Richardson (U.S. Representative from Tennessee), ed., *A Compilation of the Messages and Papers of the Presidents 1789-1897,* 10 vols. (Washington, D.C.: U.S. Government Printing Office, published by Authority of Congress, 1897, 1899; Washington, D.C.: Bureau of National Literature and Art, 1789-1902, 11 vols., 1907, 1910), Vol. 4, pp. 6-20.

7. http://supct.law.cornell.edu/supct/html/95-974.ZS.html http://ourworld.compuserve.com/homepages/JWCRAWFORD/art28.htm Prop 106, ACLU News - The Newspaper of the ACLU of Northern

California, July/August 1998 ACLU Helps Defeat Official English Law in Arizona BY MARIA ARCHULETA http://www.aclunc.org/aclunews/news498/arizona-english.html

8. http://www.washingtonpost.com/wp-srv/politics/special/termlimits/stories/052395.htm *U.S. Term Limits Inc. v. Thornton* Congressional Term Limits Struck Down By Joan Biskupic Washington Post Staff Writer Tuesday, May 23, 1995; Page A01 The Supreme Court ruled yesterday that states could not set term limits for members of Congress, saying American democracy was built on the principle that individual voters choose who governs and for how long. In a 5 to 4 decision, the court found that the states do not have the constitutional authority to regulate the tenure of federal legislators. The ruling effectively overturns term limits laws in 23 states and makes amending the Constitution the only sure means of restricting incumbency.... MAJORITY OPINION: "Permitting individual States to formulate diverse qualifications for their congressional representatives would result in a patchwork of state qualifications, undermining the uniformity and the national character that the Framers envisioned and sought to ensure." - Justice John Paul Stevens Joined by: * Justice Anthony M. Kennedy * Justice David Souter * Justice Ruth Bader Ginsburg * Justice Stephen Breyer THE DISSENT: "The Constitution is simply silent on this question. And where the Constitution is silent, it raises no bar to action by the states or the people." - Justice Clarence Thomas Joined by: * Chief Justice William Rehnquist * Justice Sandra Day O'Connor * Justice Antonin Scalia (c) Copyright 1998 The Washington Post Company.

9. http://www.migrationint.com.au/news/canary_islands/dec_1995-02mn.asp Immigration Laws: December, 1995 - Number #2 Parts of Prop. 187 Unconstitutional A federal judge in Los Angeles declared most sections of Prop. 187 unconstitutional in a 72-page ruling issued on November 20, 1995. According to the judge, "The authority to regulate immigration belongs exclusively to the federal government, and state agencies are not permitted to assume that authority."

10. http://www.nlf.net/Romer.html National Legal Foundation - Roy Romer, *Governor of Colorado v. Richard G. Evans et al* United States Supreme Court On November 3, 1992, the people of Colorado adopted Amendment 2 by a vote of 53.4% to 46.6%. In this most democratic of processes, the people of the state had spoken by referendum and enjoined their state and all lower governments from granting protected status to a group of individuals based not on an inalienable physical characteristic, but on a chosen lifestyle.... Roy G. Romer, Governor of Colorado, is on record as opposing initiatives that "deny" special rights and protection to homosexuals. ... the Supreme Court issued what may be the worst decision in the history of the court, finding that Amendment 2 did discriminate against an identifiable class of people and violated their rights to due process and equal protection under the law.

11. http://www.oyez.org/oyez/resource/case/255/ *Missouri v. Jenkins* 495 U.S. 33 (1990) Docket Number: 88-1150 Abstract Argued: October 30, 1989 Decided: April 18, 1990 Subjects: Judicial Power: Jurisdiction of Federal Courts Facts of the Case ...In order to combat segregation in public schools in compliance with court directives, the Kansas City, Missouri School District (KCMSD) sought to enhance the quality of schools and to attract more white students from the suburbs. The KCMSD's ability to raise taxes, however, was limited by state law. After determining that the District did not have alternative means of raising revenue for the program, federal district judge Russell G. Clark ordered an increase of local property taxes for the 1991-92 fiscal year. The U.S. Court of Appeals for the Eighth Circuit affirmed the decision, but ruled that the courts should enjoin state tax laws that prevented the District from raising the necessary funds and allow the state to set tax rates.

12. http://www.campaignfinancesite.org/book/html/211.html Supreme Court Reconsiders Contribution Limits Dan Manatt This selection originally was titled "In *Shrink PAC v. Nixon*, Supreme Court to Hear Challenge to Contributions Limits," from the "Recent Developments in the Campaign Finance Regulations" section of the Brookings Institution's web site (www.brookings.org). This article addresses the Supreme Court's decision to review *Nixon v. Shrink Missouri Government PAC*, in which the Eighth Circuit Court of Appeals invalidated Missouri's limits on campaign contributions.

13. [Federal] Judge will block new abortion law [MO] Posted by madprof98 On 10/09/2003 5:55 PM PDT with 3 comments Jefferson City (MO) News Tribune ^ | 10/9/03 | DAVID A. LIEB (AP) A federal judge said Wednesday he will block a new Missouri law that would have required physicians to wait 24 hours after consulting a woman before performing an abortion. Senior U.S. District Judge Scott O. Wright plans to issue the temporary restraining order against the law on Friday — one day before the abortion law was to take effect, said Wright's clerk. The decision came during a private telephone conference the judge held

Wednesday with attorneys for the state and Planned Parenthood affiliates, who had challenged the law on grounds it is unconstitutionally vague and broad. September 11, 2003, Family Research Council, State of the Family, Vol. 3, Issue 4., http://www.frc.org/get.cfm?i=SF03J01&v=PRINT#top September 11, 2003 Missouri Senate overrides MO Governor's veto of Conceal Carry Missouri passed a "Conceal Carry" bill. Governor Bob Holden vetoed it. Legislators overrode his veto, but a judge overruled. (St. L. Cir. Judge Steven Ohmer, Oct 10, 2003.) http://www.packing.org/news/article.jsp/9231 (KSDK) – A St. Louis Circuit Court decided Friday that Missouri's concealed weapons law will not go in effect Saturday, October 11. Judge Steven Ohmer made his ruling at 4:00 Friday afternoon. Opponents of the concealed carry law say the law's wording was vague and that a clause in the Missouri constitution bans concealed weapons. http://www.packing.org/news/article.jsp/9277

14. U.S. District Judge Joseph Bataillo, May 12, 2005. Bataillo an appointee of President Bill Clinton, struck down Nebraska's Marriage Amendment which was passed by 70% of the voters. (MSNBC, May 12, 2005, Alliance for Marriage, P.O. Box 2490, Merrifield, VA 22116, 703-934-1212, www.allianceformarriage.org, The Washington Times, Amy Fagan, May 14, 2005)

15. Second Circuit, July 20, 1994, Compassion in Dying filed a complaint for declaratory judgment on behalf of 3 New York physicians and 3 terminally ill patients. On Dec 15, 1994, US District Court Chief Judge Thomas P, Griesa upheld New York law prohibiting assisted suicide (penal law sections 120.30 and 125.15. On April 2, 1996, a 3-judge panel of the 2nd Circuit Court of Appeals struck down those laws as relates to physicians and terminally ill patients (*Quill v. Vacco*). The decision, and concurrence are available from Touro Law Center and Pace University School of Law.

16. Washington State On January 25, 1994, Compassion in Dying initiated a legal challenge of Washington State's prohibition against assisted suicide, RCW 9A.36.060. On May 3, 1994, Federal Judge Barbara J. Rothstein rendered a decision declaring the law unconstitutional. On March 9, 1995, a 3-Judge Panel of the Ninth District Court of Appeals overturned the District Court (2-1). On March 6, 1996 the Ninth District Court (en banc) reinstated the District Court ruling. The decision and dissent are available via Deathnet.

17. http://www.washingtonpost.com/wp-srv/politics/special/termlimits/stories/052395.htm *U.S. Term Limits Inc. v. Thornton*

Congressional Term Limits Struck Down By Joan Biskupic Washington Post Staff Writer Tuesday, May 23, 1995; Page A01 The Supreme Court ruled yesterday that states could not set term limits for members of Congress, saying American democracy was built on the principle that individual voters choose who governs and for how long. In a 5 to 4 decision, the court found that the states do not have the constitutional authority to regulate the tenure of federal legislators. The ruling effectively overturns term limits laws in 23 states and makes amending the Constitution the only sure means of restricting incumbency.... MAJORITY OPINION: "Permitting individual States to formulate diverse qualifications for their congressional representatives would result in a patchwork of state qualifications, undermining the uniformity and the national character that the Framers envisioned and sought to ensure." - Justice John Paul Stevens Joined by: * Justice Anthony M. Kennedy * Justice David Souter * Justice Ruth Bader Ginsburg * Justice Stephen Breyer THE DISSENT: "The Constitution is simply silent on this question. And where the Constitution is silent, it raises no bar to action by the states or the people." - Justice Clarence Thomas Joined by: * Chief Justice William Rehnquist * Justice Sandra Day O'Connor * Justice Antonin Scalia (c) Copyright 1998 The Washington Post Company. Supreme Court Breaks Constitutional Constraints
2003-08-08 by Sue Ella Deadwyler, Eagle Forum of Georgia, Nov. 11, 2003, http://www.georgiaeagle.org/index.php?where=articles&ID=215

18. Lincoln, Abraham. March 4, 1861, Monday, in his *First Inaugural Address.* James D. Richardson (U.S. Representative from Tennessee), ed., *A Compilation of the Messages and Papers of the Presidents 1789-1897,* 10 vols. (Washington, D.C.: U.S. Government Printing Office, published by Authority of Congress, 1897, 1899; Washington, D.C.: Bureau of National Literature and Art, 1789-1902, 11 vols., 1907, 1910), Vol. VI, pp. 9-11.

19. Jefferson, Thomas. 1821, in a letter to Mr. Hammond. Thomas Jefferson, *Thomas Jefferson on Democracy,* Saul K. Padover, ed., (NY: D. Appleton-Century Co., 1939), p. 64.

20. Jefferson, Thomas. September 6, 1819. Thomas Jefferson, *Jefferson Writings,* Merrill D. Peterson, ed., (NY: Literary Classics of the United States, Inc., 1984), p. 1426.

21. Cotton, John. Perry Miller and Thomas H. Johnson, *The Puritans: A Sourcebook of Their Writings* Vol. I (New York: Harper & Row, 1938, 1963), pp. 212-214. John Eidsmoe, *Christianity and the Constitution - The Faith of Our Founding Fathers* (Grand Rapids, MI:

Baker Book House, A Mott Media Book, 1987; 6th printing, 1993), pp. 34-35.

22. Madison, James. 1787, in a remark on the floor of the Constitutional Convention. M.E. Bradford, *A Worthy Company* (Marlborough, New Hampshire: Plymouth Rock Foundation, 1982), p. 147. John Eidsmoe, *Christianity and the Constitution - The Faith of Our Founding Fathers* (Grand Rapids, MI: Baker Book House, A Mott Media Book, 1987, 6th printing 1993), p. 102.

23. Washington, George. September 19, 1796, in his *Farewell Address,* published in the *American Daily Advertiser,* Philadelphia, September, 1796. James D. Richardson (U.S. Representative from Tennessee), ed., *A Compilation of the Messages and Papers of the Presidents 1789-1897,* 10 vols. (Washington, D.C.: U.S. Government Printing Office, published by Authority of Congress, 1897, 1899; Washington, D.C.: Bureau of National Literature and Art, 1789-1902, 11 vols., 1907, 1910), Vol. 1, p. 213-224, September 17, 1796.

24. Jackson, Andrew. 1832, *Veto of the Bank Renewal Bill.* James D. Richardson (U.S. Representative from Tennessee), ed., *A Compilation of the Messages and Papers of the Presidents 1789-1897,* 10 vols. (Washington, D.C.: U.S. Government Printing Office, published by Authority of Congress, 1897, 1899; Washington, D.C.: Bureau of National Literature and Art, 1789-1902, 11 vols., 1907, 1910), Vol. II, pp. 576-591. Richard D. Heffner, A Documentary History of the United States (New York: The New American Library of World Literature, Inc., 1961), pp. 93-96.

25. Harrison, William Henry. March 4, 1841, Thursday, in his Inaugural Address. James D. Richardson (U.S. Representative from Tennessee), ed., *A Compilation of the Messages and Papers of the Presidents 1789-1897,* 10 vols. (Washington, D.C.: U.S. Government Printing Office, published by Authority of Congress, 1897, 1899; Washington, D.C.: Bureau of National Literature and Art, 1789-1902, 11 vols., 1907, 1910), Vol. 4, pp. 6-20.

26. Acton, John Emerich Edward Dalberg, Lord. April 5, 1881, in a letter to Bishop Mandell Creighton. John Bartlett, *Bartlett's Familiar Quotations* (Boston: Little, Brown and Company, 1855, 1980), p. 615. *The World Book Encyclopedia,* 22 vols. (Chicago, IL: World Book, Inc., 1989; W.F. Quarrie and Company, 8 vols., 1917), Vol. 1, p. 31. Marshall Foster and Mary-Elaine Swanson, *The American Covenant - The Untold Story* (Roseburg, OR: Foundation for Christian Self-Government, 1981; Thousand Oaks, CA: The Mayflower Institute, 1983, 1992), p. 135.

27. Madison, James. *The Federalist No. 51, The Federalist Papers,* Clinton Rossiter, ed., (New York: Mentor Books, 1961), p. 322.

John Eidsmoe, *Christianity and the Constitution - The Faith of Our Founding Fathers* (Grand Rapids, MI: Baker Book House, A Mott Media Book, 1987, 6th printing 1993), p. 102. David A. Noebel, *Understanding The Times - The Story of the Biblical Christian, Marxist/ Leninist and Secular Humanist Worldviews* (Manitou Springs, CO: Summit Press, a branch of Summit Ministries, P.O. Box 207, Manitou Springs, Co., 80829, 1993), pp. 623-624.

28. Jackson, Andrew. December 7, 1835, in his *Seventh Annual Message to Congress.* James D. Richardson (U.S. Representative from Tennessee), ed., *A Compilation of the Messages and Papers of the Presidents 1789-1897,* 10 vols. (Washington, D.C.: U.S. Government Printing Office, published by Authority of Congress, 1897, 1899; Washington, D.C.: Bureau of National Literature and Art, 1789-1902, 11 vols., 1907, 1910), Vol. II, pp. 148, 164-165, 177.

29. http://www.marriagematters.org/ http://www.townhall.com/columnists/terencejeffrey/tj20031119.shtml http://www.cnsnews.com/ViewCulture.asp?Page=%5CCulture%5Carchive%5C200311%5CCUL20031119a.html http://www.cnn.com/2003/LAW/07/14/same.sex.marriages/

30. Jefferson, Thomas. September 11, 1804, in a letter to Abigail Adams. Thomas Jefferson, *Writings of Thomas Jefferson,* Albert Ellery Bergh, ed., (Washington, D.C.: Thomas Jefferson Memorial Association, 1904), Vol. X, pp. 50-51.

31. Jefferson, Thomas. June 12, 1823, in a letter to Justice William Johnson. Thomas Jefferson, *Memoir, Correspondence, and Miscellanies, From the Papers of Thomas Jefferson,* Thomas Jefferson Randolph, editor (Boston: Gray and Bowen, 1830), Vol. IV, p. 373. Thomas Jefferson, *Jefferson Writings,* Merrill D. Peterson, ed., (NY: Literary Classics of the United States, Inc., 1984), p. 1475.

32. Montesquieu, Baron Charles Louis Joseph de Secondat. 1748. Baron Charles Montesquieu, *The Spirit of the Laws,* 1748, Anne Cohler, trans. (reprinted Cambridge: Cambridge University Press, 1989), p. 157.

33. Alexis de Tocqueville, *Democracy in America* (1835), Book One.

CHAPTER 13: JUDICIAL ORDERED MURDER? - JAMES C. DOBSON, PH.D.

1. Mike Schneider, "Terri Schiavo Dies, 13 Days After Her Feeding Tube is Removed," Associated Press, 31 March 2005.

2. "Always to Care, Never to Kill," National Review Online, 21 March 2005.

3. Doug Bandow, "The Capitol Eye; Life and Death in Florida Corts," Copley News Service, 30 June 2004.

4. James Mostrom, "Solitary Confinement; Why You and I Should Care About Terri Schiavo," The Post-Standard, 1 March 2005; Amy Fagan, "High Court Rejects Schiavo Appeal," The Washington Times, 25 March 2005, p. A1.
5. Gary Bauer, "I Was Thirsty and You..." American Values End of Day Report, 24 March 2005.
6. Ibid.
7. "Interview with Terri Schiavo's Family Members," FOX News Hannity and Colmes, 24 March 2005.
8. "Animal Rights Law a Growing Field," CBS Evening News, 18 March 2005.
9. "A Closer Look: Terri Schiavo Case," World News Tonight with Peter Jennings, ABC News, 21 March 2005.
10. "Kevorkian Back in Prison After Temporary Release for Surgery," Associated Press, 7 February 2005.
11. "Jack Kevorkian Imprisoned Doctor Discusses Terri Schiavo," Good Morning America - ABC News Transcripts, 25 March 2005.
12. Josh Gerstein, "Schiavo's Mother Pleads for Court to Spare Terri," The New York Sun, 22 March 2005, p. A1; Jennifer Harper, "Reports, Polling Biased on Patient," The Washington Times, 24 March 2005; Fred Barnes, "The ABC's of Media Bias," The Weekly Standard, 4 April 2005.
13. "Zogby Poll: Americans Not in Favor of Starving Terri Schiavo," Zogby International, 3 April 2005.
14. James Q. Wilson, "Killing Terri," The Wall Street Journal, 21 March 2005.
15. Mitch Stacy, "Supreme Court, Appeals Court Reject Latest Appeal By Terri Schiavo's Parents," Aberdeen American News, 31 March 2005.
16. "Excerpts from Same-Sex Marriage Ruling," Associated Press, 15 March 2005.
17. "Cailfornians Vote Against Gay-Marriages, 61% to 39%," Associated Press, 8 March 2000.
18. See: www.landmarkcases.org/marbury/jefferson.html.
19. Ibid.
20. Ibid.
21. "Key Dates in the Terri Schiavo Case," Associated Press, 31 March 2005.
22. Carl Hulse, David D. Kirkpatrick, "Congress Passes and Bush Signs Schiavo Measure," The New York Times, 21 March 2005, p. A1.
23. "Key Dates in the Terri Schiavo Case," Associated Press, 31 March 2005.

24. Ibid.
25. Jules Whitcover, "Congress Ignores Separation of Powers," The Advocate, 26 March 2005, p. B6.
26. Linda Greenhouse, "Supreme Court, 5-4, Forbids Execution in Juvenile Crime," The New York Times, 2 March 2005, p. A1.
27. Tom Jackman, "Malvo Trial is Set for November," The Washington Post, 29 January 2003, p. B1.
28. Leo Fitzmaurice, "Man, 18, is Convicted in Slaying of Woman; She was Bound, Gagged, Pushed Off Bridge into River," St. Louis Post-Dispatch, 17 June 1994, p. 1C.
29. Jonah Goldberg, "Justice Kennedy's Mind," National Review, 9 March 2005.
30. "Excerpts of Supreme Court Opinion," Associated Press Online, 1 March 2005.
31. See: http://www.startribune.com/stories/1519/5269921.html
32. "Supreme Court Justice Antonin Scalia Delivers Remarks At the Woodrow Wilson Center for Scholars on Constitutional Interpretation," FDCH Political Transcripts, 14 March 2005.
33. Ibid.
34. "ACLJ Asks Supreme Court to Uphold Constitutionality of Ten Commandments in Kentucky Case," Business Wire, 8 December 2004.
35. Phone Conversation with U.S. Supreme Court Historian.
36. Bill Mears, "Ten Commandments Before High Court," CNN.COM, 1 March 2005
37. See: http://www.freerepublic.com/focus/f-news/1343936/posts
38. Valerie Richardson, "Colorado Ruling in Murder Case Angers Christians," The Washington Times, 30 March 2005, p. A5.
39. Ibid.
40. Jesse J. Holland, "Bush Sends Senate 20 Judicial Nominees," Associated Press, 15 February 2005.
41. "A Contradictory Biden," The Washington Times, 1 March 2005. http://washtimes.com/op-ed/20050228-084038-9235r.htm
42. "Meet the Press: Biden Will Oppose Scalia," NewsMax.com, 27 February 2005. http://newsmax.com/archives/ic/2005/2/27/165104.shtml
43. "GOP Jewish Group Hits Sen. Robert Byrd for Filibuster Remarks," Associated Press, 2 March 2005. http://www.freerepublic.com/focus/f-news/1354545/posts
44. FOX Special Report with Brit Hume, 1 March 2005. http://www.lexisnexis.com/publisher/

EndUserAction=UserDisplayFullDocument&org Id=574&topicId=100005814&docId=l:261749981&start=17
45. "Robert Byrd: The Minority Cannot Strangle Senate Business," The National Ledger, 4 March 2005. http://www.freerepublic.com/focus/f-news/1355962/posts

CHAPTER 16: WHEN IN THE COURSE... - MATHEW D. STAVER, ESQ.

1. The Editors, The End of Democracy? The Judicial Usurpation of Politics, First Things, November 1996, p. 18.
2. Declaration of Independence, July 4, 1776, *The Organic Laws of the United States of America.*
3. Or, as the signers of the Declaration said, "unalienable."
4. *Farewell Address* of George Washington 22 (1796).
5. Alexander Hamilton, *The Federalist,* No. 15.
6. Alexander Hamilton, *The Federalist,* No. 78.
7. *Id.*
8. James Madison, 2 *The Papers of James Madison* 1161-1171, quoting Luther Morton at the Constitutional Convention on July 21, 1787.
9. *Romer v. Evans,* 116 S. Ct 1620 (1996)
10. *League of United Latin American Citizens v. Wilson,* 908 F. Supp. 755 (C.D. Cal. 1995).
11. *Coalition for Economic Equity v. California,* 946 F. Supp. 1480 (N.D. Cal. 1996).
12. *Coalition for Economic Equity v. Wilson,* 110 F.3d 1431 (9th Cir. 1997), superseded, *California v. Coalition for Economic Equity,* 122 F.3d 692 (9th Cir. 1997).
13. *Missouri v. Jenkins,* 672 F. Supp. 400 (W.D. Mo. 1987).
14. *Missouri v. Jenkins,* 110 S. Ct. 109 (1990).
15. *Labine v. Vincent,* 401 U.S. 532 (1971).
16. *Marbury v. Madison,* 5 U.S. (1 Cranch) 137, 176 (1803).
17. *Cooper v. Aaron,* 358 U.S. 1, 18 (1958).
18. *Baehr v. Miike,* 65 U.S. L. Weekly 2399 (Cir. Ct. Hi. 1996).
19. *Romer,* 116 S. Ct. at 1620.
20. *Romer,* 116 S. Ct. at 1637 (Antonin Scalia, J., dissenting).
21. *Id.*
22. There are presently nine justices on the United States Supreme Court. The Court only needs five of the nine to make a motion.

INDEX

A

abandoned 116, 130
ABC News 117
abortion 40, 42, 75, 96, 129, 139, 146, 156, 157, 168, 170, 172, 176, 180, 195, 232, 280
above the law 62, 66, 68
absolute 65, 74
abuse 52, 70, 71, 77, 120, 154, 155, 193, 199, 210, 235
according 69, 70
accountable 71, 76, 128
acknowledge 15, 16, 18, 19, 20, 21, 23, 24, 25, 48, 56, 62, 65, 66, 68, 80, 82, 83, 90, 92, 106, 124, 126, 138, 184, 188, 192, 193, 194, 195, 212
ACLU 15, 16, 80, 81, 83, 107, 112, 145, 193
act 64, 66, 72, 75
action 61, 69, 74, 123
Adams, Abigail 102
Adams, John 106, 137, 215, 236
Adams, Samuel 99, 215
address 65, 68
Aderholt 112
Africa 125
against 124, 127
agenda 74, 118
Alabama 14, 15, 16, 19, 21, 23, 25, 45, 51, 52, 57, 58, 59, 62, 66, 67, 68, 80, 81, 92, 107, 136, 138, 145, 147, 169, 181, 188, 191
Alabama Sup. Court 68, 75
Almighty, acknowledge 15, 16
amendment 8, 19, 23, 32, 33, 41, 47, 49, 50, 57, 80, 81, 82, 86, 87, 88, 90, 92, 99, 107, 108, 112, 114, 136, 137, 138, 145, 146, 158, 160, 161, 163, 167, 169, 170, 173, 182, 189, 191, 207, 218, 219, 220, 221, 224, 227, 230, 231, 232, 235, 236, 237, 238, 239, 241, 242, 243, 244, 246, 247, 248, 249, 250
Amendment, First 19, 23, 32, 33, 47, 50, 57, 62, 66, 67, 68, 69, 80, 81, 82, 86, 87, 88, 90, 92, 107, 108, 112, 136, 145, 146, 182, 189, 191
Amendment, 14th 41, 218
Amendment, 16th 224
Amendment, 10th 23, 57
Amendment, 12th 227
America 70, 77, 121, 124, 127
American 61, 63, 64, 117, 118, 121, 124, 125, 126, 130
American Bar Association 175, 176
American Center for Law and Justice 67
American Values 116
Americans 77, 118, 120, 122
Americans United for Separation 16, 82, 83
Anan, Kofi 173, 174
anarchy 29, 104
ancient 61, 63
angels 70, 71, 77
animal rights 117
anti-religious 127
appeal 63, 65, 67, 73, 76
appointed 12, 21, 29, 30, 56, 80, 89, 98, 128, 142, 146, 159, 165, 221, 226, 240, 247
appointment 12, 55, 111, 120, 125, 171, 219, 228, 243
arbiters 77, 121
arguments 64, 73
Aristotle 153
arrest 116, 117
arrogant 120, 123, 130
article 61, 62, 122
Asia 125
associate justices 68
atheism 24, 50, 82, 192, 194
atheist 24, 43, 83
attorney general 67, 73
authorities 64, 65
authority 63, 65, 76, 121

B

babies 115, 119, 130
ballot box 128
Baptist 146, 150
Baptist, Danbury 146
Barton, David 94, 206
base 125, 126
based 63, 75, 76, 127

basic 61, 62, 63
basis 62, 65, 68
battle 130
Bauer, Gary 116
behavior 71
belief 68
believe 68, 69, 127
biases 121
Bible 127
biblical 64, 65
Biden, Senator Joe 129
bill 117, 123
Bill of Rights 70, 82, 100, 145, 153, 237
Birmingham News 67
black robed master 125, 127
Blackstone, William 36, 38, 41, 168
blind 68, 77
blind obedience 69
blood 120
body 122, 124
body of lawyers 125
bound 62, 63, 68, 69, 71, 72, 124
boundaries 30, 72, 174, 191
Bowers v. Hardwick 75, 136
brain 115, 116, 117
brain damage 117
brain dead 117
brains 119
branch 121, 122
breathing 118, 121
Breyer 125
Burke, Edmund 9, 94
Bush, George W., 52, 59, 105, 107, 111, 114, 117, 126, 128, 168
Bush, Jeb 123
Byrd, Robert 130

C

cadet 61, 62
cadre of elites 121
California 119, 120
Calley, William 63
Canada 125
capital punishment 124, 127
Carnahan, Mel 96
case 12, 15, 16, 17, 20, 21, 22, 23, 24, 25, 32, 37, 38, 41, 51, 67, 68, 73, 75, 76, 82, 83, 86, 89, 93, 111, 123, 127, 155, 157, 158, 159, 168, 170, 177, 180, 181, 184, 199, 201, 213, 219, 221, 222, 224, 227, 228, 229, 230, 232, 238, 240, 245, 248
CBS 117
censorship 16
centuries 75, 122
chain of command 63
chains 71
change 73, 75, 122, 129
characterization 73
charges 67
checks and balances 72, 121
Chief Justice 13, 14, 15, 16, 17, 18, 19, 20, 21, 22, 23, 25, 30, 45, 56, 58, 68, 69, 71, 80, 81, 82, 83, 86, 108, 110, 113, 129, 138, 145, 147, 177, 181, 189, 206, 219
children 118, 130
Christ 33, 56, 116, 186, 187, 190, 194
Christian 7, 21, 22, 27, 28, 31, 34, 35, 43, 44, 48, 58, 65, 82, 86, 87, 89, 139, 141, 147, 152, 175, 180, 186, 187, 189, 190, 192, 194, 195, 196, 197, 198, 206
Christianity 126
circumvent 120
citizen 22, 27, 31, 34, 42, 43, 44, 59, 81, 96, 97, 98, 99, 102, 103, 104, 108, 113, 131, 144, 146, 156, 158, 177, 189, 194, 196, 204, 213, 218, 219, 227, 230, 231, 239, 242, 243, 244, 248, 250
Civil Rights Act of 1964 130
civil rulers 66
civilians 63
civilization 75
claim 63, 69, 72, 115, 123, 124
Clause, Establishment 16, 19, 22, 112, 136
clauses 63
Clinton, Bill 174
cloak of legality 130
CNN 126
co-equal 122
co-equal authorities 123
cocaine addict 127
code 63
cold-blood 124, 127
colonies 38, 41, 48, 50, 63, 65, 156, 164, 198, 212, 214
Colorado Sup.Court 127
coma 116, 118
command 66, 67, 73, 76
commander 62, 63, 66
commands of God 66
commission 66, 81, 165, 166, 172, 228
committed 65, 128
communicate 123
communion 117
commuted 123
compassion 119
competing 115
complied 69
concept 121, 128
concluded 120
conclusion 69, 75
conclusively 119
condemned 115
condition 117, 118
conduct 63, 117, 118
confessed 69
confined 116

confirm 63, 72, 129, 130
conflict 62, 63, 76, 115
Congregationalist 65
Congress 19, 31, 32, 47, 49, 52, 53, 56, 57, 58, 59, 67, 68, 71, 72, 73, 82, 86, 87, 88, 89, 90, 91, 92, 96, 99, 104, 106, 107, 110, 111, 112, 113, 114, 121, 122, 123, 126, 128, 136, 145, 146, 161, 165, 166, 170, 171, 172, 174, 177, 189, 191, 192, 195, 205, 209, 214, 217, 218, 220, 222, 224, 225, 227, 228, 230, 232, 235, 237, 241, 242, 243, 244, 245, 246, 247, 248, 249, 250
congressional 123
Connelly, Chad 94, 206
conscience 62, 66, 76
consciousness 117
consensual sex 127
consent 122
consequence 75, 77, 126
conservative 128, 129
consistent 75, 123, 128
constitutes 69
Constitution 7, 8, 11, 12, 14, 15, 16, 18, 19, 21, 22, 23, 24, 25, 29, 30, 31, 32, 37, 38, 41, 42, 45, 46, 49, 50, 51, 52, 56, 57, 58, 59, 61, 62, 66, 67, 68, 69, 70, 71, 72, 73, 74, 75, 76, 77, 80, 86, 87, 88, 89, 90, 91, 92, 93, 94, 95, 96, 99, 100, 101, 103, 104, 106, 107, 109, 110, 111, 112, 113, 114, 121, 122, 125, 127, 128, 129, 131, 132, 135, 136, 137, 138, 139, 142, 144, 146, 153, 156, 157, 158, 159, 160, 161, 162, 163, 164, 165, 166, 167, 168, 169, 170, 171, 172, 173, 174, 175, 176, 177, 182, 188, 189, 190, 191, 192, 198, 199, 200, 201, 206, 212, 217, 224, 227, 228, 229, 231, 232, 235, 239, 240, 242, 243, 244, 246, 247
Constitution Corner 63, 71
constitutional 68, 76, 120, 121, 123, 124, 130
constitutional option 129
constitutional rights 74
constitutionality 121
convicted 127
conviction 48, 63, 108, 149, 183, 199, 229
conviction, religious 48
Cooper v. Aaron 24, 72, 110, 159
cooperative 118
Cotton, John 100
counter 66, 67, 118, 129
country 68, 72, 73, 76, 118, 119, 126, 128
county probate judge 123
court 9, 12, 14, 15, 16, 17, 18, 19, 20, 21, 22, 24, 29, 30, 35, 38, 40, 41, 45, 48, 49, 50, 51, 52, 53, 57, 58, 59, 68, 80, 81, 83, 88, 90, 91, 92, 93, 94, 98, 102, 103, 104, 105, 106, 107, 108, 109, 110, 111, 112, 113, 125, 126, 127, 129, 132, 136, 137, 138, 141, 144, 145, 146, 147, 156, 158, 159, 160, 161, 162, 163, 167, 168, 169, 171, 172, 175, 176, 177, 181, 182, 183, 184, 188, 191, 193, 194, 200, 223, 228, 230, 238
court 67, 68, 71, 73, 75, 76, 115, 121, 122, 124, 125, 128
court, federal 9, 15, 57, 83, 88, 93, 107, 108, 111, 112, 113, 158, 161, 169, 191
Court of Appeals 57, 58, 81, 106
Court , 9th Circuit 123
Court, 11th Circuit 67
court order 69
court, state 109, 160, 161
court system 63, 76
court-martial 63
court-martialed 63
courthouse 68, 69
courts 62, 71, 72, 73, 74, 77, 116, 119, 121, 123
create 123, 128
Creator 126
Creighton, Mandell 101
crime 66, 67
criminal 125
cronies 129
Crook, Shirley Ann 124
cruelty 117
culture 120, 122, 124

D

danger 121, 122, 124, 126
Darwin, Charles 37
Daschle, Tom 111, 128
De Tocqueville, Alexis 104, 277
De Bracton, Henry 64
dead 118
death 115, 116, 117, 118, 122, 127, 130
death penalty 124, 127
death row 117
debate 119, 124
deception 32
decided 124, 129
decision 74, 75, 116, 117, 119, 120, 121, 122, 123, 124, 126, 127
Declaration of Independence 8, 17, 18, 36, 37, 38, 39, 40, 41, 42, 51, 56, 65, 67, 79, 80, 93, 154, 164, 198, 199, 206, 208, 209
declare 64, 66, 71, 119, 127
decree 67, 121
deem 126, 119
defend 61, 63, 123, 127
defense 14, 31, 52, 63, 112, 128, 181, 217, 238
defense of marriage acts 112, 120
defied 123, 128
defy 68, 73, 75

dehydrated 115
DeLay, Tom 117
demand 123, 126
democracy 126
democratic 12, 120, 166, 198
denied 118
deny 66
Department, State 132
depicting 68, 127
deserve 71, 75, 124
desperate 128, 130
despotism 121
destroy 121, 124
determine 72, 116, 117, 124
determining 129, 130
die 117, 124, 127, 130
died 120
directive 118
disabled 115, 118
disagree 67, 73
disagreements 77
disaster 126
disciples 116
discussing 129
dishonest 69
dismayed 69
dismissed 126
disobedience 66, 67
display 67, 68, 69, 126, 130
dispute 67, 73
disregard 62, 63, 74
dissent 74
dissolution 122
distorting 118
distributed 68, 116
distributing 127
District Courts 126, 128
divided 70, 115
divine 130
divine right 64
doctrine 69, 121
document 65, 68, 72, 121
dominated 120
doubt 69, 70, 71, 120
Dr. Death 117
duct tape 124
duly 123
duties 19, 41, 42, 87, 90, 156, 193, 198, 205, 222, 225, 227, 228, 247, 248, 249
duty 25, 34, 42, 51, 55, 57, 59, 66, 67, 90, 93, 107, 113, 114, 152, 154, 155, 157, 159, 165, 166, 168, 169, 171, 176, 192, 193, 197, 199, 204, 205, 210, 224, 225
dying 117

E

earth 65, 66, 120
eclipsing 121
editorial 67
education 18, 22, 87, 148, 151, 172, 183, 204
education, sex 148
effort 117, 118, 123
elected 16, 30, 31, 56, 58, 80, 81, 90, 95, 96, 97, 110, 138, 146, 159, 162, 165, 166, 167, 171, 182, 201, 204, 211, 218, 219, 221, 226, 227, 243, 245, 246, 247
eminent tribunal 74
end 67, 116
enforcement 128
engage 75, 127, 128
England 63, 65
English 64
English Bill of Rights 64
entire 116, 123, 126
enumerate 65, 71
equal protection 158, 160, 241
essential 72, 125, 127
establish 63, 70. 122
establishment 65, 67, 68, 69, 122
establishment of religion 19, 32, 47, 57, 82, 87, 112, 136, 145, 189, 237
eternity 115
ethics 67
Europe 125, 126, 128
euthanizing 118
evil 119
evolution 29, 36, 37, 38, 137, 138, 174, 195
evolve 29, 37, 89, 121, 159, 227, 240, 245
exact 66, 75, 129
exalted 75
exception 62, 123, 128
exclusively 119, 120
excuse 63
executing 124
execution 118, 123, 124
executive 30, 58, 61, 67, 70, 90, 92, 103, 122, 146, 156, 157, 161, 168, 169, 171, 191, 198, 218, 219, 226, 228, 231, 232, 233, 241, 242, 243, 249
exercise, free 32, 47, 48, 49, 51, 57, 82, 86, 87, 136, 145, 193, 237
exist 71, 75, 119, 120
experience 70, 122
exposition 72
express 70, 122
expression, religious 43, 145
external 70
extremist 16

F

facts 75, 118
failure 63, 77
fair hearing 128
faith 10, 12, 19, 34, 35, 38, 40, 43, 48, 49, 50, 55, 80, 81, 82, 91, 126, 130, 135, 161, 162, 169, 177, 180, 181, 183, 184, 189, 190, 192, 194, 195, 228, 229, 230
fallacy 69
fallen nature 71
family 116, 120, 130
Father of Common Law 64
federal 61, 62, 68, 70, 73
federal authorities 76
federal bench 128
federal case 127

federal court 68, 72, 73, 74, 75, 76, 77, 119, 128
federal court nominees 129
federal govern 71, 72, 122
federal judge 65, 66, 69, 71, 72, 74, 130
federal judicial review 123
federal judiciary 72, 74, 122, 129, 130
federal level 128
federal obscenity laws 127
federalism 70
fellow justices 75
fiduciary 115
fiefdoms 120
filibuster 128, 129, 130
Final Judgment 68
Finney, Charles 151
First Commandment 66
five imperious justices 121
Florida 115
forbid 72, 127
Forefathers 64
forget 75, 127
forgive 117
form 69, 70, 122
former 128, 130
fornication 148
foundation 15, 18, 20, 21, 30, 36, 40, 41, 48, 64, 81, 104, 131, 132, 141, 145, 154, 160, 179, 180, 183, 192, 194, 199, 209
foundation, moral 15, 18, 20, 21, 180, 191
Founding Fathers 11, 23, 25, 56, 64, 65, 92, 93, 94, 109, 111, 120, 139, 198, 199, 200, 204
Framers 68, 70, 71, 73
Franklin, Benjamin 65
free exercise 67, 68
freedom 9, 11, 16, 21, 28, 31, 35, 36, 38, 39, 41, 42, 44, 47, 48, 49, 53, 82, 85, 90, 91, 94, 131, 135, 136, 161, 162, 179, 189, 193, 194, 195, 203, 204, 205, 206, 207, 237
freedom 62, 64, 120, 121
Frist, Bill 117
fundamental 71, 121
fundamental faw 75, 76
future 127

G

Gallup Poll 126
Gettysburg 31, 121
Gibson, Charles 117
Ginsberg , Ruth Bader, 125, 132
Glorious Revolution 64
God 7, 13, 14, 15, 16, 17, 18, 19, 20, 21, 22, 23, 24, 25, 27, 28, 29, 31, 32, 33, 34, 36, 37, 38, 39, 40, 41, 42, 43, 44, 46, 47, 48, 50, 53, 55, 56, 59, 62, 64, 65, 66, 68, 76, 77, 79, 80, 81, 82, 83, 85, 87, 88, 90, 92, 93, 94, 104, 106, 107, 112, 117, 126, 133, 136, 138, 142, 143, 144, 146, 147, 148, 150, 151, 154, 155, 175, 176, 177, 180, 181, 183, 184, 185, 187, 188, 189, 190, 191, 192, 193, 194, 195, 196, 197, 198, 199, 201, 203, 204, 205, 206, 209
God, acknowledge 15, 16, 18, 20, 24, 80, 83, 90, 92, 106, 138, 184, 188, 192, 193
God, Almighty 15, 16, 19, 25, 46, 50, 87, 192, 195
God and law 64
God, In We Trust 24, 25, 82
godless judges 120
Golden State 119
Goodridge v. Dept of Public Health. 135
Gonzales, Alberto 111
Gospel of Matthew 116
govern 28, 30, 48, 49, 53, 56, 61, 63, 64, 65, 70, 71, 74, 75, 76, 102, 105, 114, 122, 125, 154, 207, 209
government 9, 11, 13, 14, 15, 16, 18, 21, 23, 24, 25, 28, 29, 31, 33, 39, 40, 41, 43, 47, 49, 53, 56, 61, 62, 64, 70, 71, 72, 73, 74, 82, 86, 87, 88, 89, 90, 91, 92, 93, 94, 95, 99, 101, 102, 105, 110, 113, 114, 119, 120, 121, 122, 126, 131, 146, 153, 154, 155, 156, 157, 159, 162, 164, 165, 166, 170, 173, 174, 175, 177, 181, 182, 183, 190, 191, 193, 198, 199, 200, 203, 205, 209, 210, 212, 213, 223, 224, 226, 231, 235, 237, 240, 247
government, civil 15, 89
Governor 67, 119, 123
grab for power 122
graduate 65
grant 72, 115
grave 77, 124
Great Britain 63, 64, 65
Greer, George 115, 116, 118, 123

H

Hamilton, Alexander 156, 157, 169, 199, 234
hand 74, 77, 119, 122, 126
handful 74, 120
hardcore 127, 130
Harlan, Robert 127
harmless 122
Harrison, Benjamin 215
Harrison, William Henry 97, 101
Harvard 28, 36, 64, 65, 89, 163
Hawaii 120, 160
hearsay 115
heaven 66, 127
heinous 123
Henry, Patrick 35, 99
heritage 27, 28, 31, 32, 34, 36, 43, 181, 184, 187, 192, 206

high appellation 71
high school 120
higher court 76, 77
higher powers 65
history 7, 12, 27, 28, 31, 32, 33, 34, 48, 51, 55, 58, 63, 64, 79, 81, 102, 107, 111, 118, 130, 131, 144, 164, 180, 206, 210
Hitler, Adolph 130, 150
Hitler-esque 130
Holden, Bob 98
Holmes, Oliver Wendell 37, 40
homosexual 40, 42, 75, 93, 97, 102, 136, 144, 147, 158, 160, 180, 183, 184, 185, 186, 190
honest 68
horrible 119
horrors 129
Hostettler, John 112
hostilities 65
House 14, 15, 45, 56, 90, 107, 112, 113, 123, 124, 143, 145, 161, 167, 169, 174, 193, 195, 211, 217, 218, 220, 221, 226, 229, 232, 235, 237, 240, 242, 245, 248, 249
House Majority Leader 117
Houses of Congress 119
Hughes, Charles Evans 30
human being 118
human nature 70
humanity 118
hungry 116
husband 115, 116
hydrated 118
hypocrisy 130
hypothesis 74

I

idea 69, 124
ideology 75
ignore 123, 124, 125
illegal 64, 72, 130
illustrates 120
illustrious 130
imagine 127
immoral 73, 115
impeach 8, 59, 92, 93, 111, 113, 159, 161, 197, 200, 218, 219, 228, 229, 230
impeached 125
impeachment 59, 91, 92, 111, 113, 161, 200, 218, 219, 228, 229, 230
impeachments 72
impending 129
imperial power 121
imperious 120, 122
implicated 77
implications 118, 121, 127
implied 69
important 116, 124, 129, 130
impose 73, 74
imposing 128
impossible 75
improper 129
Inauguration Day 126
inconsistent 66, 69, 71
inconvenienced 118
incredible 130
independence 63, 65
independent 74, 120
infamous 75
inferior 66
influence 119
infringing 127
injunction 68
injury 64, 115, 116
innocent 63, 118, 123, 124
inquiry, judicial 81
inspire 27, 38, 39
institution 129
institution of marriage 120
instructed 117
instrument 72, 73
integrity 61, 77
intellectually 68, 69
intended 68, 72, 121, 122
intent 14, 16, 30, 40, 89, 94, 139, 206, 214, 232, 236
intent, original 30, 94, 139, 206
intentions 65
intents 66
interfering 62
internal 70
international 124
international authorities 125
international law 125
interposition 164, 165, 166, 167, 170, 172, 176
interpret 74, 128, 129
interpretation 68, 69, 70
interpreted 69
interpreting 73, 74, 77, 128
interprets 129
intervention 130
interview 117, 129
Israelites 77
issue 65, 76, 121, 124, 130
issued 68
issues 69, 123, 124, 129, 130

J

Jackson, Andrew 101, 102, 138
Jarvis, William 95, 96
Jefferson, Thomas 38, 64, 71, 74, 95, 96, 100, 102, 103, 121, 122, 126, 146, 199, 215
Jesus 116, 130
Judeo-Christian 21, 22, 62, 126, 139, 180
judge 62, 64, 68, 69, 73, 75, 76, 77, 126, 76, 77, 115, 116, 118, 119, 120
judgement 156, 160
judges 12, 14, 16, 17, 24, 25, 29, 30, 37, 39, 40, 43, 44, 48, 50, 57, 58, 62, 69, 71, 73, 75, 76, 80, 83, 85, 86, 87, 89, 90, 92, 93, 95, 96, 97, 98, 100,

102, 106, 107, 108, 109, 110, 111, 112, 113, 114, 119, 120, 121, 123, 128, 129, 135, 137, 139, 143, 144, 146, 158, 161, 162, 171, 176, 182, 184, 188, 189, 191, 197, 198, 199, 200, 201, 204, 211, 228, 229, 232
judges, federal 12, 25, 50, 57, 58, 80, 95, 96, 97, 98, 111, 123, 161, 191
judicial 8, 9, 12, 13, 14, 15, 21, 23, 24, 25, 29, 30, 31, 32, 35, 37, 40, 44, 57, 79, 81, 85, 86, 88, 89, 90, 91, 92, 93, 96, 102, 103, 105, 106, 109, 111, 114, 122, 132, 135, 138, 139, 144, 146, 157, 159, 160, 161, 168, 181, 192, 198, 199, 200, 203, 229, 230, 233, 239, 241, 242
judicial 61, 66, 69, 70, 128
judicial assault 120
judicial decisions 75
judicial decree 120, 124
judicial hostility 126
judicial nominations 129
judicial nominees 128
judicial oligarchy 125
judicial orders 77
judicial review 69, 71, 72
judicial system 119, 127
judicial tyranny 125
judiciary 11, 12, 14, 24, 32, 58, 68, 74, 80, 82, 100, 103, 110, 112, 114, 118, 121, 122, 123, 132, 156, 157, 158, 159, 162, 195, 199, 211
judiciary, independent 11, 12
jurisdiction 58, 91, 92, 100, 111, 112, 113, 137, 161, 191, 212, 213, 229, 231, 241, 244
jurisdiction 122
jurisprudence 36, 37, 42, 55, 58, 89
jury 127
justice 13, 14, 15, 16, 17, 18, 19, 20, 21, 22, 23, 25, 30, 31, 40, 45, 56, 58, 69, 80, 81, 82, 83, 86, 98, 103, 107, 108, 110, 113, 116, 118, 132, 136, 138, 144, 147, 156, 158, 159, 160, 161, 177, 181, 188, 189, 192, 193, 198, 206, 211, 214, 217, 219, 231
justice system 62
justices 62, 67, 68, 69, 119, 121, 123, 125, 126
justification 124
justify 127

K

Kennedy, John F. 88
Kennedy, Anthony 124, 125, 126
Kevorkian, Jack 117
kidnapping 127
kill 63, 116, 117, 118, 119, 127, 130
killers 123
kindergarten 120
King 12, 13, 24, 44, 56, 63, 64, 65, 66, 79, 80, 149, 164, 175, 176, 198, 210, 225, 234
King George 13, 64, 65, 79
King James 64
King John 63
Kramer, Richard 119
Ku Klux Klan 130

L

Lancaster, Gary 126, 127
Land, Richard 67
landmark 121
Langdell, Christopher Columbus, 28, 36, 89
Langdell Hall 64
law 7, 8, 9, 14, 15, 16, 17, 18, 19, 20, 21, 22, 23, 24, 25, 28, 29, 30, 31, 32, 33, 36, 37, 38, 39, 40, 41, 42, 43, 44, 45, 46, 47, 48, 49, 51, 52, 53, 56, 57, 59, 61, 62, 63, 64, 65, 67, 68, 71, 72, 73, 74, 75, 76, 77, 81, 82, 83, 85, 86, 87, 88, 89, 90, 91, 92, 93, 96, 102, 103, 104, 106, 107, 108, 109, 110, 111, 112, 113, 114, 115, 119, 122, 123, 124, 128, 130, 131, 132, 135, 136, 138, 142, 143, 144, 145, 146, 157, 159, 160, 161, 163, 164, 167, 168, 169, 171, 172, 174, 175, 176, 177, 180, 182, 183, 184, 187, 188, 189, 190, 191, 192, 193, 197, 198, 200, 201, 206, 210, 211, 212, 215, 218, 220, 221, 222, 223, 225, 227, 228, 229, 230, 232, 233, 237, 238, 241, 242, 245, 246, 249, 250
law, American 21, 36, 39, 40, 41, 43, 104
law, biblical 36, 43
law, constitutional 14, 160, 163, 182
law, federal 170, 171, 188
law, international 8, 131
law is king 64
law, moral 18, 24, 39, 40, 41, 42, 43
law, natural 14, 39
law of God 65
law of the land 122
law, scriptural 48
lawful 63
lawmaker 30
Lawrence v. Texas 75, 127, 136, 137, 141, 144, 183
laws 62, 65, 70, 71, 72, 75, 76, 121, 123, 124, 127, 128
laws of nature 18, 39, 63, 154, 209
lawyer 36, 37, 39, 72, 87, 110, 112, 113, 188, 189
leader 61, 67, 130
learning 116

Left 130
legal 9, 14, 28, 29, 36, 37, 38, 40, 41, 42, 44, 72, 86, 88, 90, 93, 97, 107, 130, 131, 132, 143, 145, 146, 158, 164, 167, 172, 175, 203, 242
legal right 71
legal scholar 64, 68
legislative 12, 30, 56, 61, 70, 89, 97, 102, 103, 106, 108, 122, 132, 146, 153, 156, 170, 191, 198, 200, 211, 217
legislature 71, 73
legitimate state interest 127
Lex Rex 64
liberal 120, 128, 129
liberal colleagues 125
liberal judges 120
liberal opponents 128
liberty 9, 17, 18, 31, 39, 41, 46, 48, 50, 51, 52, 56, 63, 64, 94, 103, 120, 126, 131, 132, 154, 155, 157, 163, 164, 172, 179, 187, 192, 193, 194, 195, 196, 204, 207, 209, 217, 238, 241
liberty interest 127
liberty, religious 17, 48, 50, 193, 195
license 72
life 12, 18, 27, 29, 30, 34, 39, 40, 41, 42, 46, 47, 48, 93, 94, 96, 103, 106, 109, 111, 115, 132, 135, 147, 148, 153, 154, 155, 159, 169, 180, 184, 192, 193, 195, 196, 204, 209, 230, 238, 241
life support 117, 118
limit 119, 122
Lincoln, Abraham 31, 36, 41, 74, 99, 121, 136, 169
litigation 74
Livermore, Samuel 88
Locke, John 23, 25
low-ranking 119, 123
lower court 77, 121
lower federal courts 123
loyalty 61, 63, 115
Lynn, Barry 82
Lyons, Champ 68, 69, 71

M

Madison, James 19, 38, 56, 70, 71, 100, 101, 157, 233
Magna Carta 63
majority 118, 120, 124, 130
Malvo, John Lee 123
man 64, 65, 66, 68, 71, 77, 124
Marbury v. Madison 71, 72, 73, 121, 122, 159, 177
marriage 40, 42, 92, 93, 102, 106, 112, 115, 119, 120, 129, 130, 137, 138, 141, 144, 147, 150, 160, 180, 183, 184, 185, 186, 187, 188, 195
Marshall, John 71, 72, 73
Massachusetts 48, 93, 102, 106, 135, 137, 138, 141, 215, 218, 234
Massachusetts Constitution 70
Mayhew, Jonathan 65
meaning 62, 70, 75, 120, 122
media 117, 118, 123
Medina, Ernest 63
Meet the Press 129
member 122, 127, 130
men 70, 71, 120, 130
mentally 115, 118
mentally retarded 118
military 61, 63, 66
million-dollar 115
ministerial 76, 77
minority 125, 130
minors 123, 124
monarchy 12, 13, 101
Montesquieu, Baron 103
monument 14, 15, 16, 17, 18, 19, 20, 21, 22, 23, 24, 57, 62, 66, 67, 68, 69, 76, 77, 81, 83, 85, 92, 107, 112, 113, 135, 136, 145, 181
Moore, Roy 14, 56, 59, 67, 77, 80, 86, 135, 136, 138, 145, 147, 169, 181, 182, 188, 192, 206
moral 15, 18, 20, 21, 24, 30, 38, 39, 40, 41, 42, 43, 55, 80, 83, 85, 87, 89, 119, 127, 135, 137, 139, 141, 142, 144, 145, 147, 148, 151, 160, 180, 182, 183, 191, 195, 199, 201, 204, 205, 206
moral foundation 77
moral relativism 122
morality 127
Moses 126
motto 18, 24, 65
movement 130
MRI 116
murder 124, 127
Muslim 43, 142
My Lai 63

N

nation 8, 9, 12, 14, 16, 18, 24, 25, 27, 28, 30, 31, 32, 34, 35, 36, 40, 42, 43, 44, 46, 48, 49, 50, 53, 56, 59, 63, 71, 74, 75, 77, 80, 81, 83, 85, 87, 88, 93, 94, 100, 104, 114, 120, 128, 126, 129, 130, 131, 132, 133, 136, 137, 142, 143, 144, 146, 147, 148, 149, 150, 151, 164, 166, 169, 170, 173, 174, 175, 176, 177, 179, 180, 181, 186, 192, 193, 195, 196, 197, 198, 199, 203, 204, 205, 207, 213, 219, 222, 227, 248
nature 116
Nature's God 63
Nazis 118
null 66, 67, 124

O

oath 19, 23, 25, 49, 50, 55, 57, 58, 59, 61, 62, 66, 69, 73, 76,

77, 93, 107, 110, 127, 145, 168, 219, 228, 233, 238, 242
obedience 63, 65, 68, 75, 76
obey 63, 65, 66, 67, 69, 73, 75, 76
obligation 69, 123
obscene 127, 128
observe 63, 74, 122
obstructionist 128, 129
O'Connor, Sandra Day 83, 125, 136
officer 61, 63, 66, 76, 77
oligarchy 7, 95, 99, 102, 104, 109, 121, 124, 126, 153, 162, 199
opinion 69, 74, 75, 122, 125
opinions 75, 121, 126
oppose 124, 126, 129
opposite 75, 119
order 62, 63, 66, 67, 68, 69, 73, 75, 76, 77, 118, 123
ordered 62, 67, 76, 77, 115, 116
orders 62, 63, 71, 73, 76, 123
Oregon 120
organic law 67
organism 125
out of control 119, 121, 128

P

Palm Sunday 123
parched 116
pardon 127
parents 116, 119
partial birth abortion 119
pass 68, 72, 77, 117, 120, 123
pastor 64, 142, 143, 150
people 62, 63, 64, 67, 69, 70, 71, 74, 75, 76, 116, 117, 120, 121, 124, 125, 126, 129, 130
permanence 74, 75
permit 74, 116, 119, 123, 126
Perry, John 77
persecution 48, 50, 190
person 75, 118, 127, 129
personal beliefs 68
philosophy 28, 29, 30, 40, 42
plaque 61, 63
pledge 18, 40, 79, 106, 108, 112, 123, 136, 147, 214
police 116, 117
policy 74, 121
political 123
politically correct 128
poll 117, 118
pollster 117, 118
polygamy 48, 184
porn 43, 108, 127, 130
position 68, 125, 129
positivism 28
post-modern nonsense 124
power 64, 70, 71, 74, 77, 122, 126, 130
power, judicial 23, 103, 161, 229, 239
power, legislative 56, 103, 106, 170, 211, 217
powers 71, 72
practices 63, 64
prayer 128, 130
pre-born 124, 129
preamble 31, 63, 173
precedent 30, 37, 69, 101, 112, 132, 146
Presbyterian 64
president 64, 66, 119, 121, 122, 123, 128, 129
press 118
prevent 62, 128
primary 64, 70
prince 65, 66
principle 61, 63, 64, 66, 72, 74, 128
prison 117
pro-family 130
procedure 119, 129
process 120, 123, 127, 129
prohibit 16, 19, 32, 43, 57, 82, 86, 87, 91, 92, 136, 145, 158, 160, 163, 164, 166, 168, 189, 224, 237, 239, 244, 246
prohibited 69, 124
prohibiting 67, 68, 119
promise 76, 126
property 18, 41, 98, 135, 158, 204, 231, 238, 241
protect 70, 75, 123, 128, 129, 130
protest 127
provisions 62, 69, 121
Pryor, Bill 67, 73, 74
psychological 130
public 67
public buildings 126
public officials 68
public opinion 124, 126
public property 126
public sense of morality 127
public spaces 68
public square 128
published 65, 66, 67
purpose 61, 62, 64, 66, 119
pursuit of happiness 39, 40, 41, 94, 154, 155, 209

Q

qualifies 116
question 67, 74, 117, 118, 121

R

rape 127
ratification 70
ratified 126
rational 119, 120, 124, 126
re-interpreting 125
re-nominating 128
Reagan, Ronald 24
receive 116, 120, 128
recognize 62, 66, 68, 77, 116, 121, 130
refuse 67, 73, 76, 117, 119, 123
regime 24, 49, 50, 108, 110, 190, 192
Rehnquist, William 113, 129

rejected 63, 65
relativism 28, 119
religion 14, 19, 23, 32, 35, 38, 47, 48, 49, 57, 67, 68, 69, 82, 86, 87, 88, 90, 104, 107, 112, 136, 145, 152, 183, 189, 190, 191, 237
religious 67, 126, 128
religious community 127
Religious Liberty Commission 67
remove 62, 66, 67, 68, 76, 77, 117, 123
repeat 64, 67, 117, 121, 128
representative 120, 123, 124
republic 12, 55, 59, 92, 95, 102, 104, 138, 151, 162, 166, 231
Republicans 123
respecting 67, 68, 69
respirator 116, 118
responsibility 115, 122
revival 151, 195
right 62, 66, 67, 75, 76, 124, 128
right to abortion 125
right to sodomy 125
righteousness 65
rights 13, 17, 29, 36, 41, 42, 48, 51, 52, 56, 82, 88, 90, 93, 94, 97, 100, 106, 108, 110, 145, 148, 153, 154, 156, 157, 158, 162, 180, 184, 185, 191, 192, 193, 198, 201, 203, 204, 205, 209, 211, 235, 237, 239
rights 63, 64, 71, 76
rights, inalienable 94
Riley, Bob 67
Roe v. Wade 40, 55, 75, 107, 111
Romans 65
Romney, Mitt 138
royal monarchs 120
rule 63, 64, 65, 67, 73, 74, 120, 121, 126
rule of law 62, 63, 65, 67, 69, 71, 72, 73, 74, 75, 77
rule of man 63, 77
rule of men 69, 72, 74
ruling 72, 75, 76, 121, 124, 125, 127
Runnymede 63
Russert, Tim 129
Rutherford, Samuel 64

S

sabotage 129
same-sex 106, 137, 141, 142, 147, 160
same-sex Marriage 119, 120
San Francisco 120, 123
San Francisco Supr.Ct 119
sanction 119, 120
satan 28, 32, 33, 142, 176
Scalia, Antonin 125, 129, 144, 160
Schaivo, Michael 115, 116, 117
Schiavo, Terri 115, 116, 117, 118, 119, 123
Schindler 118
school 14, 28, 33, 36, 37, 47, 48, 49, 58, 82, 87, 89, 106, 108, 136, 143, 146, 148, 172, 175, 176, 181, 183, 192, 193, 205
school, public 108, 120, 128, 136, 141, 143, 181, 183
Scott, Dred 41, 98
Scottish 64
seal 65
secular 22, 50, 131, 184
Sekulow, Jay 67
self-government 53, 56, 105, 110, 114, 182, 193
Senate 12, 56, 111, 112, 123, 128, 129, 156, 167, 170, 172, 173, 175, 205, 217, 218, 221, 222, 226, 227, 228, 232, 235, 240, 243, 245, 248, 249
Senate liberals 129
Senate Majority Leader 117
Senate rules 129
senator 128, 129, 130
Sensenbrenner 112
separation of church and state 16, 32, 40, 46, 81, 82, 83, 87, 127, 151, 182, 183, 184, 188, 190, 207
separation of power 11, 70, 71, 102, 109, 114, 123, 198
Sergeants at Arms 126
sermon 65, 66
sex partners 119
sex videos 127
Simmons, Christopher 124
smear 130
So Help Me God 77
socialism 128
socially 120
sodomy 75, 83, 136, 141, 144
sole determiner of rationality 119
Son of God 176
Souter 125
South America 125
Southern Baptist 67
Southern Poverty Law Center 16, 83
Sovereign 7, 14, 16, 17, 18, 19, 20, 21, 22, 23, 24, 25, 30, 48, 49, 55, 56, 66, 165, 174, 192, 194
standard 28, 29, 76, 147, 170, 171, 199, 201
state 61, 62, 69, 70, 71, 119, 127
state legislatures 72, 73
state official 73, 75, 76
states 61, 62, 65, 120, 123
Stevens 125
strict constructionist 128, 129
suffer 77, 117, 130

support 61, 63, 69, 73, 74, 75, 76, 117, 126, 129
supremacy 25, 106, 109, 111, 114, 162
supreme 62, 72, 74, 77
Supreme Court 14, 16, 17, 24, 29, 38, 40, 41, 48, 52, 58, 59, 67, 69, 72, 73, 74, 75, 80, 81, 83, 94, 98, 102, 103, 104, 107, 108, 109, 110, 111, 119, 120, 121, 123, 124, 126, 126, 136, 137, 138, 144, 156, 158, 159, 160, 161, 163, 167, 168, 169, 171, 172, 175, 181, 184, 188, 194, 223, 228, 229, 230
Supreme Court Building 126
Supreme Court Justices 122
Supreme Court of the United States 124
Supreme Court precedent 127
Supreme Judge 65, 67
supreme law 72, 71, 74
supreme legislator 66
swear 61, 73
sworn 63, 69, 73, 74, 76, 127
system 70, 72

T

tactics 128, 130
Taney, Roger 98
taxes 108, 157, 158, 170, 212, 218, 222, 243
Ten Commandments 14, 15, 16, 17, 19, 21, 22, 24, 33, 40, 45, 50, 52, 53, 55, 56, 57, 62, 68, 76, 80, 81, 92, 104, 107, 108, 112, 126, 135, 141, 143, 169, 180, 182, 188, 191, 194
terminally ill 118
terminate 129
testimony 18, 160, 230
Texas 117
text 69, 71, 76, 125
thief 122
thing of wax 74, 122
Thompson, Myron 15, 56, 57, 62, 66, 67, 68, 69, 73, 76, 77, 135
Thompson, William 68
torture 130
tradition 19, 30, 48, 51, 80, 125, 132, 133, 142, 184, 188
truth 9, 13, 25, 33, 51, 56, 58, 73, 79, 85, 92, 146, 150, 151, 154, 155, 179, 180, 182, 184, 187, 194, 195, 205, 207, 209
tube 115, 117, 118, 123
tyranny 8, 13, 23, 24, 25, 37, 40, 44, 48, 49, 63, 64, 65, 77, 79, 80, 113, 114, 135, 138, 139, 146, 153, 155, 160, 162, 177, 195, 200, 210, 213
tyrant 13, 16, 22, 25, 52, 65, 66, 146, 167, 210, 213

U

unconstitutional 16, 21, 86, 87, 88, 90, 106, 109, 113, 119, 127, 136, 137, 138, 142, 144, 146, 158, 160, 161, 175, 182, 189
understand 116, 126, 127, 128
unelected 30, 97, 120, 162
union, civil 184
United Nations 173, 174, 175
United States 65, 66, 67, 69, 70, 71, 125, 126, 127, 128, 129
unjust 116
unking 66
unlawful 62, 63, 66, 67, 69, 77
uphold 69, 76, 124, 127
USA Today 126
usurp 65, 122

V

vacancies 128
vacant positions 128
values 80, 85, 88, 89, 130, 145, 147, 149, 198, 199, 201, 203
victim 118, 122
Vietnam 62, 63
violate 62, 66, 67, 69, 71, 73, 74, 76, 123, 127
violation 65, 66, 67, 71, 77
vital 74, 75
void 66, 67, 71, 72
vote 119, 120, 128, 129

W

Wall Street 131, 166
War, Civil 36, 104
War, Revolutionary 137, 195
warned 77, 121
Warren, Earl 108, 110
Washington, George 25, 61, 101, 155, 233
water 116, 117, 118
welfare 31, 115, 158, 217, 222
West Point 61, 62, 63
Whittemore, James 123
wife 64, 115
will 67, 119, 121, 122, 123
William of Orange 64
women 115, 118, 120, 124. 127, 130
Word of God 27, 34, 47, 53, 150, 176, 177, 184
world 65, 67, 71, 125
Wright, Scott O. 96, 98
writing 124, 125
written 72, 115, 118, 124, 128, 129

Z

Zechariah 77
Zogby, John 118